The Little Audio CD Book

Bob Starrett and Josh McDaniel

Peachpit Press • Berkeley, California

The Audio CD Book
Bob Starrett and Josh McDaniel

Peachpit Press
1249 Eighth Street
Berkeley, CA 94710
(510) 524-2178
(800) 283-9444
(510) 524-2221 (fax)

Find us on the World Wide Web at: www.peachpit.com
Peachpit Press is a division of Addison Wesley Longman

Copyright ©2000 Bob Starrett and Josh McDaniel

Editor: Clifford Colby
Copy Editor: Stephen Nathans
Production Coordinator: Lisa Brazieal
Interior Design: Robin Williams
Compositor: Owen Wolfson
Cover Design: John Tollett with Mimi Heft
Cover Illustration: Lisa Brazieal
Indexer: Cheryl Landes

Notice of Rights
All rights reserved. No part of this book may be reproduced or transmitted in any form by any means, electronic, mechanical, photocopying, recording, or otherwise, without the prior written permission of the publisher. For information on getting permission for reprints and excerpts, contact Gary-Paul Prince at Peachpit Press.

Notice of Liability
The information in this book is distributed on an "As is" basis, without warranty. While every precaution has been taken in the preparation of the book, neither the author nor Peachpit Press shall have any liability to any person or entity with respect to any loss or damage caused or alleged to be caused directly or indirectly by the instructions contained in this book or by the computer software and hardware products described in it.

Trademarks
Throughout this book, trademarked names are used. Rather than put a trademark symbol in each occurrence of a trademarked name, we state we are using the names only in an editorial fashion and to the benefit of the trademark owner with no intention of infringement of the trademark.

ISBN 0-201-70897-3

9 8 7 6 5 4 3 2 1

Printed and bound in the United States of America.

To Dana.
—Bob

To Mom and Pop.
—Josh

Acknowledgments

We wish to thank Cliff Colby, astute wordsmith, obscenity sieve, and editor extraordinaire. We're really sorry if our foul mouths made your life difficult. Along those same lines, we'd like to thank Steve Nathans for crafting and honing our occasionally awkward use of the language. As always, Steve, you make us look many times better than we actually are—right on, brother. The patient and kind production staff, Lisa Brazieal in particular, deserves endless thanks for getting this book into aesthetically pleasing shape. Finally, we're shooting thanks out Dana Parker's and Jason McDaniel's way, as they patiently attended to a few ambiguous paragraphs for us. Oh, and honorable mention goes to Anheuser-Busch Inc., for its inspiration-in-a-can; Wesley Willis, for his incisive commentary; and Mojo Nixon, for sustaining us throughout the writing of this book. If we forgot someone, consider this sentence redeemable for an apology and a six-pack.

Table of Contents

Introduction . . . . *xi*

Chapter 1 Compact Discs and Recording   1

Save those LPs and 45s 4
   From vinyl, tape, or disc 5
Analog and Digital 6
Issues in Audio Recording 7
   What recorder? 7
   What media? What color? 9
Recorded History 9
   X confusion 11
Why Use CD-R? 11
   Two hundred songs on a disc? 12
So Sue Me 13

Chapter 2 Sources of Digital and
               Digitizable Audio   15

First Things First 16
   Getting music 19
Where Is the Good Music on the Internet? 19
   FTPs: Don't waste your time 19
   Music on the edge 20
Music Download Sites 22
Getting the Music 26

Chapter 3 Audio Recording and Ripping Software   29

Beware the BIOS, a Necessary Digression 31
    Back to the story 33
Recording Software for Windows 33
Recording Software for Mac OS 37
Audio-Only Recording Programs 40
Jukeboxes that Record 41
High-End Audio Recording Software 42
Specialized Software for Extraction 42
Ripping Without WAVs—CDFS.VXD 44
    Simple burning 45
    Other CD programs of interest 46
    Freedom of choice 47

Chapter 4 CD-Recordable and CD-Rewritable Drives   49

CD Recorder Interfaces 50
Selecting a Recorder 53
    Recorder features 54
The X Factor 54
CD Recorders—What's Inside? 58
    Random access time 59
    Hardware requirements 60
    Standards, history, and writing modes 61
    CD-R standards 63
    CD-R data structure 64
CD-R Writing Modes 66
    Disc-at-Once (single-session) 66
    Track-at-Once 66
CD-R Incompatibility 67
    CD-R hardware 67
    CD-R media 67
    Dyes 68

Chapter 5 General Hardware   71

Sound cards and USB sound devices 72
Phono preamplifiers 78
The RIAA Curve, a quick digression. 79
Stereo peripherals. 82
Additional CD-ROM drives 83
Hard disks 83

Chapter 6 Recording and Troubleshooting   87

Recording with Windows—
    It's a Wonder It Works at All 88
    Auto Insert Notification. 89
    Sync data transfer. 90
    Disconnect. 90
    Microsoft's FindFast 91
    Read-ahead optimization 91
    IDE busmaster drivers 92
    autoexec.bat and config.sys 93
Sure and Stable Mac Recording...
    and iMac Limitations. 93
Recommendations for IDE Recorders 94
Rules and Regulations for SCSI Recorders 94
    SCSI on the Mac. 97
Troubleshooting Recording Problems—
    Causes of Buffer Underrun. 98
CD-R Media 100
Using Your Computer While Recording 102

Chapter 7 Highway 61 Restored   103

Making Connections 104
Stuff You Need on the Outside. 105
    Connecting your stuff. 109
Stuff You Need on the Inside 111
Recording 120
    Restoration. 124
    The high-pass, or rumble, filter 125
    The declick, or impulse noise, filter 126

    Median filter. 128
    Dehiss, denoise filter. 129
    Dehum, debuzz, notch filter 129
    Reverb. 131
    Equalizers. 131
 Preparing for the Burn 132
 The Burn. 133

Chapter 8 Restoring and Recording Cassette Tapes   135

 Unplug and Plug In 136
 Recording 137
 Taking a Noiseprint 141
 Track Splitting 146
 Dehissing 148
 The Burn. 155

Chapter 9 Copying CDs   157

 The Ubiquitous but Sometimes Nefarious
    Copy Utility. 158
 How Bob and Josh Copy CDs. 164
 The Burn. 176

Chapter 10 Recording MP3s to CD   177

 In the News 178
 Now Let's Go Get Some of These Things 180
    Napster 183
 Requisite Software. 186
 Getting Your MP3s Ready for CD. 189
 Burning Your Former MP3s to Disc 196

Chapter 11 Compilation Discs   197

 Track 1, from a CD 198
 Track 2, from a Tape 199
 Track 3, from Vinyl 200
 Track 4, from an MP3 201

Equalization. 202
Fade-Ins and Fade-Outs. 205
Normalization 209

Chapter 12 Mixed Discs — 211

The Making of Multisession 212
    The audio session 213
    The data session. 218
    The deleterious autorun.inf file 221

Chapter 13 Home Recorders — 225

Home Burning Basics 227
The Audio Home Recording Act of 1992 (AHRA) 232

Chapter 14 Legal Issues: A Quick Overview — 235

The Law 236
Think Practically. 236
According to the RIAA 237
According to the HRRC 239
    The effect of the Betamax case on CD burning 239
Go to Jail?. 241
Where Are We Now?. 242

Appendix A CD Recorder Manufacturers — 243

Appendix B What Are MP3s? — 245

Appendix C Web Resources for CD Recording — 249

Glossary 251

Index 265

Introduction

When you truly enjoy an activity, it is easy to forget that others may not share your interest. For instance, although millions of folks enjoy basketball, we can think of many reasons that we don't play basketball. First, we don't watch basketball on TV. We don't watch the pickup games in the park. We really don't understand at all the Final Four, whatever that is.

And even if we tried, we don't understand the rules. We are afraid we would not be very good. We would likely get all hot and sweaty, and we don't like to do that. We could get hurt, and we have had enough physical pain while writing this book to last us awhile. (Nothing serious—a knee for Bob and a shoulder for Josh. Josh even threw away his sling in a valiant effort to push forward and bring you the finest audio restoration advice available. Three hours after knee surgery, Bob was laying in his bed with his laptop, furiously writing Chapter 2, telling you where to find music to record.)

If you are reading this, then we suspect that you care about recording your own audio CDs. (You may even care about basketball, and we hope we didn't offend you with our aversion to it.) We truly enjoy making our own CDs, but maybe you have never done it and have never seen someone else do it. Or maybe you have seen it done but didn't understand how it worked. Or maybe the whole idea of creating your own discs is frightening.

In this book, we will try to help you understand the rules of audio CD recording so you will not be afraid to dive right into it. We guarantee that you won't get hot and sweaty and that you will not get physically injured. With a little practice, you'll get good at recording your own CDs and will easily impress your friends and family with your computing prowess, even if you have none on the basketball court.

We'll walk you through the whole process of recording your own audio CDs, from picking out and setting up the recording equipment, to finding and using audio recording and restoration tools, to burning a perfect CD.

If you've been putting off getting a CD recorder or are hesitant to record audio CDs with a recorder you already have—like we hesitate to step onto the court—worry no more. A little knowledge about the rules and a pioneering spirit are all you need, other than a CD recorder and blank media. You can create your own compilation CDs with whatever source of music you have, whether its another CD, a tape, an LP, or an MP3 file. In this book we hope to show you how with clear explanations and concrete examples.

Bob Starrett
Josh McDaniel

Compact Discs and Recording

We've all been through this: You hear a cool song on the radio, and in imagining that the bounty of creativity in that song will surely spill over into other tracks by the band, you shell out $14.99 for the CD that contains it. Unfortunately, that one song is the only good song on the disc. Your CD collection probably includes more of these one-hit wonders that you'd like to admit—ours certainly do. Not all discs have only one cool song, many have several, but only a rare few CDs are good through and through.

If your CD player holds only a single CD, you have to do a lot of disc swapping to get a continuous musical experience. If you have, say, a five- or six-disc changer, then you can program it to play the best selections from several discs, but when you swap out the discs, you have to program the changer all over again. If you're lucky enough to have a 100- or 200- or even a 300-disc changer, you may never have to swap discs, but you still must program playlists, and it's anyone's guess which will run out first—the number of playlists you're allowed or your patience with the programming. It's a hassle, and a needless one at that. Listening to CDs is supposed to be fun, right?

CD recorders to the rescue! With a CD recorder, you can extract the tracks you want to your computer's hard drive and easily proceed from there to cue them up in a CD recording program—in absolutely any play order you like—and then burn your own CD. You can label the CD with a nice black-and-white or color label and even make inserts for the jewel case. For about a buck, you can make your own "Greatest Hits" compact disc. And, because you made it for yourself, it's quality-assured—in fact, in that sense, it's better than anything any record company could produce.

What about software?

Traditionally, CD recording programs for Windows were built for recording data—audio was usually only there as an afterthought, mainly because it was easy enough to implement, since CD-ROM is based on the CD Audio format. Today, most companies with programs that were originally designed for data recording have enhanced and simplified their software's audio recording functionality and, in many cases, highlighted it (see **Figure 1.1**).

At one time, Mac users had many choices for recording data and audio. But as the Mac's popularity flagged toward the end of the '90s, most of these tools disappeared. Today Mac users have just a couple of choices: Adaptec's Toast (see **Figure 1.2**) and Charismac's Discribe (see **Figure 1.3**). But with all the new users coming to Apple because of the iMac, look for more Mac programs to appear.

For Linux users, the road to recording is a little more difficult, but the tools—although less well known than their Mac and Windows counterpart—are now available in increasing numbers (see **Figure 1.4**). Many of the Linux tools are merely graphical front ends placed over a core command line recording program.

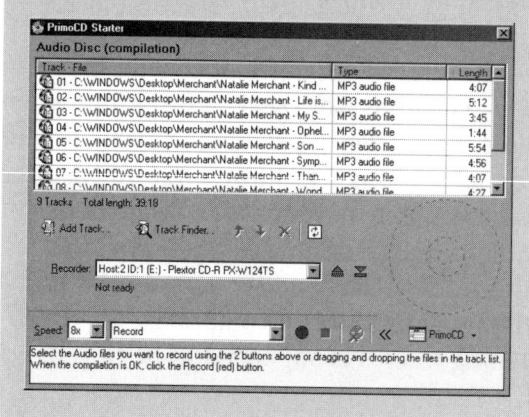

Figure 1.1

Figure 1.2

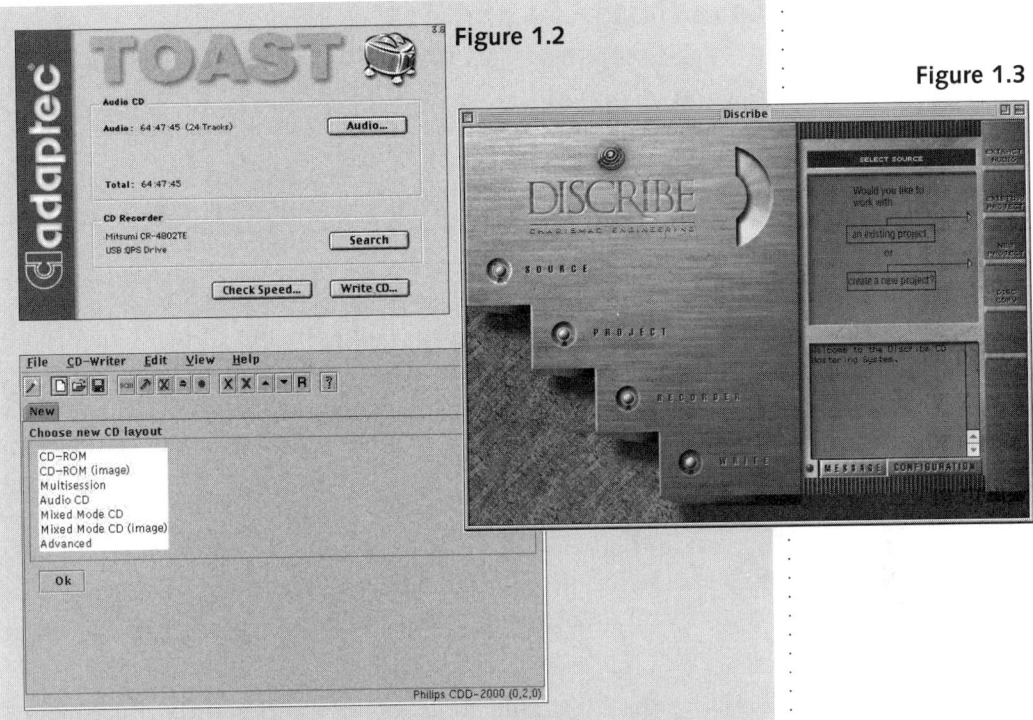

Figure 1.3

Figure 1.4

Computer not required

Even if you don't have a computer you can still make compilation CDs with one of the new low-cost home recorders. A home recorder is a CD recorder that looks like the CD audio player in your home stereo system but plays and records CDs, in much the same way computer software and a CD-R drive do (see **Figure 1.5**). The recorder's speed is limited to 1x or 2x, and the media costs a little more than the standard-issue CD-R media you'd use in a CD recorder, thanks to a percentage-of-sale-price tariff imposed by the recording industry to provide for royalty distribution. (Since regular CD-R media is multipurpose, it's not really fair to apply this surcharge, which only pertains to duping copyrighted music.)

Once you have produced your masterpiece compilations, you can play them in any standard audio CD player, in any CD-ROM or DVD-ROM drive, and even on some DVD players. (We will have more on that and some of its implications later.)

Figure 1.5

Save those LPs and 45s

For many of us, an even better use of a CD recorder than editing and reconfiguring our CD collections is the ability to copy and preserve our LPs, 45s, and tapes on indelible CD-R. A lot of that old vinyl and tape is either irreplaceable or would be exorbitantly expensive to replace with store-bought CDs. Moreover, moving your vinyl and tapes to CD gives you a chance to preserve a delicate piece of the past.

And if you are looking to replace an out-of-print recording, remember that all that old vinyl and tape does not always end up at the used record store selling for five times what the proprietor paid for it. Garage sales and flea markets are pregnant with some precious pieces of vinyl (and you can sometimes find collector's items for cheap). Even if your find is dented and scratched, ruined beyond audibility even, today's software will not only help you salvage it but also bring it up to your listening expectations—including correcting that hopeless skip.

Audio restoration tools are available from many software manufacturers; some are even built for restoring record albums (see **Figure 1.6**). You will see them as freeware, shareware, and retail products, and most of them can turn a poor album or tape into a solid source file for recording to CD. We'll cover these products in Chapter 7, "Highway 61 Restored," and Chapter 8, "Restoring and Recording Cassette Tapes."

Figure 1.6 Audio restoration tools can turn poor quality source materials into pretty good quality files for recording to CD.

Equipment on the cheap

If you have old vinyl and need a turntable, check out garage sales. Although you can still buy turntables new, from the basic to the professional model, you may find a top-quality (and many times barely used) table at a garage sale for a song. Another way to scheme a turntable if you don't have one or gave yours away—shame on you!—is to check with family and friends. You may find a nice old turntable just sitting in a friend's or relative's basement or garage, collecting dust and free for the asking.

As far as tape decks go, if you have reel-to-reel tapes, you probably still have a reel-to-reel tape recorder, and this will work just fine for transferring those tapes to your hard drive for later recording to CD. If you have cassette tapes, you may have an old cassette player around, but make sure that it is in top shape for transferring your tapes to hard disk. If you don't, you can buy a new one for just a few bucks.

From vinyl, tape, or disc

Making copies or compilations from vinyl or tape is more time consuming than making copies or compilations from CD and requires some patience, but the results are certainly worth the effort. We cover such issues as track splitting and editing and audio restoration in Chapter 7 and Chapter 8. Making compilation discs from CDs, on the other hand, is usually straightforward; the content is digital, so the transfer is digital. No quality loss or interference will creep into the process, except in certain cases—we'll look at those specific instances in Chapter 6, "Recording and Troubleshooting."

Audio origins

The audio compact disc was first released as a product by Philips and Sony in 1982 and has been called the most successful consumer electronics product in history. Obviously, many years of development were involved, and if you know the details of how these CDs actually work, you will quickly realize why. It's a bizarre affair if you think about it, this laser shining on a piece of spinning polycarbonate, reflecting light off of microscopic bumps, and turning the results—that is, the diffusion of the light from the surface of the disc—into clear, crisp music. Of course, the whole crazy scheme was preceded by many other developments, mechanical, theoretical, electrical, and optical.

Subsequent developments, such as the transistor, lasers, and improvements in manufacturing processes, allowed Sony and Philips to begin development of the compact disc in 1979. Both original prototypes—Sony's and Philips's—were large-diameter discs. The final size of the disc came in at 120 millimeters, and the disc held 74 minutes of digital music. You will often hear the story that the compact disc ended up holding 74 minute of music because the wife of Sony's chairman, Akio Morita, insisted that it be long enough to hold Beethoven's Ninth Symphony, her favorite piece. And that is all that it is, a story. To see why the compact disc is the physical size that it is, take a CD and lay a cassette tape on top of it. Do you still believe the Ninth Symphony story? The key here is compact. The cassette tape had been a great success because of its size. The marketing people at Philips wanted to continue that success with the compact disc.

Analog and Digital

Tapes and records produce analog music. CDs produce digital music. There are a couple of exceptions, most notably digital audio tape (DAT) and the digital compact cassette (DCC). DAT is still employed in many recording studios, but its widest use is as backup tape for computer applications. DCC was almost a total failure in the marketplace, and these devices, championed by Philips, are not even manufactured anymore.

We'll explain the difference between analog and digital sound in Chapter 2, "Sources of Digital and Digitizable Audio," but for the moment, the best way to differentiate between digital and analog music is to remember that analog music is the transmission of the audio signal itself and digital music is the transmission of the audio signal using numbers.

Issues in Audio Recording

Since this is the first chapter, we should also touch on issues that arise in CD recording and in audio CD recording. (We'll cover each of these in more detail later in the book.) The three most commonly asked questions you will see on the newsgroups dedicated to CD recording are:

- "What recorder should I buy?"
- "What media brand is best?" and finally,
- "What color media is the best?"

An ongoing and unresolved debate rages around these questions, but for the first time, here, in this book, we'll present the definitive—if not quite satisfying—answer.

First, however, let's quickly outline the issues.

What recorder?

Taken in turn, the primary query on the newsgroups and among friends and enemies and brand loyalists is, "What recorder should I buy?" Being that we're craven cowards, here is our answer: It depends.

Sony, Philips, TEAC, Mitsumi, Yamaha, Ricoh, JVC, LG Electronics, Samsung, Sanyo, and Plextor all manufacture recorders. The first question to ask yourself for each is, has Company X ever made a bad product? The answer for each is yes: every multinational corporation issues a cruddy product from time to time. The next question to ask is, does Company X generally make good products? The answer is yes again. Every company that's survived in this competitive industry has done so by generally issuing good products. What are the differences between the products that these companies make? Well, some make generally higher-priced products and some generally make lower-priced products. Some are priced in the middle. Does price equal quality? Does price equal features? Many times it does not. As with any complex product, price is only one factor in a well-informed purchase.

Now, we just named the handful of companies that *manufacture* CD recorders. But if you've studied the retail shelves for recorders, you've probably encountered a host of other names. You may ask, what about Smart and Friendly? What about Hi-Val? What about Mitsubishi? What about AOpen? What about the dozens of companies that sell CD recorders? The operative word is *sell*. CD recorders are a hot commodity. Everybody wants to be in on the action, to gain some brand-name recognition and be known as a top supplier. To the best of our knowledge, other than devices from the manufacturers we just named—the Big Eleven as we'll call them—every CD recorder sold is not manufactured by the company whose name is on the box.

But make no mistake, it is manufactured by one of the Big Eleven. For example, Hewlett-Packard used to sell recorders manufactured by Philips. Now, Hewlett-Packard sells Sony recorders—many, many more, in fact, than Sony itself. Mitsubishi recorders were at one point manufactured by Ricoh. Hi-Val recorders come from whatever source can supply the company's needs at the right price. This means that the mechanism that Hi-Val ships this month may not be the one that it ships next month. And this applies to many other resellers.

Here's a good example of why it's sometimes hard to tell the origin of a recorder. We were at a computer store, hanging around the CD recorders section as we often do, to see who is selling what and at what price. A couple of guys were holding a generic-looking box, no colors, no flashy artwork, no wondrous claims—it was some final remnant of a sale or promotion. The others had apparently moved quickly. One guy asked us if we were looking for the drive on special, indicating that he had the last one in his hands. The price? $169. That was quite a deal at the time. But there was hesitation. He had also been looking at a Ricoh recorder, in a flashy box with all kinds of award seals pasted on it. The price? $399. It seems he was about to hand over the last of the sale drives to us and pay the extra $230 to get the Ricoh name, surely feeling more comfortable buying a name-brand product with a well-established company behind it. We looked at the box, and, sure enough, the generically packaged recorder was—dig this—a Ricoh! Not just any Ricoh, mind you, but exactly the same model as the expensive Ricoh-branded recorder. We told him to compare the pictures and finally convinced him that he was getting a great buy. The buyer and his friend walked away happy, feeling good about saving $230.

Now, the generic package and the Ricoh-branded one had a few differences, such as the level of technical support and the versatility and power of the included software, but not enough, in our minds, to justify the price difference. This story will become increasingly important as you read through Chapter 4, "CD-Recordable and CD-Rewritable Drives," where we will discuss recorder buying tips, how to choose one that fits your needs, and how to save a lot of money when you do buy a recorder.

What media? What color?

The second big question is, "What blank media should I use?" Theoretically, all brands of blank CDs should work in all brands of drives. For the most part they do, although you may find some incompatibilities now and then. Simply put, CD-R media is a polycarbonate disc, coated with dye and a reflective metal on one side. Polycarbonate is the base material of a blank disc, as it is in a pressed or stamped disc. Now, different manufacturers may use different dye formulations and different metal reflective layers, usually gold or silver. The dyes are of three categories, generally: cyanine, pthalocyanine, and metal azo. Each of these has variations, but those are the three basic categories. The combination of the dye type and the reflective layer type gives CD blanks their distinctive color. Some are blue, some are green, and some are gold, and there are many different shades of each. And some recorders will seem to work better with some brands or colors of disc.

But our answer to the question of what media to use is simple: Use what works. Our answer to what color dye is best is this: None is best. (Don't worry: We'll discuss CD-Recordable and Rewritable media in more detail later.)

Recorded History

A little history on recordable CD might put things in perspective.

A dozen years ago, you had to be Howard Hughes to afford the equipment needed to record your own audio CDs. A Yamaha PDS 101—a rack-mounted two-piece unit produced in 1988 and used for professional audio recording—cost about $50,000. But interestingly, it was not audio recording that brought us to the present point in time, the age of $150 CD recorders and media for less than a buck a pop.

The interest in CD recording was pushed by the need to record data CDs, or CD-ROMs. With a new disc from America Online arriving daily in your mailbox, it's easy to forget that that disc—delivered free, as a promotion, at a cost to AOL of less than 75 cents—cost significantly more than that ten years ago. The practice at the time for making CD-ROMs was to deliver what is called an image (the source data to be reproduced on disc) to a mastering company on nine-track tape. The mastering house would then make as few as 100 or more than 100,000 discs for you. If your CD-ROM data was complete and working, then this was a viable option, even if each disc cost $5 or so, plus a $2,000 or $3,000 mastering fee.

If you needed to test your CD-ROM before replicating it, you had to place a minimum order of 100 discs and pay the mastering fee in addition to the cost of the discs. Then you tossed out ninety-nine discs and tested the remaining one, unless you had a lot of testers, in which case you only threw away ninety discs. If something was wrong, of course, you had to fix it and go through the process again, paying thousands of dollars each time around. This could get expensive, and it explains why a few dozen companies were willing to pay upward of $100,000 for a machine that would record single CD-ROMs for testing.

In the late 1980s, a CD recorder wasn't a half-height device that fit into a computer's drive bay or attached to a printer port. A full recording system—consisting of a computer (an 8-MHz IBM 286 with 640K of RAM), a hard-disk subsystem, and a recorder fitted with a special encoding board—weighed 600 pounds, and the first of these behemoths sold for $150,000. Sony released a two-piece desktop unit for the bargain price of $30,000 in 1991. Shortly thereafter, Philips introduced a desktop recorder for $12,000 and Sony countered with a one-piece unit for $10,000. JVC made the first half-height recorder in 1992 at a cost of $11,000 or so, including a hard-disk subsystem. Most of these were 1x recorders that wrote discs in real-time—that is, 74 minutes for a full, 74-minute, 650-MB CD. Yamaha really got the half-height and speed trend going with its $5,000 CD-R100 4x-speed recorder in 1994. Kodak was the leader in the speed race back then, producing a 6x recorder as early as 1993. But at $28,000, the cost-to-speed ratio was a little steep. Finally, Hewlett-Packard broke the $1,000 price barrier in 1995 with its SureStore 4020i (manufactured by Philips), and prices have been dropping ever since.

Advances in that last few years have included the introduction of erasable CD, known as CD-RW or Rewritable, and the ability to record at speeds as fast as 12 times (12x) that of the first recorders. *X!* That magic letter…

X confusion

You'll see recorders advertised in what seems at first to be a confusing string of Xs. And you'll see terms such as 4x2x24 and 6x4x32.

CD recording, in the beginning, was done in real time, that is, at 1x. At that time, CD-ROM drives read data at 150 kilobytes per second, and that was the speed you recorded CDs at too. CD drives have a variable rotational speed, from 200 rpm at the beginning of the disc to 530 rpm at the outer edge of the disc. When the CD is playing and recording, the first song starts at the inside of the disc and subsequent songs follow toward the outside of the disc. This is the X factor. A drive that spins at 400 to 1,060 rpm is a 2x drive. The same holds true for recording. Recording at 2x, of course, means that a full disc can be recorded in 38 minutes instead of 76 minutes. Recorder speeds have increased to 12x, meaning the drive records 12 times faster than the first recorder's speed; CD-R write speeds for drives you'll see today are typically 4x, 8x, 10x, or 12x.

The numbers in advertisements and drive specifications reflect these speeds. So, in a formula such as 4x2x24, the first number is the recording speed for CD recordable (CD-R) media. The second number is the recording speed for CD-RW media, which is usually 2x or 4x but is getting faster, too. The third is the maximum reading speed for any CD disc, except an audio disc. Audio discs are never played at more than 1x, unless you want Bruce Springsteen to sound like Alvin and the Chipmunks.

Why Use CD-R?

Adding to your computer the capability to record audio discs gives you other bonuses. Of course you can create CD-ROMs or make backups of your software discs, but you can also back up your hard disk to a CD-R or CD-RW disc.

A CD drive is now the third most popular computer storage peripheral in the world, behind, of course, the floppy-disk drive and the hard drive. Many other storage peripherals have taken a run at becoming universally used and available, but none has had the success of CD-ROM and CD-R and CD-RW devices. For example, Iomega's Zip drives had a good chance of becoming a standard storage format, but the Zip's capacity was soon outstripped by user needs. Even Iomega has joined in: Its latest product is a CD recorder called ZipCD. Magneto-optical (MO) drives also had a good chance to become a universal storage medium, but continuing high prices and a lack of standards precluded their success. Even promising new technologies such as DVD-RAM have struggled, despite their large capacity of 2.6 to 4.7 gigabytes per side. DVD-R—that is, recordable DVD—is still too expensive for the average user.

Two hundred songs on a disc?

Continuing developments in the MP3 industry make your recorder useful for a whole new audio purpose. MP3 (short for MPEG 1, Layer 3; MPEG itself is short for Moving Picture Experts Group) is a compressed format you are probably familiar with. The compression ratio, depending on the recording bitrate, or amount of compression, is about 10 or 12 to 1, which means the size of an audio file can be reduced as much as twelve times via a coded compression algorithm that eliminates redundant information and data that represents inaudible sound.

Some manufacturers are introducing stereo-component CD players that will play MP3 files through your stereo from a CD drive connected to a special decoder board. Most of these are smaller companies, but you can expect to soon see this capability in CD players from the major electronic manufacturers (see **Figure 1.7**). Since you can get 100 to 200 MP3 songs on one CD in the CD-ROM format, you can really compress your music collection down to just a few discs. Or if you just want to have your collection available to play on your computer, this is a great way to do it with a minimum of trouble. We'll talk more about MP3 compression in Chapter 10, "Recording MP3s to CD." And in that chapter we'll also look at Microsoft WMA (Windows Media Audio), audio compression and decompression, and other compressed audio formats.

Figure 1.7 The Brujo MP3 player was one of the early players that used a CD-ROM drive to play MP3 files directly from a data CD-ROM.

So Sue Me

Several of the things that you do when you make your own CDs—such as copying audio CDs, extracting tracks from disc to hard drive (which is also called ripping), and compressing CD tracks into MP3s—bring up what's legally permissible and what is not under the copyright laws of the United States. The issues are complex, constantly changing, and will ultimately be resolved by the Supreme Court. In Chapter 14, "Legal Issues: A Quick Overview," we will introduce you to some of the legal issues, but that chapter and this book are not meant to give you any legal advice.

> **Compakt disc**
>
> Throughout this book, when we refer to CDs, we spell *disc* with a *c* and when we refer to magnetic media, or hard disks, we spell *disk* with a *k*. You'll see arguments over this all the time. Publications that should know better—such as *PC Magazine, the New York Times,* and *the Wall Street Journal*—continue to spell *compact disc* as *compact disk* simply because their stylebooks tell them to, and everyone knows, the stylebook is always, absolutely, monolithically, and undeniably correct, bow before its majesty!
>
> As usual, you're best off trusting the tale, not the teller. So don't take our word for it either. Simply consult your own music collection for the proper spelling: Every CD-ROM drive and every CD recorder ever made and every disc that carries the logo clearly says *Compact Disc.* So CDs are compact discs, not compact disks, despite what *PC Magazine* and *the New York Times* seem to think.

Sources of Digital and Digitizable Audio

We know we can record audio to CDs, but where do we get the music? The most popular way is to make audio CDs from our own CD, LP, or tape collection. Non-long-playing records—45s and 78s—provide good source material as well. Many of these recordings may be out of print and hard to find and perhaps will never be available again.

From your collection, you can pick and choose favorite songs or gather tunes of a common theme or genre. When an artist or group records an album, they does it as they like it, we suppose, although it's just as likely that pressures exerted by a record company or contract dictate some recorded content. In any event, whoever chose the songs or sequence, it wasn't you, and odds are that only a portion of what's on it appeals to you. Or if the album is appealing to you as a whole, perhaps the order of the songs is not; that can be changed easily enough, in just a few minutes.

Another source of music, or even spoken-word material, is your own creations, if you are a musician or poet. (Maybe you are neither and would just like to scream into a microphone and then listen to yourself.) But if you are like most people, the music made by others, in many varieties, is likely what you will want to use as source material for the audio CDs you make.

First Things First

The first step in making your own CD is, of course, deciding what to put on it. That is completely up to you, and that's the best part of audio CD recording. So the first step is to think about what you want to make, what songs you want to put on your disc. Once you have gathered the materials together—the CDs, that is—you have what we call source materials. These are the CDs that you are going to put into your CD-ROM or CD-R drive so that you can extract, or rip, the songs to your hard disk. Although you can make compilation CDs directly from the source discs to your recordable disc, or destination, doing it that way can create problems. We cover that in Chapter 9, "Copying CDs."

If you are into preservation, you will find all you need to know in Chapter 7, "Highway 61 Restored," and in Chapter 8, "Restoring and Recording Cassette Tapes," which cover recording and restoring vinyl and tape, respectively.

If using your own music collection is the most common way to make a CD, the most controversial source of music is MP3 files on the Internet. Many applications will play MP3 files for you, including Winamp (see **Figure 2.1**).

Figure 2.1 Winamp is the most popular MP3 player. Unlike some others, though, it does not allow you to record MP3s to CD.

MP3 stands for MPEG-1, Layer 3, and is a standardized compressed audio format. The algorithm used in compressing the audio was codified by the Moving Picture Experts Group (MPEG), an organization that also sets video compression standards, including that used in DVD (MPEG-2 Video). The MP3 compression algorithm can compress WAV files at a ratio or 10 or 12 to 1 with hardly any loss in quality. At roughly 10 MB per minute of CD-quality music, WAV files are way too hefty to distribute via the Web with any kind of reliability, speed, or efficiency. However, because of the small size of WAVs compressed into MP3 format, MP3s are a natural file format for downloading music from the Internet.

You'll see other compressed audio formats, such as Microsoft's WMA (Windows Media Audio; see **Figure 2.2**), which is becoming pretty popular now, and Yamaha's VQ (see **Figure 2.3**). And you'll also see RealAudio files, which have RMA and RAM extensions (see **Figures 2.4** and **2.5**). The Liquid Audio format is popular because you can put various protections into it (see **Figure 2.6**). AT&T had a compressed and secure format, too, called a2b music (see **Figure 2.7**). Finally, you'll see WAV files on the Internet, but these are so large that they are hardly worth downloading. WAVs are for recording to CD, not downloading. For our purposes, the only WAV files you will work with will come from your hard drive, whether converted MP3s or files extracted from CD tracks.

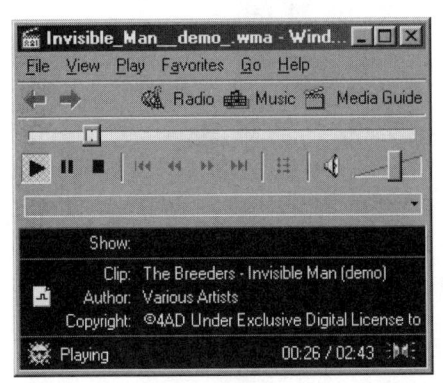

Figure 2.2 The Windows Media Player is rather plain in appearance compared to most other players.

Figure 2.3 Though not often seen, the Yamaha VQ format makes small and great-sounding files. But proprietary formats never go far, whatever their merits.

THE LITTLE AUDIO CD BOOK

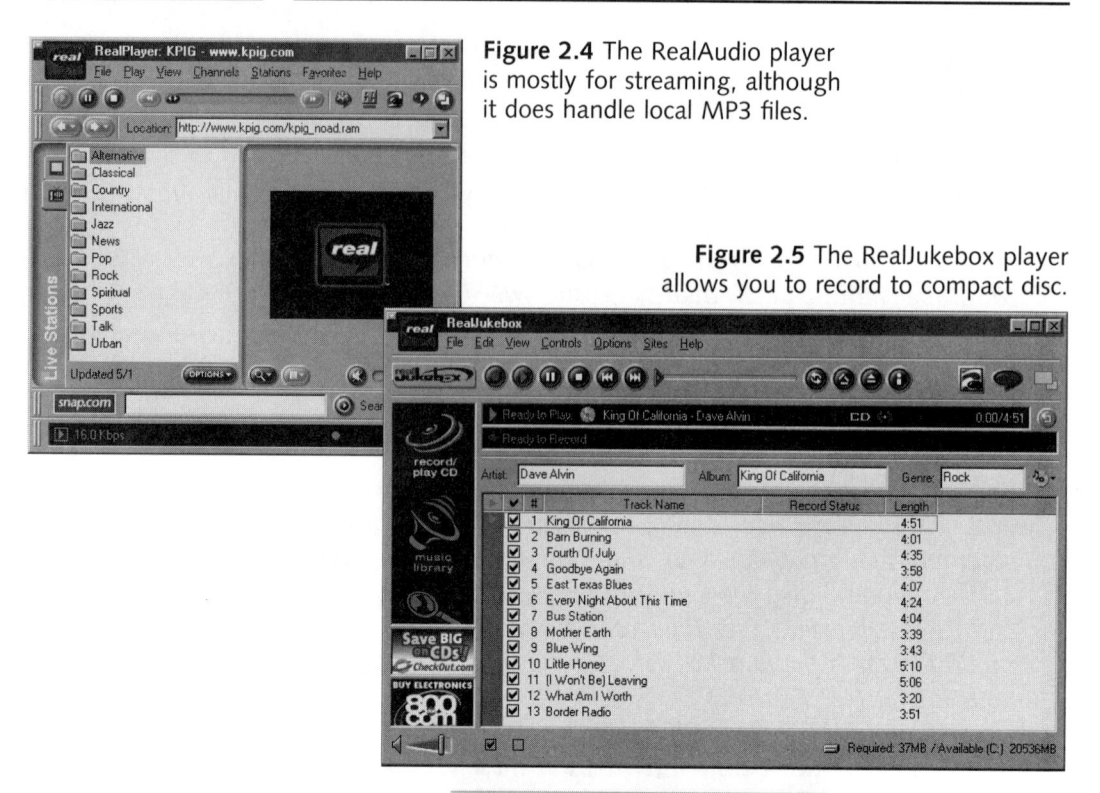

Figure 2.4 The RealAudio player is mostly for streaming, although it does handle local MP3 files.

Figure 2.5 The RealJukebox player allows you to record to compact disc.

Figure 2.6 The Liquid Audio Player makes it easy to download a song. Simply press the Download button on the player.

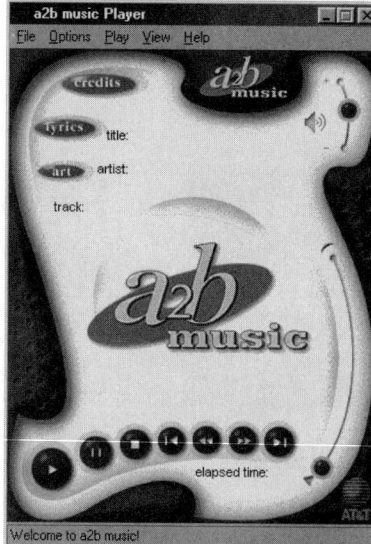

Figure 2.7 The a2b player will play the secure a2b file format. Its other claim to fame is the ugliest interface of any player we have seen. Reminds us of Elvis, somehow. It must be the pink.

18

Getting music

Since the point here is to make your own custom CDs, luckily, there are sites that offer free downloads of MP3 and WMA and Liquid Audio files that you can later cut to disc. Sites such as Listen.com, ArtistDirect.com, Launch.com, GetMusic.com, Rioport.com, CDNow.com, and Emusic.com also allow you to purchase and download single tracks, usually for about 99 cents each. Chances are that you will find artists you like in these venues since not all good music-makers are under contract to the big record companies and many well-known artists allow some of their music to be downloaded for free or track-by-track at a small cost. You'll also find stuff from independent record companies (indies) with enough sense to realize that the future of music distribution is on the Internet.

We'll look at just a handful of the most popular sites here, because there are so many of them around. For more music download sites, poke around the Internet a little; you will find a lot of them.

> *A good way to get started is to look at the site of the player you are using to play files. Most of these sites have music or links to music in their format. It is best to stick with the MP3 format, if you can, to save yourself the time of conversion. Most recording programs support MP3 files, a few support WMA, but very few support direct recording of any other compressed format to CD.*

Where Is the Good Music on the Internet?

Although you are unlikely to find legitimate music from the Top 40 charts available for download, either for free or for a fee, thousands of free or inexpensive legal tracks are available. You need to do a little snooping, though, to find them. Later in this chapter, we gather some sites that are likely to have some of the music you want.

FTPs: Don't waste your time

Before Napster and programs like it came along, the way to download MP3 files from the Internet was by FTP, or File Transfer Protocol. You could download an FTP program and look for servers hosting the songs you were seeking. Then, using the protocol, you simply, in theory, downloaded from the directory that you found out on some server somewhere. One of the troubles with FTP servers is that many are "ratio" servers. That means that you have to upload a song before you can download anything. You will see different ratios, such as five to one or six to one, which means that you can download five or six songs for every song that you upload. Don't get caught in this trap. Uploading a copyrighted song is a copyright infringement if you do it, and you are just contributing to the problem of unauthorized music on the Internet.

This activity was largely underground and unknown to most until portals began putting up their own MP3 search engines, so you didn't even need an FTP program to find or download the songs. Lycos caused some controversy when it was the first of the major portals to add this feature. Nice as it sounds, this type of download strategy is a waste of time. We won't even waste space on it here. Go over to www.lycos.com or www.altavista.com and try to download some MP3 files. You will quickly see what we mean.

Music on the edge

Much easier, but less likely to be legitimate, is to use file finders such as Napster, iMesh (see **Figure 2.8**), Scournet (see **Figure 2.9**), CuteMX (see **Figure 2.10**), and for the Mac, Macster (see **Figure 2.11**) to quickly and easily locate MP3 files on the Internet. Unlike the Web sites we mention later, which will only post authorized music files for download, Napster and its ilk will yield plentiful results, but you will have no way of knowing whether the poster of the files you find has the right to make them available to others for no charge. You can easily make assumptions, however, from looking at the results that you get. To be safe, stick with authorized sites for downloading licensed music.

Figure 2.8 iMesh is similar to Napster and is just as easy to use. Like Winamp, it has many skins available so you can tailor its looks.

2: Sources of Digital and Digitizable Audio

We know that you can use Napster and the other programs like it to download illegal copies of music over the Internet. But we also know that Napster has legitimate uses, such as being used to find and download music posted by its owners. So we won't ignore Napster at all. It is efficient and simple to use.

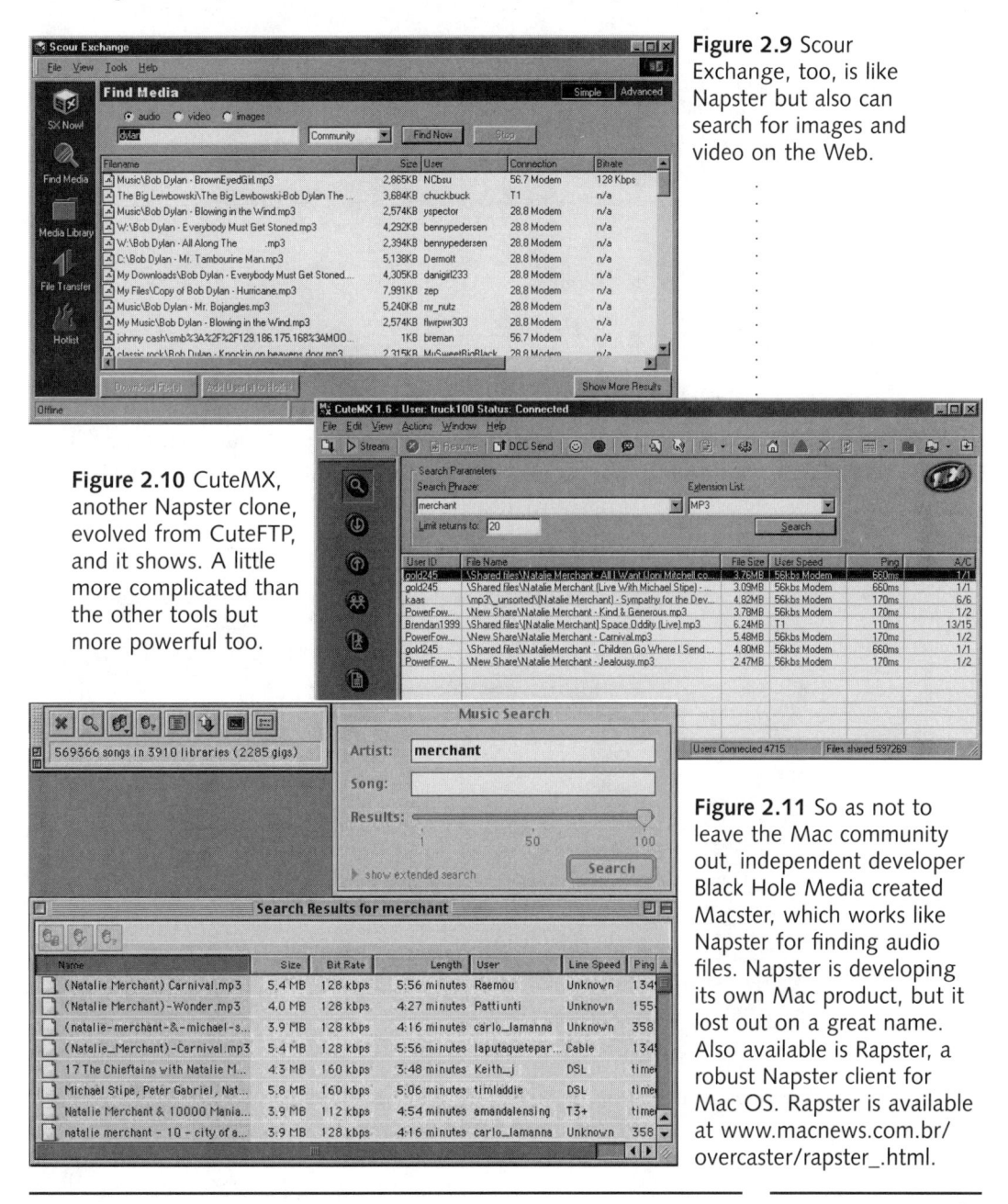

Figure 2.9 Scour Exchange, too, is like Napster but also can search for images and video on the Web.

Figure 2.10 CuteMX, another Napster clone, evolved from CuteFTP, and it shows. A little more complicated than the other tools but more powerful too.

Figure 2.11 So as not to leave the Mac community out, independent developer Black Hole Media created Macster, which works like Napster for finding audio files. Napster is developing its own Mac product, but it lost out on a great name. Also available is Rapster, a robust Napster client for Mac OS. Rapster is available at www.macnews.com.br/overcaster/rapster_.html.

Music Download Sites

As promised, here's our collection of Web sites where you can find music and related information.

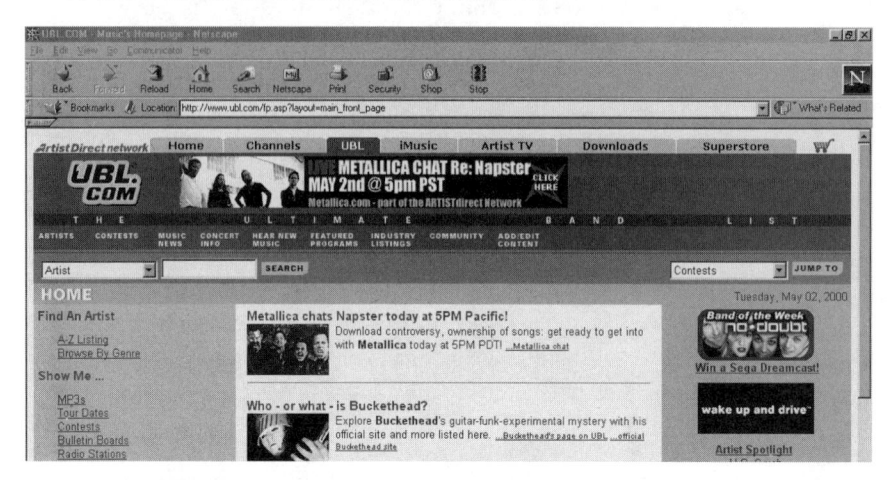

ArtistDirect.com *www.artistdirect.com*
The best part of Artistdirect.com is the Ultimate Band List. Lots of downloads here, plus the latest news. We can't wait to chat live with Lars and the boys. We just hope we're not on the band's Napster list.

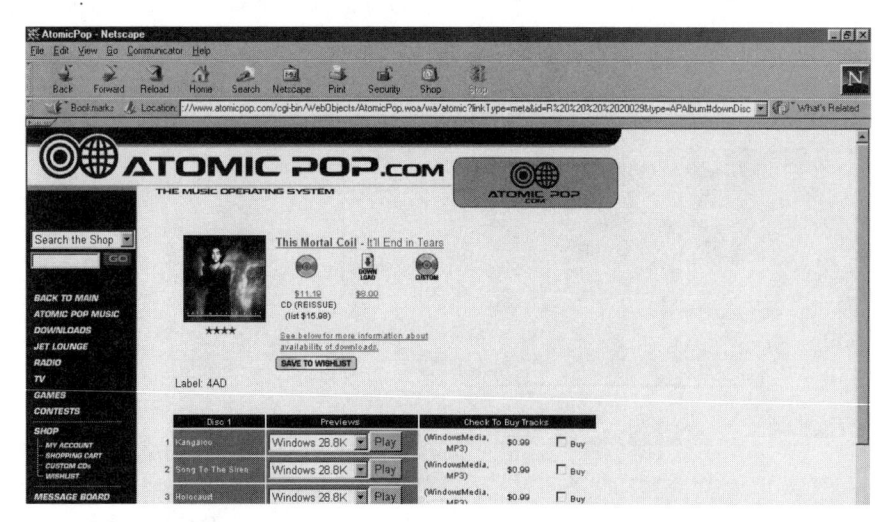

AtomicPop *www.atomicpop.com*
AtomicPop.com covers most of the bases, offering MP3, WMA, and Liquid Audio downloads.

CDNow.com *www.cdnow.com*

CDNow will sell you standard CDs, make custom CD compilations for you, or let you buy and download music to make your own. We have a problem, however, in understanding how selling a single track at $2.99 constitutes a sale or special offer. That's 30 bucks for enough downloads to make a ten-track disc. We'll go buy two discs retail for that.

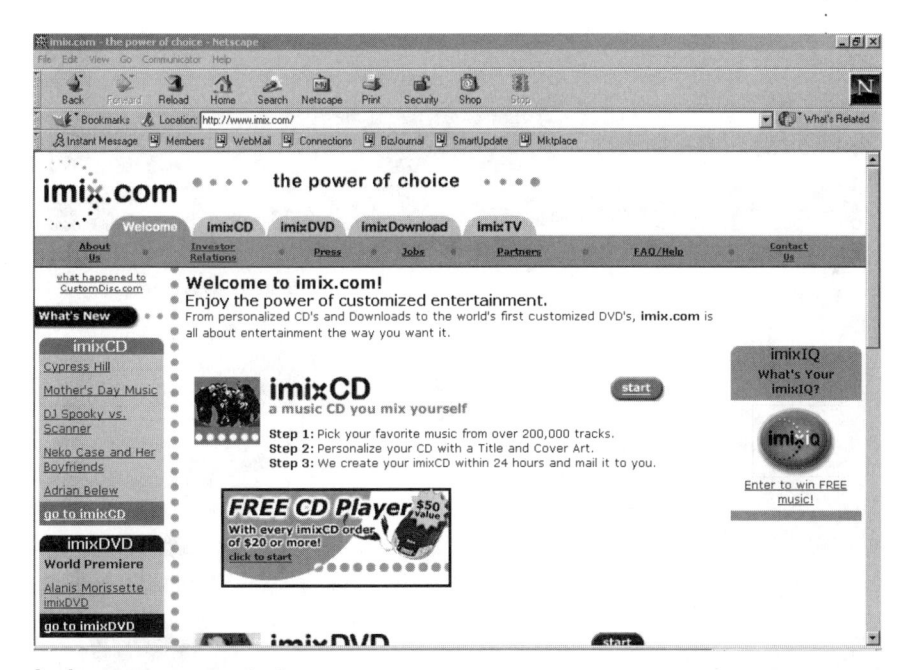

Imix.com *www.imix.com*

Imix started out making custom audio CDs for its customers but recently added downloadable Liquid Audio tracks to its site. It has a pretty good selection of free songs and a great (and growing) catalog of songs you can buy for 99 cents.

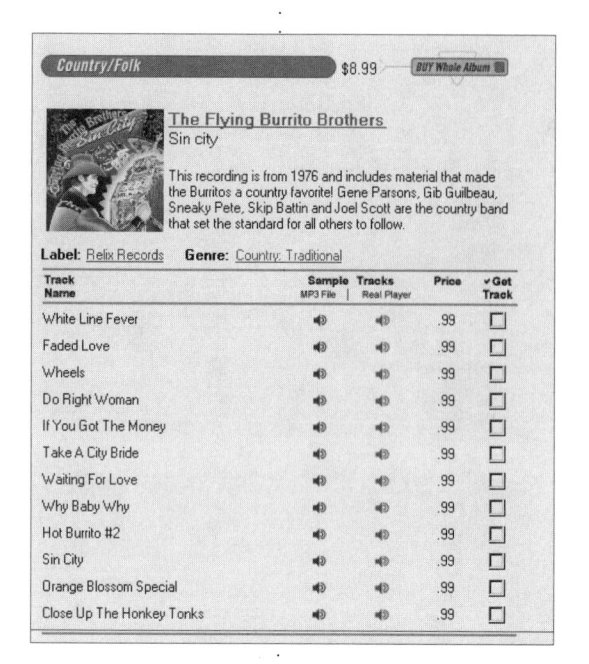

Emusic.com *www.emusic.com*

Emusic is one of the top online music destinations. It has licensed content from many record labels and sells it for a small fee, usually 99 cents to $1.49 per song.

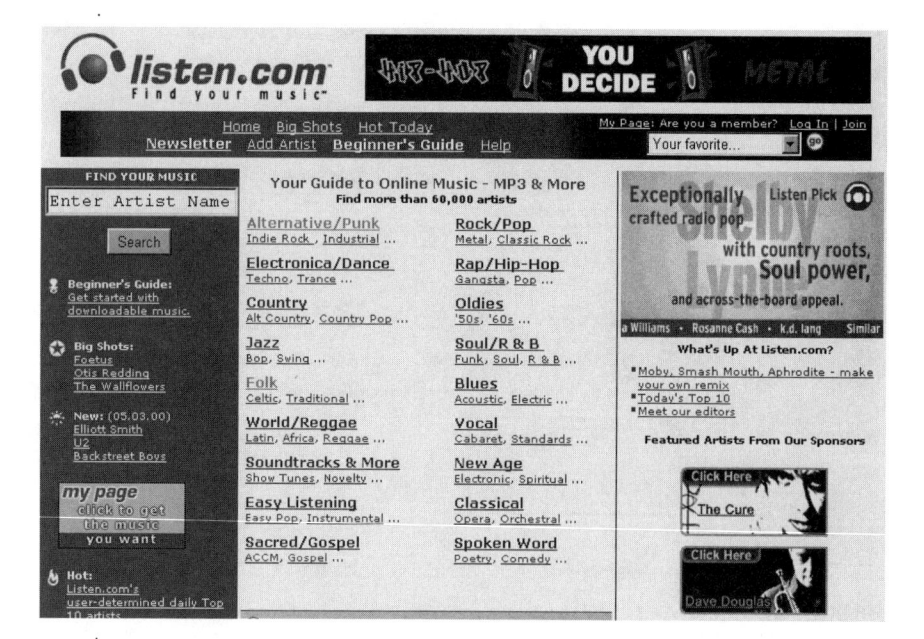

Listen.com *www.listen.com*

Listen.com is a good place to find tracks, both free ones and low-cost single downloads. Listen.com does not host its own songs but, rather, points to other sites that do.

MP3.com *www.mp3.com*

MP3.com is a great place to get music because all of it is free—unless, of course, you want the folks to make a disc for you. Still, that only costs six bucks, and it includes audio tracks, MP3 files, and a copy of Winamp. There is a lot of good music here... and a lot of bad. Any artist may post his or her songs to MP3.com, so with the wheat comes the chaff. You can listen to any song in lo-fi or hi-fi and then easily download the ones that you like for later recording to CD.

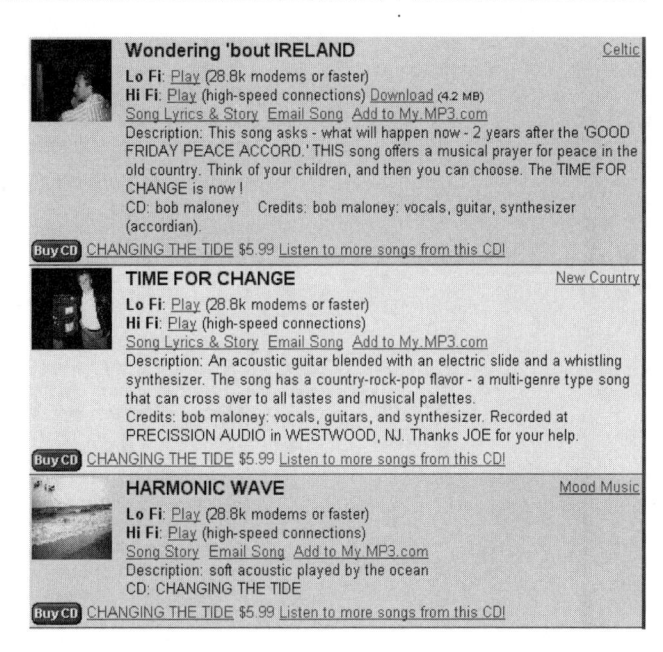

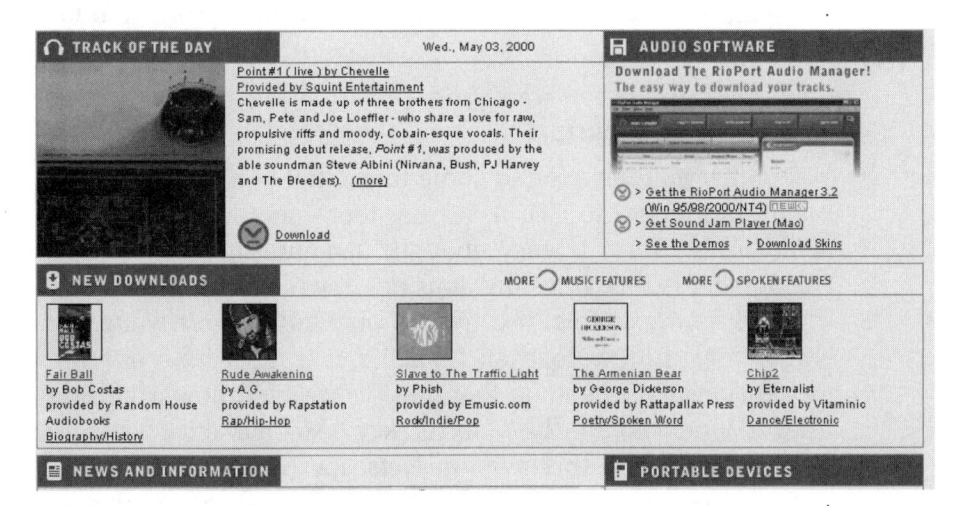

RioPort.com *www.rioport.com*

RioPort was started to support owners of the Diamond Rio portable MP3 player. It has evolved into an excellent destination for finding free and low-cost downloadable music.

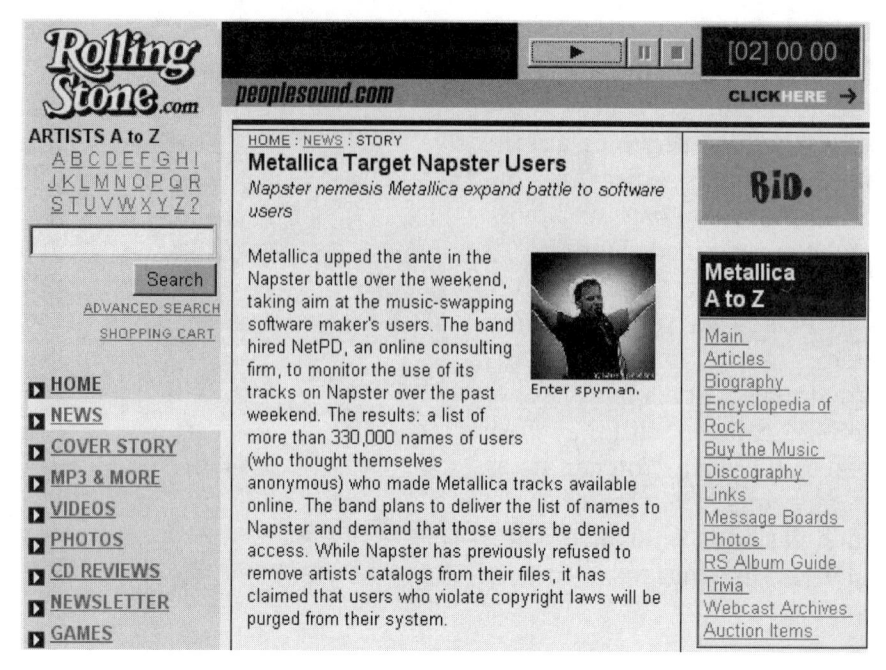

Rollingstone.com *www.rollingstone.com*
Rollingstone.com offers information on various artists and lots of free downloads.

Getting the Music

Now that you have found some tunes that you want to download and record to CD, acquiring them and converting them into usable form is easy enough, usually. The first thing to remember is this: If a song does not download when you click its link—for example, if it tries to play but doesn't, your software tries to download an html file or a file with a different extension than the song that you want—hold down the Shift key (Windows) or the Control key (Mac) and click again. Or you can do it this way: in Netscape Navigator right-click (Windows) or Control + click (Mac) and choose Save this Link as. Internet Explorer handles these files without any special machinations. Just click the song link, and IE will download it to your hard disk.

The bottom line is that there is a lot of legal free and low-cost music out there to be had. It takes a little poking around, but you are bound to find many new artists that you like and many of your favorites, too. Obviously, if you are going to be downloading a lot of music, a fast Internet connection is helpful but not necessary. You will be surprised to see that your 56-Kbps modem will download MP3 files pretty quickly, and you won't even notice if you are downloading in the background or away from your computer. Using one of the download programs, you can cue up what you want before bed and the songs will be waiting for you in the morning. Drag them into your recording program, and you'll have a CD in time to play it on the way to work.

> *For the most part, your computer, hard drive, sound card, and other peripherals you use are probably sufficient for audio recording from any source and to any recorder, unless your computer is very old and slow. We want to urge you to get a 56K modem if you don't already have one. Anything slower that that is just too painful to deal with when downloading music files. If DSL or cable modem is available in your area, you may find that it is cheaper than you think. It varies from location to location. But beware—once you use DSL, you will be hooked and you will never be able to stand a 56K modem again. Ever.*

What is SDMI?

In December, 1998 the RIAA launched SDMI, or Secure Digital Music Initiative. The purpose of this plan was for record companies and others to come together and design and choose a copy-protected or watermarked format for Internet music files, one that would disallow copying or be able to control what could be done with a downloaded song.

Audio Recording and Ripping Software

You have lots of choices for software for recording audio CDs, from the cheap hack to the professional package that costs hundreds of dollars. What is important to you in a CD recording package? The No. 1 consideration, in our opinion, is that the program has the features that you need and works well on your machine. Traditionally, CD recording software has notoriously misbehaved. Luckily, that's not so much the case today: Many great packages will do the job reliably and efficiently.

We always look to Sonic Spot for the most comprehensive and organized collection of audio tools, whether they be rippers, editors, encoders, or recorders, unless we are looking for just the traditional recording packages as we categorize them later in this chapter. In that case, www.cdpage.com is a better source for finding them. Visit Sonic Spot at www.sonicspot.com, and you'll also find reviews of many of the products we mention here.

The ability of the user's machine to keep up with the demands of the recording process has always been a problem. To get around these system limitations, many programs use proprietary drivers to try to keep the process stable but end up causing recording conflicts and problems. For one thing, the drivers themselves are often unstable. What's more, some programs have trouble coexisting with one another. So if you have three recording packages installed on your machine you might have some problems. For the safest recording experience, stick to one program each for ripping, editing, and recording. You may find a program that performs all three functions well, and if that is the case, and it works for you, stick with it. We are not discouraging you from experimenting with many programs, however, nor are we suggesting that you must necessarily limit the programs that you keep handy on your hard disk. Just keep in mind that the possibility of conflict is high, probably more than with any other type of software.

To circumvent any of these potential hang-ups, figure out exactly what you need to rip, edit, and record, and make your decision from there. To help you, we are going to look at the types of programs and categorize them as best we can.

Chances are that you got some recording software when you bought your recorder. Most recorders come with software for recording data and music, although many times it is a "lite" edition and does not have all the features that you might want. (Easy CD Creator is a good example of that—although the bundled version basically does the job, you have to upgrade to the "Deluxe" edition to get all the audio recording features.)

The good news here is that most of the other software you may need to acquire to round out your audio tool set is free or inexpensive. Of course, you can find high-end tools. But few of us need to make a major investment in software to get good-quality audio discs.

> **Traditional recording software**
>
> Much of the current audio recording software has been around for only a short time. Until recently, CD-Recordable was not all that popular for recording audio. Most of the original recording packages, which have been around for half a decade or longer, were initially written for those who wanted to write computer data to CD-R for software prototyping and business applications. These programs also usually included the functionality to write audio, just because it was fairly easy to implement.
>
> The implementations in the early days were usually pretty crude, however. The surviving packages, now well established and fairly reliable, have gained more audio features, and almost all of them can make good audio discs. They also are coming with new features such as built-in wave editing, track splitting, and automatic MP3 and WMF conversion. They still record data, of course, and in most cases can make some of the more exotic CD formats such as Enhanced CD, CD-Text, Video CD, and Bootable CD (El Torito). If you plan to record data as well as audio, these packages—Easy CD Creator, WinOnCD, Toast, Primo CD, Nero, and the others listed in this chapter—are the best bet for all-round CD recording.

Beware the BIOS, a Necessary Digression

The programs we're speaking of here we'll call traditional recording packages. (You might also see them referred to as premastering software, which hearkens back to the days when CD software was mainly used by CD-ROM publishers to make tapes with images of CD-ROMs on them to send to replication plants as sources for mastering and pressing.) These programs are usually a little more expensive than some of the excellent shareware available, but they make up for some of that with better-staffed support desks, good help files (available with the application and online), and excellent recorder support.

What's this about recorder support, you ask? Not all recording software supports all recorders. Sometimes the recorder is too old or too new; other times it's a recognition problem—

the software could work with the recorder, but it thinks it can't because it misidentifies it. As we discussed in Chapter 1, "Compact Discs and Recording," with a handful of recorder manufacturers and scores of resellers and distributors, you're likely to see what's basically the same recorder sold in many boxes and under many names.

But what if you don't like the software bundled with the recorder? You look elsewhere, maybe for something with more audio capabilities. But what happens when you fire up your new program and it says "no supported recorders found?" Well, this happens a lot and has to do with the value-added concept. When these recorder resellers and distributors go about putting their own faceplate and label on the outside of the same recorder, they also change some things inside the recorder. The thing they change that has the most impact on the user is the BIOS (Basic Input/Output System) ID string. You see, these resellers don't want you to buy and install their branded recorder and then, when your computer boots up and shows what devices are attached, have it say the original maker's name. That just wouldn't be good marketing.

It may seem odd that we're talking about the guts of a recorder while we are in the software chapter, and you're thinking you don't care about this BIOS stuff—you just want to record CDs. But you must care. Otherwise you might get frustrated and think this whole CD recording thing is a bust, which it isn't—but it could be if you don't pay attention to BIOS issues.

When recording software starts, it too looks at the recorder BIOS string to see if it works with that make and model of recorder. So a recording program can work with a recorder with the one BIOS string but not work with the same recorder with another BIOS string, even though they are the same recorder. Sounds silly, but it's true and it happens all the time.

So when buying recording software, make sure the software supports your recorder. If it doesn't, then you're in a bad way.

Back to the story

Now, back to traditional recording software. Usually, it's not great practice to list a bunch of software in a book if you want the book to continue to be current. That's because software comes and goes and names and versions change and companies get bought and sold. But the CD recording market is pretty stable, and if new companies or applications do come on the scene, you can just go to the book's Web site at www.peachpit.com/littleaudio/ and find the updates we'll have there. You can usually count on any of the stuff from our list of traditional CD recording software to be reliable and well supported—you really can't go wrong with any of these programs for data or audio recording. Some will have more audio-specific features than others, but all will record audio CDs from WAV files and many support MP3 and WMA files too.

Recording Software for Windows

In 1996 and 1997, Adaptec, a company best known for making SCSI cards that connect CD recorders, hard drives, and other devices, purchased two leading CD recording software tools, Corel's CD Creator and Incat's Easy CD Pro, and began a disturbing trend toward consolidation in the recording software business. (Which isn't necessarily to knock the excellent consolidated product that resulted, Easy CD Creator.) In 1999 Adaptec also acquired CeQuadrat, whose WinOnCD has been top of the pops in Europe, and that might suggest that the trend toward a no-competition, reduced-option market has continued. But the good news is, it's not so at all—you've still got a great range of choices, especially on the Windows side.

CDRWin, Golden Hawk Technology, *www.goldenhawk.com*
A great tool for the technically minded, CDRWin will perform many low-level operations such as subcode editing and inter-track indexing that many other programs cannot (see **Figure 3.1**). Definitely for the advanced user. It's popular in part because it can copy Sony Playstation discs, which many programs cannot.

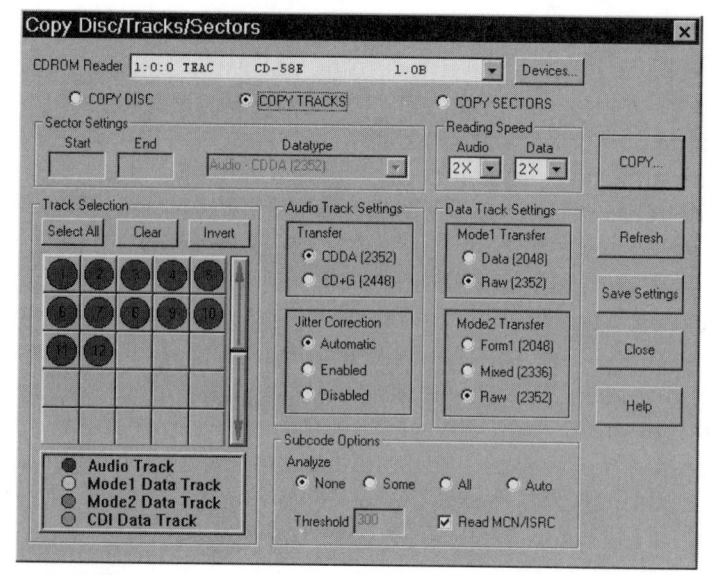

Figure 3.1 Along with Feurio, CDRWin is probably best for the advanced user.

DiscJuggler, Padus, *www.padus.com*
DiscJuggler handles audio well but is at its best in simultaneous copying and jukebox recording.

Easy CD Creator, Adaptec, *www.adaptec.com*
The most popular recording program, Easy CD Creator has lots of features and extras. CD Spin Doctor (see **Figure 3.2**), included in the deluxe version, is a great program for the beginner. It lets you record from analog as well as digital sources and offers track splitting and denoising.

Gear Pro, Command Software, *www.gearcdr.com*
Command Software has just upgraded Gear Pro to include new audio handling features, among other enhancements.

Hot Burn, Asimware Innovations, *www.asimware.com*
Hot Burn does on-the-fly resampling and byte ordering, removes pops and clicks, and allows for intertrack index marks.

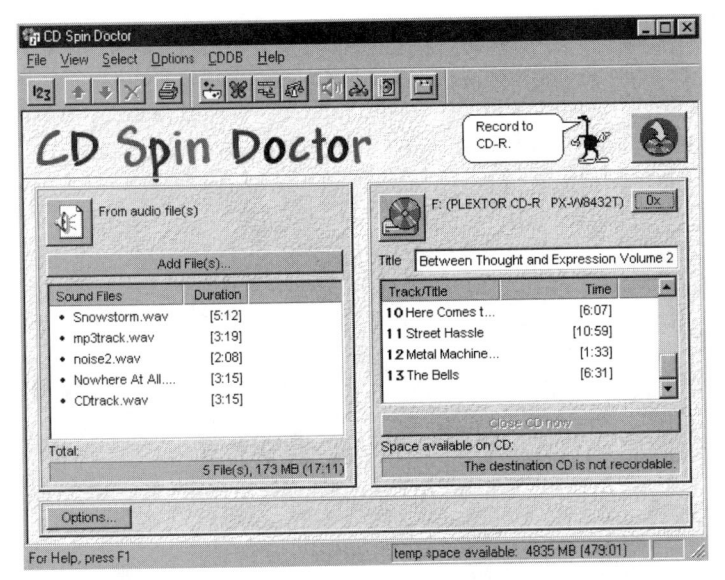

Figure 3.2 You are likely to get Easy CD Creator if you buy a recorder bundle. Unfortunately, the A/D-converting audio program Spin Doctor, shown here, only comes with the deluxe version, which is sold at a reduced price to registered users of the bundled version and is rarely found in CD recorder bundles.

Nero Burning ROM, Ahead Software, *www.ahead.de*

With excellent audio capability, Nero Burning ROM also will handle all CD data types. Powerful and complete, it is best for advanced users, although beginners can learn it quickly enough (see **Figure 3.3**).

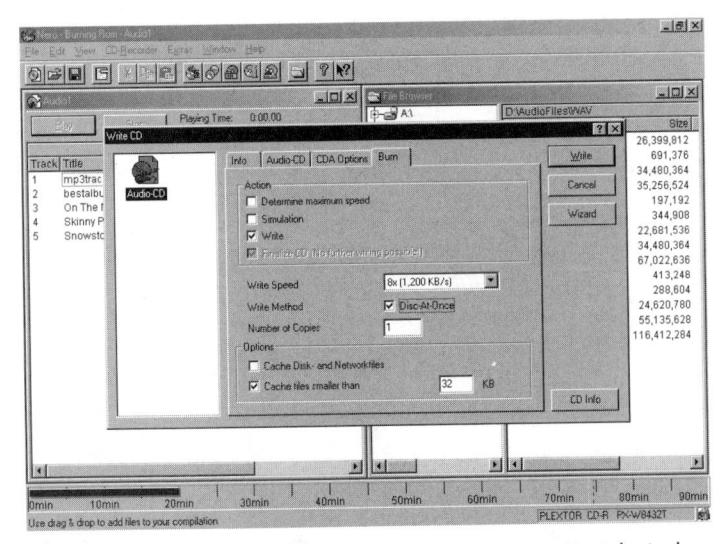

Figure 3.3 Nero Burning ROM wins the name contest but also competes for the most powerful and complete recording software award.

NTI CD-Maker, NewTech Infosystems, *www.ntius.com*
CD-Maker now supports MP3 files in addition to WAV. With its automatic hardware setup and clean interface, this program is easy to use (see **Figure 3.4**). The latest version supports live recording.

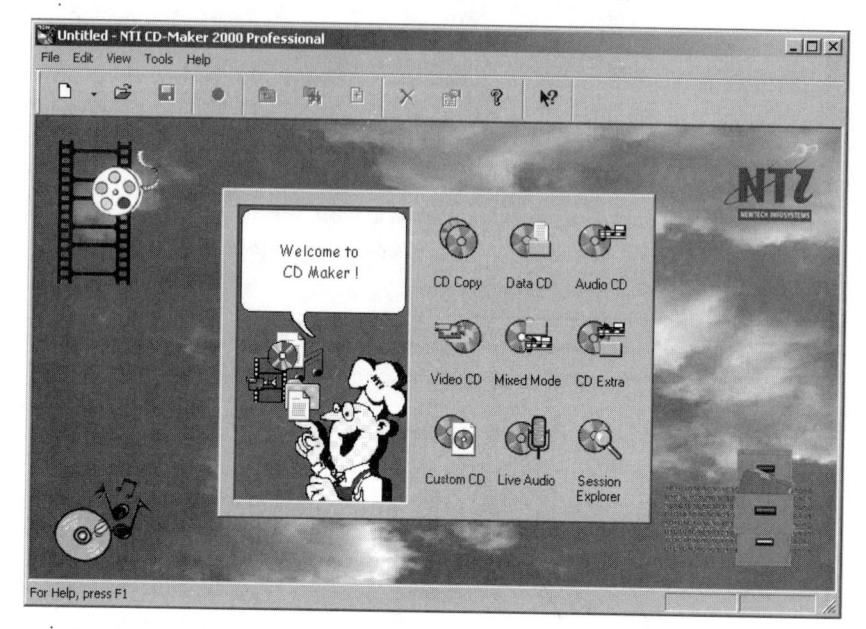

Figure 3.4 CD-Maker is rock-solid and the addition of MP3 capability in the latest version makes it a good choice for overall audio and data use, including live recording.

Primo CD Plus, Primo CD Pro, Prassi Software, *www.prassieurope.com*
Primo CD Plus is an excellent recording program with good support for ripping and recording (see **Figure 3.5**). It lets you mix WMA, WAV, and MP3 files in the same job. Geared for professionals, Primo CD Pro is best suited for multiple simultaneous copies and jukebox recording.

WinOnCD, CeQuadrat/Adaptec, *www.cequadrat.com*
Popular in Europe, WinOnCD is packed with special features for the audio enthusiast, such as a built-in WAV editor. Also available is Just Audio, which will rip, burn, and record from CD or analog input and split and clean tracks (see **Figure 3.6**).

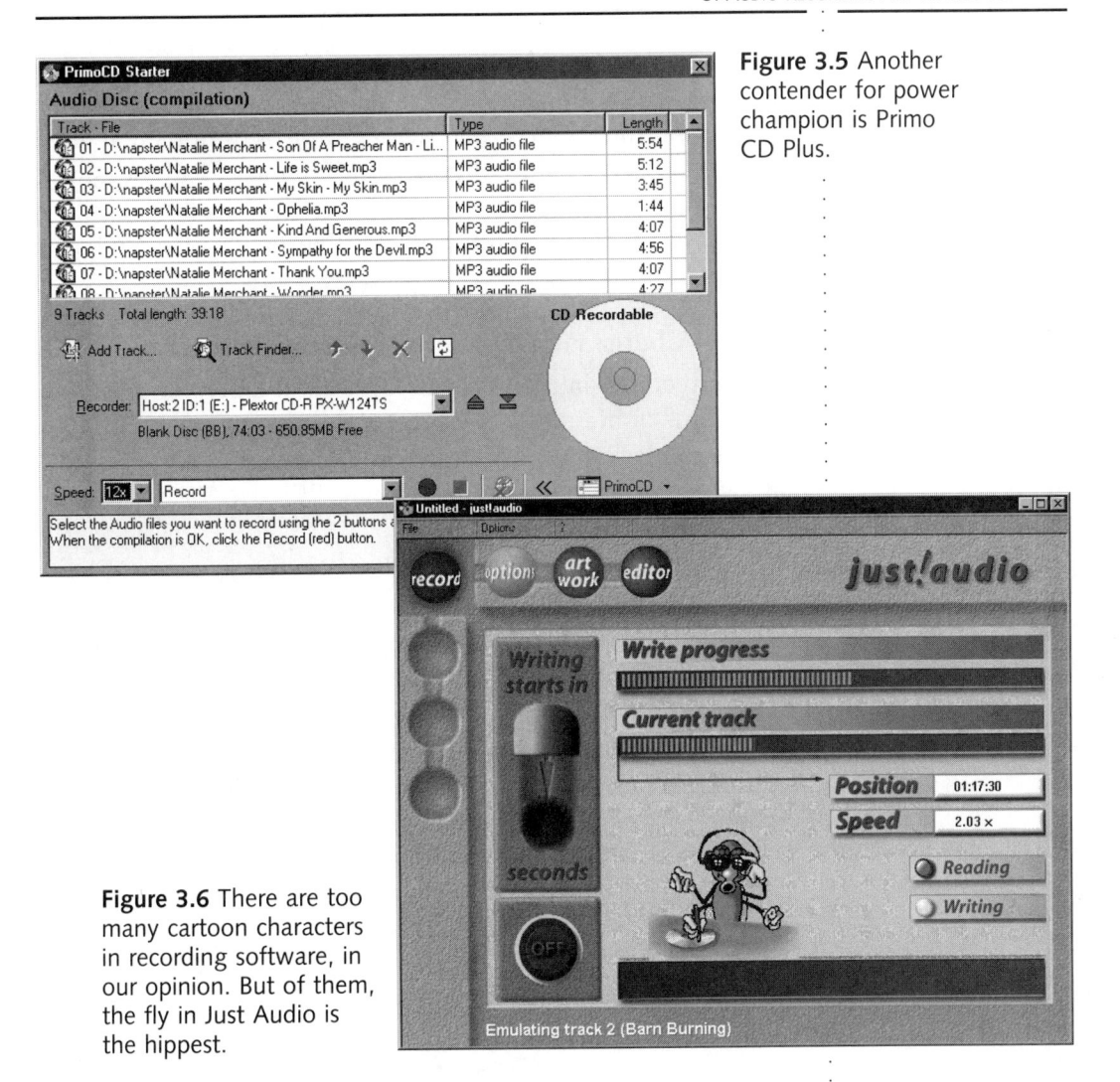

Figure 3.5 Another contender for power champion is Primo CD Plus.

Figure 3.6 There are too many cartoon characters in recording software, in our opinion. But of them, the fly in Just Audio is the hippest.

Recording Software for Mac OS

Things aren't quite so diversified on the Mac side, but then again they never were. Time was when nearly every company in the Windows market had a Mac version, but these were mostly afterthoughts, mere shells of their Windows counterparts. The good news was, this didn't make much difference to Mac users—for one thing, Mac recording was always pretty straightforward and predictable (much more so than Windows recording), and the dominant tool, Toast—then an Astarte product and now sold by Adaptec—was bundled with most Mac drives and did the job as well or better than the rest. With Apple's recent resurgence on the strength of the iMac and Power Mac G4, and the parallel (and demographically similar, at least on the iMac side) rising interest in MP3 and CD-R audio, the Mac CD-R market may be on the upswing. If you're thinking of jumping on that bandwagon, you've got a nice troika of software options.

Discribe, Charismac Engineering, *www.charismac.com*

Discribe records data and backs up and compresses files and also records audio discs. It works with ATAPI, SCSI, USB, and Firewire CD-R/RW drives. It also supports the AIFF audio format (which Macs typically use where PCs use WAV files).

Toast, Adaptec, *www.adaptec.com*

Easy to call Toast the premier recording package for the Mac, since it is one of only a handful (see **Figure 3.7**). The most recent edition of Toast, Version 4.1, added a Mac version of Spin Doctor, MP3 conversion capability, and support for FireWire recorders (it also works with IDE, SCSI, and USB devices). If your Mac has a FireWire connection in addition to USB, you can now get it to really scream with a FireWire recorder.

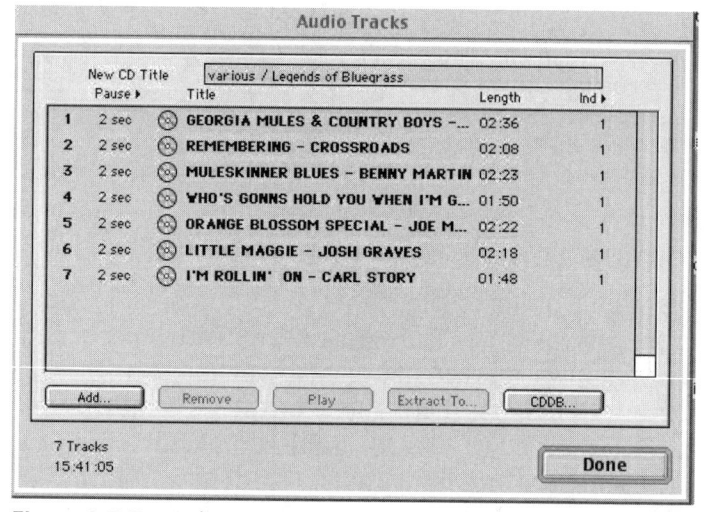

Figure 3.7 Toast that CD. Toast is clearly the popularity leader in recording for the Mac, partly because of the small Mac field.

WaveBurner, Emagic, *www.emagic.de*

WaveBurner supports CD-Text, recording from digital or analog sources, and Sound Designer II and AIFF file formats. It also offers nondestructive editing, PQ editing, and all the other desirable features for professional recording on the Mac.

> **Recording software for Linux**
>
> The newest craze in CD recording is doing it with Linux (see **Figure 3.8**). Not many tools are available yet, but here the ones we know of so far (all are available for online download).
>
> **XCDRoast,** www.fh-muenchen.de/rz/xcdroast
>
> **BurnIt,** www.imada.ou.dk
>
> **CD Record,** www.fokus.gmd.de/research/cc/glone/employees/joerg.schilling/private/cdrecord.html
>
> **Figure 3.8** Linux users, don't despair. A little downloading and setup gets you a recording program with a GUI.

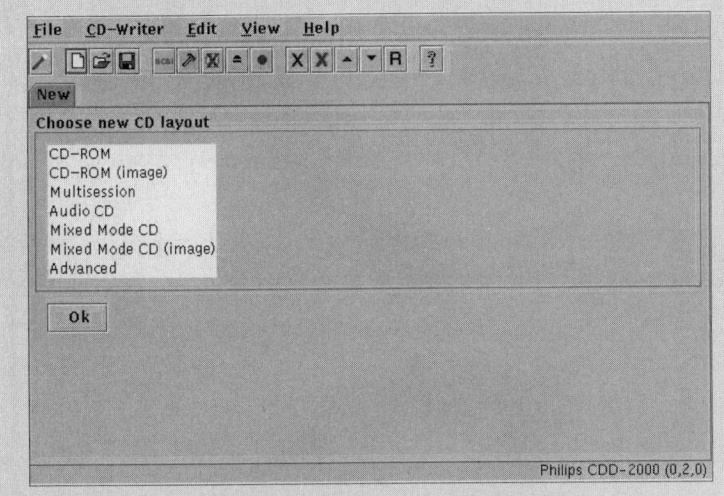

Audio-Only Recording Programs

The next category of recording programs are written specifically to record audio and do not record computer data to CDs. Most are fairly new. Some are mature and some are not. Some started as MP3 jukeboxes and later added CD recording functionality. Drive support will vary with these programs, so make sure your drive is listed in the support list on the program's Web page.

- **AudioCD MP3 Studio 2000,** *www.ashampoo.com*
- **CD Copy,** *http://members.aol.com/mbarth2193/titel.htm*
- **CD Recording Studio,** *www.ashampoo.com*
- **CD Studio,** *www.dialog-medien.de/CDS/*
- **CloneCD,** *www.elby.de/english/corp/index.htm*
- **Dart CD Recorder,** *www.dartpro.com*
- **Fireburner,** *http://mariettabros.com/bob/CDRPortal/downloads.htm*
- **Feurio,** *www.feurio.com* (see **Figure 3.9**)

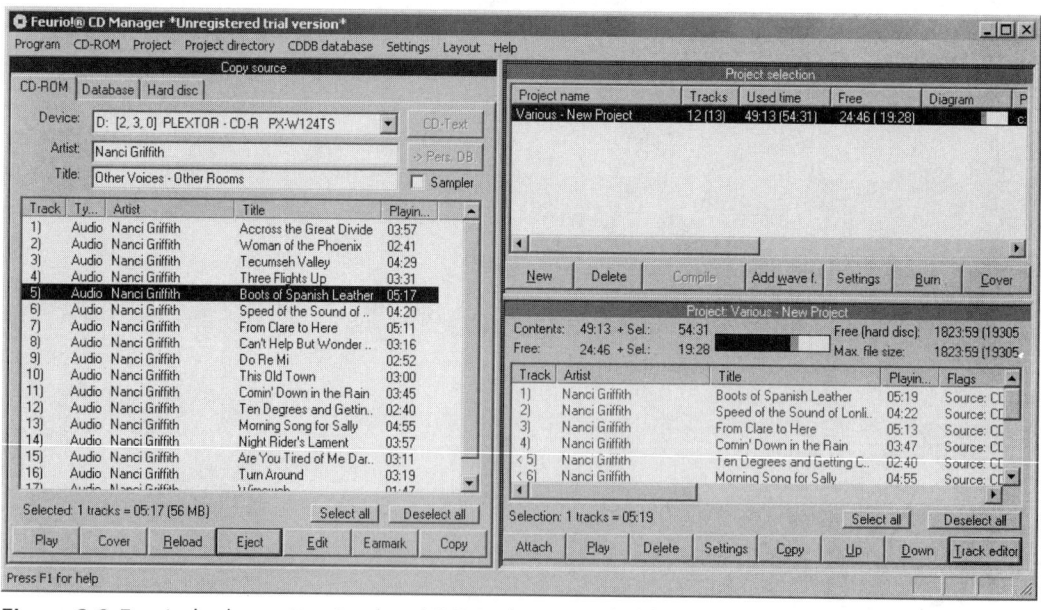

Figure 3.9 Fuerio looks pretty simple, eh? It is, but it probably has more options and features, including low-level capabilities, than any other recording program.

- **Gear Audio,** *www.gearcdr.com*
- **LAVA Burn,** *www.dialog-medien.de/lava*
- **Liquid Player,** *www.liquidaudio.com*
- **MP3 CD Maker,** *www.zy2000.com*
- **MP3 Wizard,** *www.databecker.com/p_mp3wiz.htm*
- **MP3 Liquid Burn,** *www.orionstudios.net/liquidburn/*

Jukeboxes that Record

Finally, there are the programs that originally started as MP3 jukeboxes and players and later gained CD recording functionality or were designed as jukeboxes with CD-recording functionality.

Some of these may be familiar to you if you have worked with MP3s. MusicMatch Jukebox is one of the most popular MP3 players.

- **EarJam,** *www.earjam.com* (see **Figure 3.10**)
- **MusicMatch Jukebox,** *www.musicmatch.com* (see **Figure 3.11**)
- **RealJukebox,** *www.real.com*

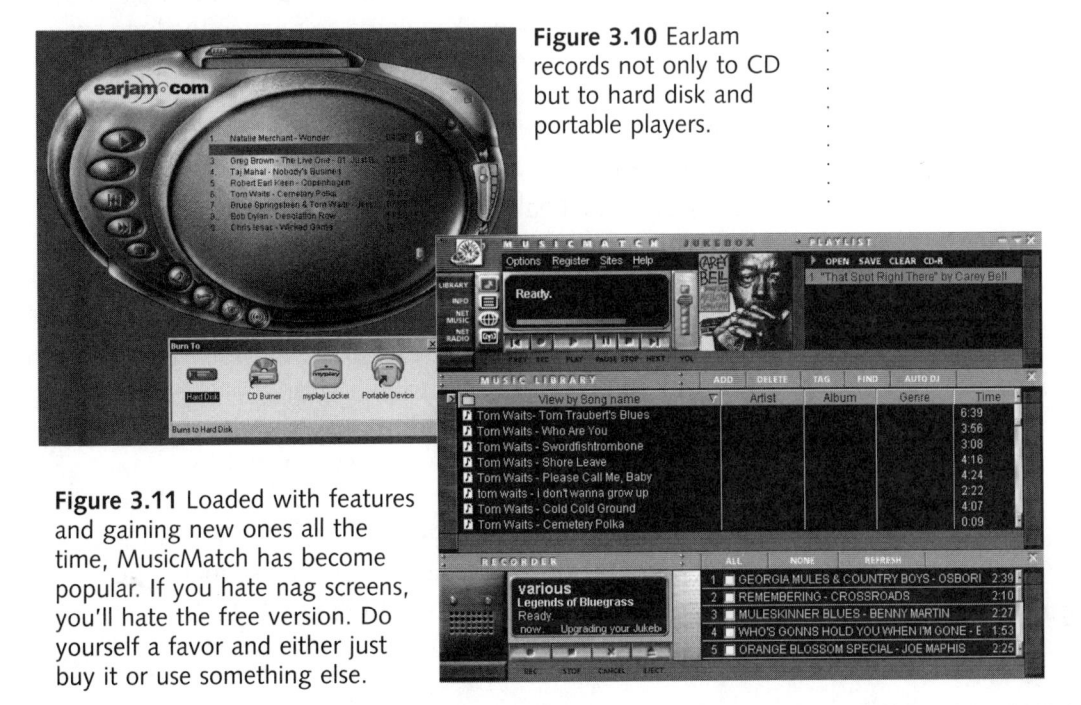

Figure 3.10 EarJam records not only to CD but to hard disk and portable players.

Figure 3.11 Loaded with features and gaining new ones all the time, MusicMatch has become popular. If you hate nag screens, you'll hate the free version. Do yourself a favor and either just buy it or use something else.

High-End Audio Recording Software

Moving up the ladder of features, complexity, and cost, professional recording programs have more features than you could ever need and probably cost a lot more than you want to spend.

- **Media Jukebox,** *www.steinberg.net*
- **CD Architect,** *www.sonicfoundry.com*

Specialized Software for Extraction

Although most recording software will perform digital audio extraction (also known as ripping), and many do it well, in troublesome situations you might be better advised to look to some of the extraction tools that can specifically deal with the problems of extracting audio. The products range from the simple to the complex.

Easy CDDA Extractor, *www.poikosoft.com/cdda*

This program is fairly sophisticated, offering synchronization, manual entry of track offsets, and support for the Compact Disc Database, or CDDB. The main interface clearly shows the track name, track number, start time, length, and the size the extracted file in megabytes. You can also reverse the byte order, and swap left and right channels for drives that mix them up.

CD Copy, *http://members.aol.com/mbarth2193/titel.htm*

CD Copy will output to several file formats, including WAV, MP3, Yamaha VQF, and Real Audio (see **Figure 3.12**). It supports CDDB and lets you set a track's start and end sectors.

Audiograbber, *www.audiograbber.com*

The full-featured Audiograbber extracts files quickly and easily (see **Figure 3.13**). It can extract using the ASPI layer or MSCDEX, lets you set the ripping offset, and has a buffered burst mode and fixed and dynamic synch widths.

Audio Catalyst, *www.xingtech.com/mp3/audiocatalyst*

Audio Catalyst is Xing's version of Audiograbber. The same features are there, but Xing has integrated its MP3 encoder into the program and changed the interface slightly.

Figure 3.12
CD Copy can use several reading modes to achieve accurate extraction.

Figure 3.13
Audiograbber works with CDDB and can link to an external MP3 encoder.

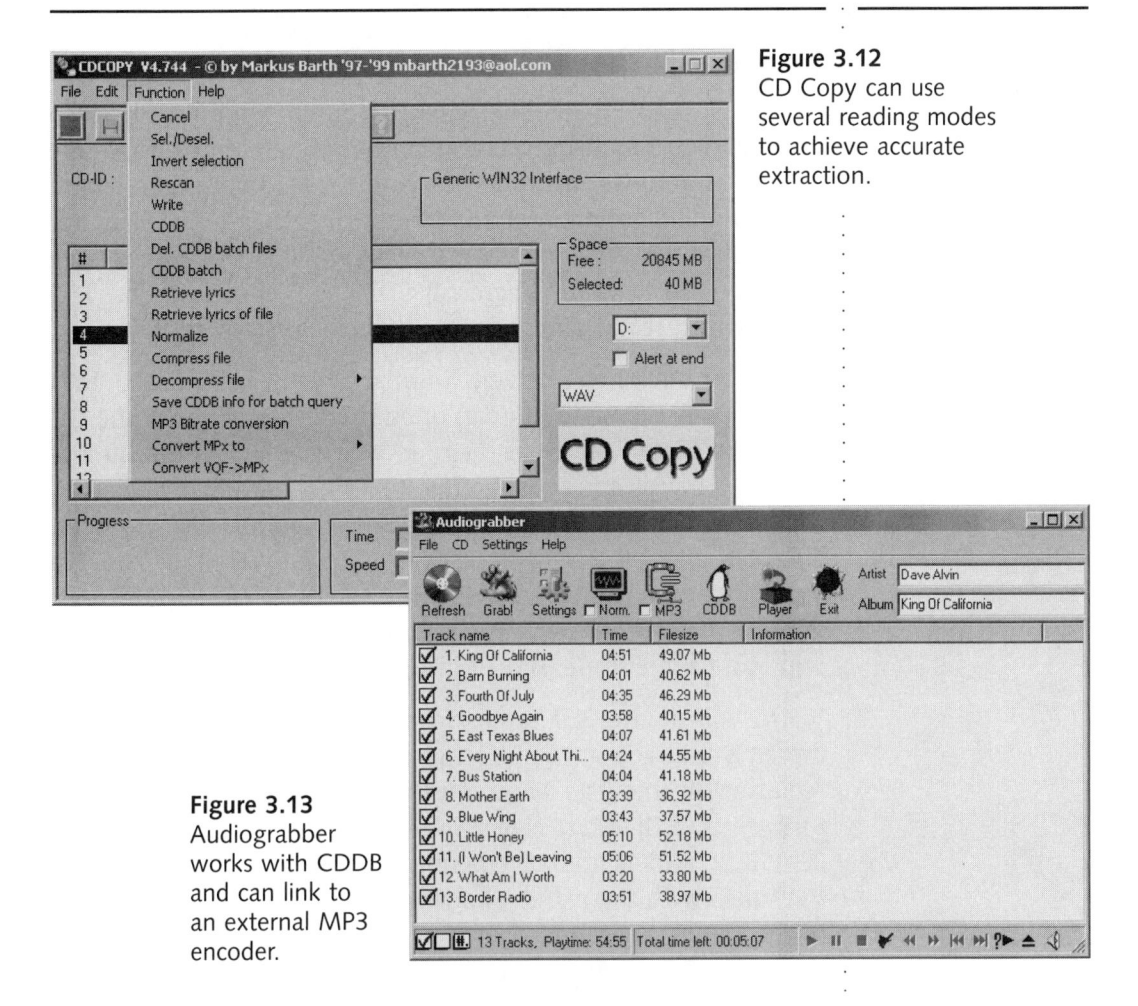

Exact Audio Copy (EAC), *www.exactaudiocopy.de*

In its most secure mode, Exact Audio Copy almost guarantees a perfect extraction, but this can be painfully slow. Using fast and burst modes usually give good results, however. This program—with its capability to adjust track offset; extract in secure, fast, and burst modes; and determine the capabilities of drives—is likely the best extraction program ever written. And it is only in .8 beta.

Many more rippers are available. Check the listing at www.sonicspot.com. Also check Compact Disc and DVD news, reviews, and in-depth technical information at www.cdpage.com. The book's Web site—www.peachpit.com/littleaudio/—also has links and updates for ripping programs.

Ripping Without WAVs—CDFS.VXD

If you plan to create MP3 files or other compressed audio formats, you might be wasting some time creating a WAV file on your Windows machine first and then compressing it into the secondary format. A handy piece of software bypasses the creation of a WAV altogether. CDFS.VXD is a freeware device driver that replaces the Microsoft CDFS.VXD (Compact Disc File System) in the subdirectory c:\windows\system\iosubsys.

Once you install the driver, Compact Disc Audio files (.cda) appear as WAVs, and you can open them directly from the CD in a WAV editor and treat them as WAV files. Opening the file in a WAV editor and then saving it to your hard disk gives you the same result as extracting the track from the disc. You can also use any WAV-to-MP3 converter to convert the .cda file directly from the audio CD to MP3 (or other compressed format) without having to extract it to a hard disk first. This driver will work with some, but not all, drives.

When you open a CD after you've installed this replacement driver, you'll see, in addition to the audio tracks, two subdirectories on the disc: Mono and Stereo. Under each subdirectory, you will find three more subdirectories: 11,025Hz, 22,050Hz, and 44,100Hz. Opening these directories reveals the WAV files with the usual Windows WAV icons. Right-click one of the WAVs, and choose Properties. If the file properties box shows the preview tab, then the drive is supported by this driver. If only the general tab is showing, then the drive is not capable of working with the new driver (see **Figure 3.14**).

You can get the driver from www.maz-sound.com/cd-rippers.html. To install the driver, go to the windows\system\iosubsys directory and rename CDFS.VXD to anything you want. Then unzip the file and copy the new cdfs.vxd into the directory. CDFS.VXD is also available at www.sonicspot.com/alternatecdfsvxd/alternatecdfsvxd.html.

Simple burning

If you want to start with the simplest recording application, try MP3 CD Maker, at www.zy2000.com.

This program will not do much, other than record MP3 files to CD-R, but it works and it's about as simple as you can get. It does has a few more, less-obvious features: Right-click any MP3 and you will see that the application will export to WAV, always handy. We are not going to say it is cheap, because it is not, but you can have some of the full-featured offerings we've listed for about twice the price of this program. But it does have something going for it that the larger programs do not. It is written and supported by a small developer, and we like to support small developers and the shareware concept. Throwing a few bucks their way now and then will surely get you into heaven.

Another program that deserves a good look for its simplicity is HyCD Play and Record. This program uses the Copy and Paste functions reached through the right mouse button to decode CD-Audio tracks to MP3 and to burn them to CD-R. Simple to use and highly rated. Get it at www.hycd.com.

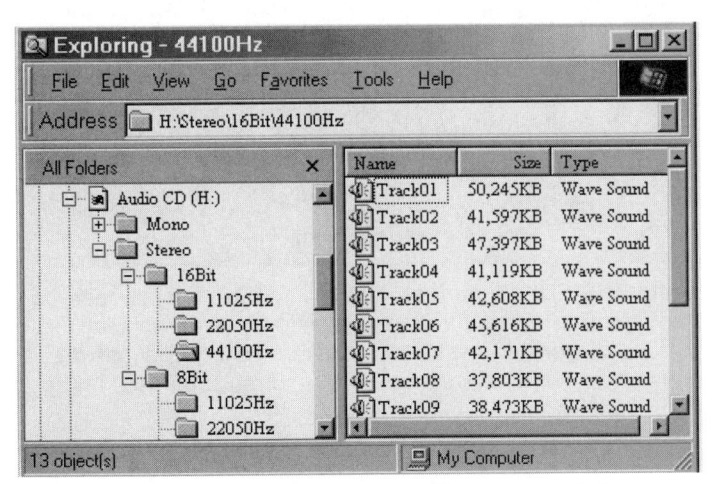

Figure 3.14 This is how the directory of an audio CD looks after you install the alternative Compact Disc File System (CDFS) driver.

Other CD programs of interest

A few more software utilities might be helpful to you from time to time, not for recording but for just having around. The first is CDR Identifier, which tells you who made a piece of media, or rather who made the stamper used to make the media. It will also tell you what kind of dye is used in a piece of media. It works with both blank and recorded discs and is freeware (See **Figure 3.15**). You can download CDR Identifier at www.gum.de/it/download/english.htm.

Another useful utility is CD Speed, which tests CD-ROM drive performance and a drive's ability to perform Digital Audio Extraction. Download it here: http://come.to/cdspeed.

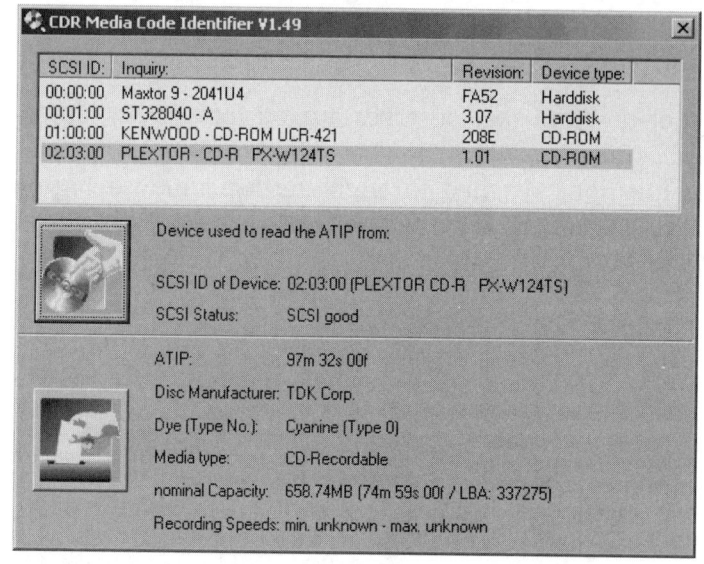

Figure 3.15 CDR Identifier is a handy tool for finding out who made the CD-R media you're using—a good way to spot cheaper versions of disc brands you like—and for identifying elements of the discs such as the dye formulation used in the recording layer.

Freedom of choice

You can have your choice from the stable and growing set of tools for audio CD ripping and recording. If you're just going to rip your CDs to WAV and burn new CDs, you need only a single package. If you are really into restoration and recording, you may want to use separate tools for each step of the process. You may find that you like one program for ripping, another for analog recording, a third for audio restoration, and a fourth for recording the CDs themselves. That's OK. That is the whole point of being able to make your own CD-Audio discs. Like the music that you choose, you can do it any way that you like.

CD-Recordable and CD-Rewritable Drives

Just the title of this chapter makes us squirm, because, as purists, we'd rather leave CD-Rewritable out of the book entirely, since it has very little to do with making audio CDs. But we must contend with the marketing types who invariably confuse things by sticking CD-Rewritable where it doesn't belong.

Most of today's writable CD drives write to two kinds of media, CD-Recordable (CD-R) and CD-Rewritable (CD-RW). The obvious advantage of CD-RW is that you can write to it multiple times, whereas you can write to CD-R once. But for our purposes, the benefits end there. For one thing, you can usually pick up CD-R media for $1 a disc or significantly less in bulk, and a CD-RW disc usually costs $3 or more. What's more, you can write a CD-R disc significantly faster than a CD-RW disc, and reinitialization times for reusing RW discs are interminable. Most important, since our goal is to make discs that we can play on our stereos, CD-R is the obvious choice. Scant few audio CD players will play back CD-RW discs, whereas nearly all audio players can playback CD-R discs. So although we realize that many companies now use the term "CD Recorder/Rewriter"—or worse, persist in describing their offerings only as CD-RW drives—we'll stick with the horses that got us here. From this day forward, we will refer to the drives that write CDs only as CD recorders, or, in looser moments, as burners. In the audio recording context, at least, the world will be better for it—marketing people be damned.

CD recording technology can be rather complicated, but fortunately, you don't need to know how it works at the lower levels to use it efficiently. We'll go into many of the actual details in this chapter, but you don't need to know most of it to make your own CDs. For many years, you had to pay careful attention to the components you used, both system and drive, because there was a lot of room for error. Early recorders for Windows machines were SCSI-based, and you could spend hours configuring the SCSI card and recorder and drivers. With the Mac and its built-in SCSI, things were a bit easier. Plus, in the early days of recording, a Mac or PC system barely had enough horsepower to write a disc at single speed. Hard disk space was at a premium, and the thought of tossing a 40-MB WAV or Mac-formatted AIFF file on there for temporary storage was heresy.

CD Recorder Interfaces

SCSI (Small Computer System Interface) drives are still widely available and are a good choice if your system is based on SCSI or if you plan on adding other SCSI devices. However, if you are buying a PC today, you will likely end up with an IDE recorder, one that uses the same interface as your hard drive; in fact, it may plug into the same cable, depending on how many IDE devices you have in your computer. Or if you are using a Mac, options will vary by model—SCSI for early Power Macs and the first Power Mac G3-based systems; USB-only for most iMacs; USB and FireWire for more recent iMacs; and USB,

FireWire, IDE, and SCSI for Power Mac G4s. PC users can use USB and FireWire, too, although IDE still accounts for the majority of recorders on the PC side.

The last couple of years has also seen the introduction of recorders designed for the notebook market in parallel and PCMCIA (otherwise known as PC Card) configurations—the interfaces traditionally used to connect peripherals to portable PCs. These recorders are significantly slower than the fastest IDE and SCSI drives, but they do the job if you need recording on the road or, more likely given the cost of portables, if your notebook is your only computer. Speed variations aside (see "The X Factor" section), whatever connections your system supports, you can find recorders to suit them—just make sure you buy one that matches it.

Name that connection

When we say IDE, we mean IDE, EIDE, ATA, and ATAPI because they are all generally the same thing, just an interface specification. The terms are bandied about haphazardly enough, generally by marketing types, that it's easier and just as useful to say IDE (Integrated Device Electronics) than to distinguish this from EIDE (Enhanced Integrated Device Electronics) and ATA (AT Attachment) and ATAPI (AT Attachment Packet Interface). Anything we say here in reference to IDE will apply no matter which of these acronyms you happen to encounter when you're researching various CD recorders.

In whatever incarnation, and whatever it is called, IDE is just a simplified way of connecting hard drives, CD-ROM drives, CD recorders, and other peripherals to a computer. Let's do it this way: On a PC, look at the cable that connects to your hard drive. That's an IDE cable. Your motherboard usually has two IDE connectors. You can plug two IDE devices (hard drives, CD-ROM drives, CD recorders) into each cable. With one other step that we'll get to in a minute, that's all you need to know. Plug that cable into your recorder. Forget ATAPI, ATA, EIDE. The only other thing you need to do, and do this first, is to set the Master/Slave jumper on the back of the recorder. The back of an IDE recorder has three jumpers: Master; Slave; and Cable Select, sometimes marked C/S. Forget Cable Select altogether. Never think of it again or inquire as to its use.

Since the IDE cable will take two devices, make sure that one is set to Master and the other is set to Slave. To be safe, set your recorder as Master on the second IDE cable, if you can. This procedure applies to all desktop PCs and the most recent Power Mac G4s, which all use IDE as the primary interface for attaching recorders.

Connecting a recorder to the Mac

Attaching a CD recorder to a Mac should be pretty straightforward. All Macs that predated the iMac (680x0-based models including Performas and Quadras, early Power Mac models, and first-generation nontower G3s) use SCSI connectors for peripherals. And plenty of SCSI CD recorders are available. The Mac system pretty much always recog-nized them; you may sometimes need an additional driver, but these should come with your drive. If you have an iMac, you don't have SCSI, because Apple dropped it, which a lot of people say is a mistake. We agree, but there's not much to be done about it. If you have one of the first-generation of iMacs, then you'll attach your recorder to the USB port or to a USB hub, if you have one. (You may also have to visit Apple's Web site, www.apple.com, to get your firmware for CD-R. USB recorders for the iMac, such as QPS's Que! should ship with this update on the software CD.)

We like USB; it makes a lot of things a lot easier, but it does cause some limitations when recording CDs. USB, or Universal Serial Bus, is a way that you can connect your system to most peripherals, including mice, keyboards, scanners, printers, and of course, CD recorders. But when recording CDs, and especially when recording audio CDs, USB has a limited data transfer rate. So if you have only a USB port to use, you probably will end up recording audio at 2x. You might get lucky and have it work at 4x, depending on your system, although there's no guarantee of this, even with drives that bill themselves "4x." It is that same problem that you will read about elsewhere in this book, data transfer rate. The USB port cannot transfer data fast enough to record at over 4x. If you have one of the second-generation iMacs, you will also have, in addition to the USB port, a FireWire port. This type of connection is much faster than USB, so your speed limitations go away. FireWire CD recorders have recently entered the market, and we suggest that these might be a better choice than USB recorders unless you are comfortable with the recording times supported by USB.

If your Power Mac is a recent G4 model, you have several interface options, including IDE, which means you can choose among most of the recorders in the market today. Although Power Mac G4s don't include the built-in SCSI connection of earlier Macs, the boxes can be opened just like PCs, so you can pop in a SCSI card if it's SCSI you prefer.

You may occasionally see FireWire drives listed under the interface's official name, IEEE 1394—not the easiest string of letters and numbers to remember. For the most part, recording audio doesn't require that you know any numbers except one. That number is 99 and that is the maximum number of Red Book audio tracks that you can put on a CD-Audio disc. You only need to know one color, too. That's red, as in Red Book, which is the color of the cover of the binder in which the CD-Audio specification was released.

Finally, you may be tempted by parallel-port-connected drives because of their ease of setup and portability. This is fine, but these recorders, which are just IDE recorders with a parallel-to-SCSI converter inside the case, are hobbled by data transfer speed issues. A parallel port can't sustain what an IDE or SCSI interface can take, so unless you have some special circumstance, you should probably avoid parallel port recorders.

Selecting a Recorder

You have a lot to think about when selecting a CD recorder, but fortunately, you have fewer variables to consider now than a few years ago. The interface is the first one, we suppose, and whether you get an IDE or SCSI or USB or FireWire recorder doesn't matter to us; our advice in this book applies equally to all. You will see drives from major electronics manufacturers on the shelves of the retail store and on e-tailers's Web pages. Some names are very familiar—Yamaha, Ricoh, Sony, Sanyo, Philips, and JVC. Others are not so familiar if you are new to CD recording. Mitsumi and Plextor, for instance, don't make a lot of other things—such as TVs and stereo equipment—that you see in the electronics store, but they should not be ignored as recorder choices just because the name is new to you. Big Japanese, Korean, and Taiwanese companies make a lot of things. Mitsumi probably makes cranes and road graders, for instance, and though you will never see a Plextor TV, when it comes to CD-ROM and CD recorders, many consider Plextor to be the finest brand available. And although you will never see its name on them—at least not on the front—Panasonic, too, makes CD recorders, and nice ones at that. But if you want a Panasonic, you will have to find one that is sold by someone else under its own brand name. If you stumble upon a recorder made by Matsushita, that's a Panasonic, because Matsushita is Panasonic's parent company.

Recorder features

What features should you look for in a CD recorder? Today the answer is speed and speed. Most current recorders write at a minimum of 4x, and the fastest will record at 12x. We discussed the X factor in Chapter 1, so we'll touch on it briefly again here.

When you are playing music, the drive mechanism in your CD player spins the disc at different speeds, depending on where on the disc the head is positioned. The songs are arranged in a spiral track, much like an LP, except that an LP tracks from the outside to the inside, a CD tracks from the inside to the outside. When the drive is reading from the inside of the disc, it spins at 200 rpm as the disc starts and gradually picks up to 530 rpm at the very end of the last song, assuming the disc is a full 74 minutes long. The reason for the speed change is that the track must pass under the read head at a constant speed.

> *If you really want to know, that speed is 75 sectors per second. A full disc has 333,000 sectors. Since the spiral track becomes longer per rotation of the disc as the head moves from the inside to the outside, playing the songs in sequence, the drive must spin faster and faster as it plays the music to keep reading 75 sectors each second. This type of activity is called Constant Linear Velocity, or CLV. The discs sectors always move under the read head at a constant velocity.*

The X Factor

In the case of playing your audio CD on your home player, the drive is playing at 1x, 75 sectors per second. Music is never played at faster than 1x, of course, because it doesn't sound quite right, to say the least. Recording, on the other hand, can be done at any speed, from 1x to 12x, and soon, we expect, 16x and 20x. So when you record music, you can record it at any speed that your recorder will support. You will read here and there that discs recorded at slower speeds sound better, but that is just not true. The way a disc sounds is largely dependent on how many errors it has on it. All discs, whether pressed commercially or recorded via CD-R, have errors, and discs and players are equipped to correct errors to a certain degree. CD audio error correction comes in the form of Cross Interleaved Reed Solomon Code (CIRC), another thing that you don't need to know anything about, but again, another term that you can throw around if you want. Whether it will impress anybody we don't know.

> *What CIRC does is this: When an audio CD player encounters an error, it uses either blanking or interpolation to mask the error. Remember that in audio playback, the affected bits are 1/75 of a second of sound. When blanking, the player simply does not play that 1/75 of a second of sound where the error is. Alternately, using interpolation, the player looks at what data came immediately before the error occurred and what data comes immediately after and plays something that is close to both the previous sound and the following sound, thus masking the error.*

Now, we heard all this talk about recording speed having an effect on the quality of a disc, so we decided to see if there was anything to it. We fired up all the machines at the lab and recorded a bunch of discs at a bunch of speeds. Then we tested all the discs for errors. The differences between discs recorded at slower speeds and those recorded at faster speeds were statistically insignificant. We also tested a bunch of store-bought discs, the pressed kind rather than the recorded kind. Man, those things had lot of errors (see **Figure 4.1**)! You'll be glad to know that the discs you make at home, at whatever speed, will have tons less errors on them than the discs sold in music stores (see **Figure 4.2**). Even with the higher error rates, though, the pressed discs were still well within the specification for allowable errors, so don't go crying down to your record store complaining about how lousy its discs are. If you buy or make a disc that is way out of spec, you'll know it—you'll hear it (see **Figure 4.3**).

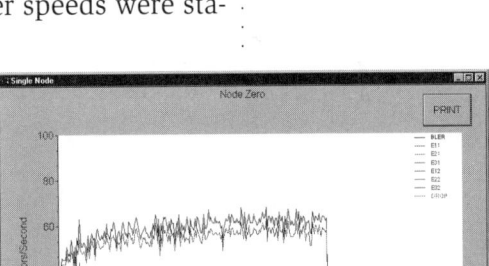

Figure 4.1 Pressed CDs from the record store generally have higher error rates than the CDs you make yourself. This commercial CD even has E32, or uncorrectable errors on it. That is the spike you see at the bottom at the 23 minute mark.

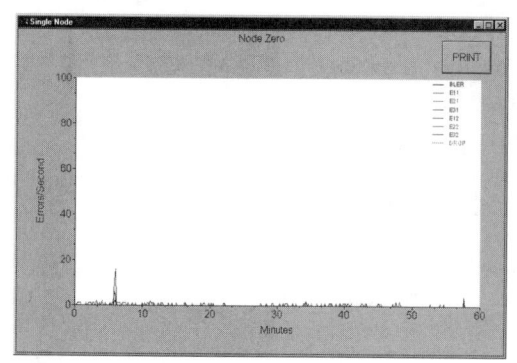

Figure 4.2 As you can see, CD-R discs have extremely low error rates.

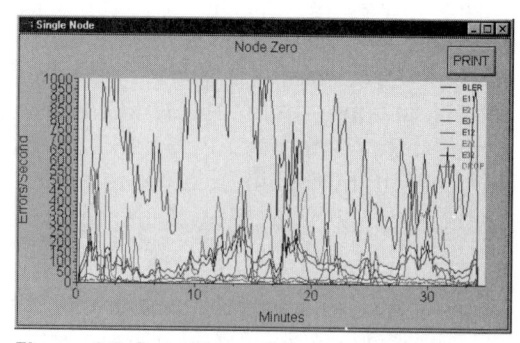

Figure 4.3 Sometimes things go seriously wrong. This is the result.

> *Now, sometimes people ask—and this is not a stupid question if you have never worked with CD recorders—whether a disc recorded at 12x, for instance, can be read by a drive that only reads at 8x or in an audio player that plays at only 1x. The answer is yes, no matter what speed a disc is recorded at, it can be read at any other speed in the case of a CD-ROM. With an audio disc, it will play in any audio player at 1x, no matter what speed was used to record it.*

When you are looking for a CD recorder, you will have a lot of speed choices, from 2x to 12x. Let's look at that in practical terms. The faster the recorder, the faster you can record your discs, Let's assume that the disc we are recording is full, that is, it has 74 minutes of audio on it. How long will that take to record at different speeds? At 1x, it will take about 76 minutes: 74 minutes to write the music and a couple of minutes to write the table of contents and finalize, or close, the disc. We'll get into the TOC, closing, and other things such as Disc-at-Once and Track-at-Once a little later, but for now, let's just stick to time for recording. That 76 minutes is a lot of waiting around, especially if you cannot do anything else on your machine while all this is going on, which is sometimes the case on slower machines. We'll get into that, too, in a minute. Double-speed recording will take about 38 minutes, so we can easily calculate it out for faster and faster recorders:

- 4x = 19 minutes
- 6x = 12 minutes, 42 seconds
- 8x = 9 minutes, 30 seconds
- 10x = 7 minutes, 35 seconds
- 12x = 6 minutes, 20 seconds

You can see that the faster the recorder, the less time you have to wait for your recording to finish, naturally. When looking for a recorder, balance the time differences with the recorder cost and get something that is comfortable for you. Anticipating the future, because recorders with these speeds have yet to be produced, we will really be ripping out those CDs at a record pace soon:

- 14x = 5 minutes, 30 seconds
- 16x = 4 minutes, 45 seconds
- 18x = 4 minutes, 12 seconds
- 20x = 3 minutes, 48 seconds

With speed, however, comes the potential for problems. For a long time, anything you read about CD recorders would include a reference to "buffer underrun." You'll still see it today, but many people mistake it for other problems. CD recording, by its nature, must be done, in most cases, in one continuous stream; the data that is going on the disc must be transferred from the computer to the recorder in a continuous, uninterrupted stream. If the stream is interrupted for too long, for whatever reason, you get a buffer underrun and the disc you were making is ruined. Simply put, the computer streams data to a recorder's buffer and the recorder retrieves the data from the buffer and writes it to the disc. However, if the recorder goes to the buffer and finds no data—if the computer can't supply it consistently enough or fast enough—the recording process is stymied by having no data to write. Hence, buffer underrun.

This is not such a big deal today, since discs cost about a dollar, but ten years ago, when they cost $100, or five years ago, when they cost $25, it was quite a big deal to ruin a disc. Ruin enough of them and you could ruin your career or your financial well being! There is little joy in watching twenty-five bucks go down the tubes, just like that; there is not a lot of joy in watching a buck go down either, especially if it happens several times in a row. And that doesn't include the time you spent setting up the recording job or the time it took to record the disc to the point where the error occurred. Fortunately, the speed, reliability, and capacious storage of today's PCs has made buffer underrun much less common. We'll look at buffer underrun and how to avoid it in Chapter 6, "Recording and Troubleshooting."

> *Blank CDs, with a couple of exceptions, hold 74 minutes of music. So, when we record at 1x, it takes about 76 minutes because, in addition to the music, the recorder must record lead in and lead out. You don't really need to know about lead in and lead out to make good audio discs, but we'll explain it briefly here because you may see, from time to time, some recording software that will issue the messages "writing lead in" and "writing lead out." You can also impress your friends at parties and such by throwing those terms around.*
>
> *Lead in is simply blank space at the beginning of a disc that lets the player know that it is at the beginning of the disc. Lead out, similarly, is blank space at the end of the recorded portion of a disc that tells the player that the disc is over. In between, you have your songs, or tracks, however many you put on the disc (as many as 99). In between your songs, or tracks, are silent (to the ear) spots, 2 seconds long, usually, that let the player know that one song has ended and another is about to begin. In these spots between songs are index points. These contain information that lets the player skip from track to track. There can also be index points within a song.*

CD Recorders—What's Inside?

Internally, a CD-Recordable drive is similar to a standard CD-ROM drive. Since all CD recorders today not only write but also read discs, much of the mechanics are similar. A CD-Recorder physically consists of an optical head, a turntable for the disc, a controller, and a signal-processing system. The optical head, which shines the laser on the disc surface, is mounted on a sled or swing arm and includes a laser diode, a lens, and a photodetector that reads the laser reflections from the disc (see **Figure 4.4**). The laser is capable of different power settings: a low setting (.5 milliwatt) used when reading a disc and a high setting (4 to 8 milliwatt) used when writing to CD-R media. The photodetector contains several photodiodes that ensure the laser beam is in focus and following the disc track, or pregroove.

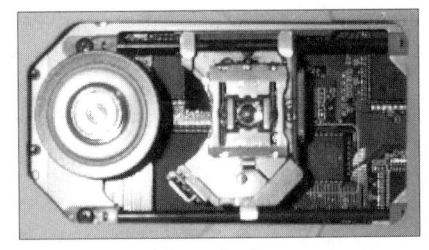

Figure 4.4 Although the mechanisms can use various designs, the core of a CD recorder is an optical head that moves back and forth on a sled.

A pregroove is a microscopic spiral track on the disc that guides the laser as it writes data. Drive electronics direct the laser beam to focus on a portion of the disc. As the laser pulses according to the data being fed to the recorder, the heat generated by the laser causes the organic dye on the CD-Recordable disc to deform, creating optical marks that are interpreted by a CD-ROM or CD audio player as the pits that would be formed had the disc been injection-molded. These marks are read by a CD-ROM drive or audio player in the same manner as pits on mass-replicated discs, even though they are created by a different process. A multifunction controller in the drive handles the focus, tracking, turntable motor rate of spin, and input from user controls.

Random access time

Seek time, or random access time, refers to the speed at which a drive can get to requested data. Because the disc is spinning at a variable rate of speed, depending on the location of the optical read head, seek time includes speeding up or slowing down the disc and moving the optical head to the desired location on the disc. The fastest CD recorders claim 180 millisecond seek times, though most recorders are in the 200 to 300 millisecond range, very much slower than modern hard drives that seek at 10 millisecond or less. Luckily, seek times don't come into play much in CD recording or in playing an audio CD. During recording, all laser movement is linear and the recorder makes no random seeks. Playing audio CDs is also a linear process, so seek times are not important. If you plan to use your recorder

59

for reading CD-ROMs, however, seek time does become a consideration, so the faster the better, although the read-speed differences between recorders should be a relatively minor factor.

Hardware requirements

CD-R drives can generally run on any speed computer, the only limitation being the recording speed you can obtain. As long as you have a 386 or faster PC or 680x0-based Mac, you can record CDs, but you may have to do it at lower speeds. If your PC has a Pentium running faster than 300 megahertz with at least 32 megabytes of RAM, your system should be powerful enough to record at the top speeds of any of today's burners. And all Macs made in the last few years should be able to do the same job. The problem, of course, is the possibility of buffer underrun. CD recording can often prove a real computer resource hog, depending on the recording software you use and the options you set. So, the more resources you have, the more you have to use and share.

> **I've only got one drive bay!**
>
> PCs have changed. The shelves of retail stores brim with Aptivas, Prolineas, Brios, Pavillions, Jornadas, and all the other over-the-top names attached to these machines. In spite of their silly monikers, they're usually pretty good systems, and odds are if you bought one you're pretty happy with it. The problem with some of these PCs is that they only have one drive bay and it usually contains a fast CD-ROM drive or a DVD-ROM drive. So what if you want to use a CD recorder? Are you stuck with an external one? Remember that many of these machines are small to save desktop space, part of the reason they only have one drive bay. Adding an external drive means two things. First, you will lose whatever desktop space that you saved when you bought the thing in the first place. Second, unless you can stand to record at a 2x or 4x maximum, using a USB recorder, you will have to get a SCSI drive, which means you will need to get a SCSI card, and that starts getting expensive. There is one solution, however, currently offered by Ricoh, but soon to be seen from the other recorder manufacturers (Toshiba should be next). Ricoh has come to the rescue of all the bayless folks who want internal DVD-ROM, CD-ROM, and CD-R/RW capability. The new drive is the MP9060A, an ATAPI drive that uses two laser diodes in a single pickup to read and write. The drive features 6x recording, 4x rewriting and, 24x reading for CD-ROM and 4x reading for DVD.

Standards, history, and writing modes

The history of CD-R begins with the creation of the audio compact disc. In 1980, Philips NV and Sony Corp. unveiled CD-DA, or Compact Disc-Digital Audio. In the twenty years since its announcement, the prerecorded audio compact disc has all but eliminated the use of turntables and vinyl records and become one of the most successful consumer electronics products of all time. The audio compact disc is the culmination of a unique sequence of technological breakthroughs in digital audio, mathematics, optics, lasers, electronics, galvanics, plastics, and manufacturing methods.

The two ingredients most responsible for the success of the compact disc are standardization and versatility. The compact disc is simultaneously the most standardized and the most versatile storage medium ever developed: standardized, both in how the discs are manufactured and in how data is read from them, regardless of who made your disc or player; and versatile, in the wide variety of digital data that the discs can store.

Storing audio digitally places huge demands on the capacity of a medium. For example, 60 minutes of music, recorded in stereo at a sampling rate of the standard 44.1kHz, 16-bit quantization, plus the essential error correction, modulation, and synchronization data for CD-Audio, requires a capacity of 15 billion—that's 15 thousand million—bits. Compact Disc-Digital Audio was designed with this requirement in mind. This built-in capability to store enormous amounts of data was not lost on the creators of the compact disc.

However, the versatility of the compact disc did not always extend to the means of placing information on the disc. Before 1988, the only possible way of placing information on compact discs was to create discs by injection molding, which required equipment found only in sizeable manufacturing plants and production shops. This was a problem for software developers: They had no way of testing CD-ROM applications without ordering a short run of mass-produced discs. This was an expensive proposition, since pressed compact discs then cost about $3 a disc and because the minimum order accepted at most manufacturing plants was for 200 discs, with additional costs—often to the tune of $2,500 or more—assessed for the mastering of the information.

Costs could only go so low in part because the creation of the stamper used to form the discs was the most expensive part of the process and because the time required to set up a replication line for a run of 200 took almost as long as it did to press the discs. Many software developers were forced to do their testing by recording their data to tape, sending it to the manufacturer with an order for a short run of discs, testing the discs, fixing problems, recording the changes to tape, and sending that tape in for another run for more testing. This made software development more costly and time-consuming and limited CD-ROM publishing to those companies that could afford the expense.

In 1988, Philips and Sony released the specification for CD-Recordable discs, called the System Description CD-WO, or Orange Book Part II (see **Figure 4.5**). We said before that you had to remember the color red. Now we suppose you should remember orange too. The specification defines "a disc which contains a recording material which shows a reflection decrease due to recording" and which, when recorded, "can be played back on conventional CD players." Before we delve into the Orange Book, its limitations, and its possibilities, however, let's look at standards.

Figure 4.5
The first CD recorder was the Yamaha PDS (Programmable Disc Subsystem) 101. The recorder is on the top, the encoder is on the bottom.

CD-R standards

Two types of standards for data storage media exist: physical and logical. A physical standard, simply put, defines the "container," and a logical standard, just as simply expressed, defines the way the container's "contents" are arranged and sometimes the "contents" themselves.

A good analogy is a sheet of lined notebook paper. The paper, usually white, made from wood pulp, and 8 1/2 x 11 inches in size with three holes punched along one edge, would be the container, or the physical standard. The lines printed on the paper might also be part of the physical standard. The way the contents of the paper are arranged—in sentences, paragraphs, or outline form—would be the logical standard. The contents themselves might be fiction, notes, drawings, or a musical score. A 3 1/2-inch floppy disk, for example, is a physical standard and can be used in both Macintosh and Windows PCs. The logical standard—the file format of the contents—can be specific to one or the other platform, something well-known to any computer user who has experienced the frustration of trying to read a disk formatted for Macintosh on a PC.

The Red Book specification for CD-Audio defines not only the container (the disc itself and the way data is arranged) but also the exact type of information that it contains (digital audio recorded at 44.1kHz). This guarantees that every disc will play in every player, and it allows disc and player manufacturers to achieve economies of scale that have been passed on to CD-ROM and, now, to CD-Recordable.

Although CD-Audio standards established the compact disc as a successful technology for audio recordings, the standards were adaptable for other types of content. CD-ROM is an extension of the CD-Audio specification, intended for storage of information in general.

The physical format and manufacturing processes of the two types of discs are identical. Only the contents, or the file format and type of data, are different. The same holds true for CD-R discs; the physical format of the CD-R discs, whether CD-ROM or CD-Audio, are identical, no matter what type of information the disc contains when it has been recorded.

A CD-R disc can be recorded in any of the logical CD file formats and with any type of data that can be stored on a pressed compact disc. The Orange Book standard defines only the media and does not specifically define the drives used to record or play it. Therefore, the CD-R drives that record the media may use slightly different ranges of laser powers and may offer some features and not others. The media itself can be in any of four states: a blank unrecorded disc that is pregrooved and time-stamped; a partly recorded disc; a closed multisession disc; and a finalized, or fixed, disc.

CD-R data structure

CD-R discs can be recorded in any logical file format. However, the Orange Book specification does support different physical methods of writing data to a CD-R disc: Disc-at-Once, Track-at-Once, multisession, and packet writing. To help explain each of these writing modes, let's first look at the underlying specifications that make them possible and also limit them.

> *In audio recording, we will be using only Disc-at-Once and Track-at-Once recording. Multisession and packet writing are not appropriate methods for writing audio discs.*

The Red Book specification for CD-Audio allows audio data to be placed in separate tracks on a disc with two seconds between each track. Data on an audio disc is organized into frames to ensure a constant read rate; each frame consists of 24 bytes of user data plus synchronization, error correction, and control and display bits. This data is not arranged in distinct physical units; one frame is interleaved with many other frames, so that a scratch or defect in the disc will not destroy a single frame beyond correction. Rather, a scratch will destroy a small portion of many frames, all of which can be recovered.

The disc itself is divided into three areas: Lead In, Program Area, and Lead Out. Each track's location, or address, is recorded in the disc's Table of Contents, which is stored in the Lead In area. With pressed CDs, the number and location of the audio tracks to be recorded are known, so the Table of Contents is written to the disc (or more accurately, to the glass master that will be used to create metal stampers to mold discs) in advance of writing the actual audio data. An audio disc can contain as many as 99 tracks, which are stored in the Program Area. Following the Program Area is the Lead Out area, which is simply 90 seconds of silence, or blank sectors. The Lead Out area on an audio disc is essentially just a ham-fisted way to let CD audio players know the music is over.

Red Book architecture is entirely sufficient for playing CD-Audio because music is generally accessed in only one way: sequentially. Randomly accessed data, however, needs another type of structure. Frames, at 24 bytes, are too small to hold useful addressable records, and the limited number of tracks, 99, makes them unsuitable for units of data storage. To accommodate recordability, the Orange Book specifications further divided the disc. A CD-R disc is divided into the System Use Area—which contains the Power Calibration Area (PCA) and the Program Memory Area (PMA) and the Information area, which itself contains one or several sessions with Lead In, Program area, and Lead Out.

The PCA Section of every CD-R disc is reserved for, as the name implies, a test area for power calibration of the laser of a CD recorder and a Count area, which keeps track of the available space in the test area. Each time a disc is inserted into the drive for the addition of more data, the CD recorder performs a calibration (OPC, or Optimum Power Calibration) to determine the ideal laser power to use in writing to the disc. The OPC can differ over the life of a disc and is determined by recording speed, atmospheric conditions such as temperature and humidity, and the condition of the disc itself. The power calibration consists of writing to the disc at different laser powers and then reading the written data back to determine which laser power is best for recording. Each time a power calibration is performed, it takes up space in the Test area of the PCA and bumps up the number in the Count area. The PCA can be written to only 99 times. The PMA is reserved for recording track numbers and their start and stop times. Each time a track is written to the disc, this area is updated with its number and location, as many as 99 times.

CD-R Writing Modes

Knowing the difference between Disc-at-Once recording and Track-at-Once recording will help you determine whether you will be able to fill unused space on a disc at a later time if you want to add more music tracks to it. Plus, if you are making a disc that will ultimately be mass-produced by a pressing plant, you must use Disc-at-Once recording.

Disc-at-Once (single-session)

Disc-at-Once, single-session, is the most common, and the simplest, method of writing data to a CD-R disc. The recorder assembles, or stages, the data to be written and then writes it to the disc in one uninterrupted session, beginning to end, without ever turning off the recording laser. When it has written the data, it closes the session and finishes the disc by writing the requisite 1.5 minutes of null data (the Lead Out).

Disc-at-Once requires the premastering software to create a "cue sheet" of the data to be recorded, so that the TOC is written to the disc *before* the actual data. The data structure is like that of a mass-produced audio disc and consists of a Lead In (which contains the TOC), Program area, and Lead Out. This type of disc can be read on any CD-ROM drive or played on any CD audio player. This writing mode should be used to create a "master disc" that can be sent to a disc manufacturer as input for mass replication.

Track-at-Once

The Track-at-Once method of writing is similar to multisession and is related to Disc-at-Once writing. As the name implies, a recorder writes a single track or multiple tracks of data to the disc but writes the data in the Program area before the Lead In (including TOC). The recorder then fixes, or closes, the disc, which cannot be written to again.

With Track-at-Once, the order of writing is this: reserve space for Lead In and TOC, write data, return to reserved space, write track start and stop locations and TOC, return to end of data and write Lead Out. This type of disc is considered a single-session disc, but it is not suitable for input for mass production.

Track-at-Once recording is useful if you want to make a compilation audio CD but don't have all the material at hand. You can record a track, or two or five and then later go back and record more tracks to the disc. You can record more tracks because the disc is not closed, or finalized. The downside of recording in this mode is that you cannot play the CD on a CD audio player until it is closed. You can, however, play it on your CD recorder.

CD-R Incompatibility

There are incompatibilities in CD-R technology, just as there are in any technology. Not all floppy disks, for example, are readable in all floppy disk drives, and occasionally a floppy disk is so incompatible that it is only readable in the drive that wrote it. Perhaps incompatibility seems more serious with CD recording because the compact disc has become so standard so it might help to understand what causes them and what can be done to avoid or correct them.

CD-R hardware

The Orange Book specification defines CD-R media, but it only partly defines the hardware that records the media. Each CD-Recordable hardware manufacturer must follow the specification to an extent to be able to record to the media, but even with that limitation, there is plenty of room for differences between recorders.

Standards for CD recorders are defined as ranges, not as absolutes. Different CD recorders use lasers of different intensities (but within the prescribed range of 4 to 8 milliwatts), which in turn create differences in the optical marks formed in different dye polymers used by the different manufacturers. Other features, such as buffers, interface type, command set, and even writing modes, are entirely up to the manufacturer to implement or not.

CD-R media

The Orange Book specification for recordable media defines the standards to which the discs must conform, but does not determine the process by which the blank discs are manufactured.

Manufacturers may use different, often proprietary, processes to create the media. Manufacturers are constantly experimenting with the formulas for the organic dye polymers in the discs; and even with the same formula and even under stringently controlled conditions, there can be variation between production batches of dye polymer.

There are also variances in how well different brands of media perform in different brands of CD recorders. Although rare, it still happens. The same drive that produces flawless recorded discs with one type of media sometimes produces a "coaster"—that all too descriptive term for a failed CD-R disc—from another type of media. It is also possible to create a CD-R disc that works on one CD-ROM drive or audio player but not another.

Dyes

CD-R makers use three kinds of organic dye when creating the recording layer of CD-R media: cyanine, phthalocyanine, and metal azo. You can recognize cyanine-based media by its bright emerald green color (that is, when it is on media with a gold reflective layer—the dye itself is blue). Phthalocyanine-based media is yellow-green in color (again, on a gold-backed disc—otherwise, it's just pale green). Metal azo dye is identified by its deep blue color (this time if it's on a silver-backed disc—it is green otherwise). A variation, the aqua-hued advanced phthalocyanine, is also now in wide use. You can easily identify CD-RW media by its gray color. Manufacturers use two types of reflective layers on recordable discs, gold and silver. Yes that's real gold and real silver there on the disc, but don't be fooled: Although not as painful as scooping out your fillings to sell the precious metals therein, trying to scam gold or silver from CD-Rs is just as pointless. However much gold or silver a CD-R may contain, it's not enough to make them cost—or be worth—much more than a buck each.

Using CD-RW media for audio discs

There's a great question that we thought you'd never ask, so we waited until the end of the chapter to answer it. Can you use CD-RW media to make audio discs? Sure you can. You can make them all day long and play them all day long in your CD-ROM drive. But when it comes to playing them in your car stereo or on your home stereo, you are probably in for a surprise. They won't work. Why not? Because the reflectivity of a CD-RW disc is much lower that that of a CD-R disc and CD audio players, except for some very recent ones, do not have the correct laser to read the disc properly. Sometimes you can get lucky and a well-made player will actually pick up on the disc despite the reflectivity difference, but we don't think that either you or we are really that lucky, neither having yet won the lottery.

CD-RW can be useful for setting up an audio disc without making a lot of CD-R discs that you don't quite like, however. With CD-RW, you can make your disc, listen to it on your computer, erase it if you are not happy and then do it again until you get it just right. Then you can just copy the CD-RW disc to CD-R and have a nice finished product. But if you follow the other advice in this book and carefully extract, clean, and listen to your audio files before committing them to disc, then you usually can get it right on CD-R the first time around.

You notice that we said you have to erase the disc and do it over. Why can't you just erase a single track and replace it? The answer is that you can, but only if it is the last track on the disc. Once you erase the last one, the next to the last one becomes the last one and you can erase that, too, all the way down to the first track. Why can't you erase something in the middle? Because whatever you put in its place is unlikely to be the same length as what you took out and there is no provision for shifting things around like you can with a MiniDisc, for instance.

General Hardware 5

Now that you're versed in the ways and means CD-R drives, we want to fill you in a little on the computer that houses these drives as well as some of the other things you might want for digital audio projects. Here's some good news: You already have everything you need, with the possible exception of a few stereo peripherals. You have software that will extract digital audio to your hard disk for editing or preburn storage—the software that came with your CD-R drive will do that. You probably have a Web browser—if not, let us remind you that this is the year 2000, and it might be time to break down and get one—and that browser is sufficient for acquiring music from the Internet. You have a line input somewhere on your computer, maybe in the form of a mic jack, maybe in the form of a line-in jack, or even maybe in the form of a digital connection. With those connections you'll be able to capture music to your hard disk from an analog source, such as a record album or cassette tape.

The only things you may not have laying around are record and cassette tape players and a phono preamplifier for your record player. No sweat there. You can acquire turntables, preamps, and tape decks inexpensively these days, simply because CD has effectively replaced those formats. And you can find very powerful, inexpensive audio restoration software packages—we'll discuss those in detail in Chapters 7, "Highway 61 Restored," and 8, "Restoring and Recording Cassette Tapes"—that can compensate for most of the faults your stereo peripherals might have.

Look back to Chapter 1, "Compact Discs and Recording," for more information on stereo equipment, but you don't need to go out and buy a Digital Audio Labs sound card or a Well Tempered Super turntable or an NAD C160 stereo preamp. That's not to say these costly items won't render really high quality sound in both your stereo system and the CDs you make—they will, absolutely—but rather that everyone with a burner and a few peripherals of whatever quality can participate in the projects we talk about in this book.

In this chapter, we're going to look at some of these wonders of modern science, so you have an idea of what the various elements of the project of burning an audio CD actually do and where they can be upgraded.

> Here's a rule we'll ask you to stick to every time the upgrade issue comes up: Try what you have first—for computer and stereo equipment—and then if you're unhappy with the CD you end up burning, upgrade to better stuff.

Sound cards and USB sound devices

As the name indicates, a sound card is a card—fitting into either a PCI slot or an ISA slot in your PC (PCI is the small one, ISA the big one)—that issues and receives sounds. More simply, it's that thing at the back of your Windows PC you plug your speakers, microphone, and joystick into. When you're capturing music from an analog source, such as a record or tape, you'll be plugging in from your source to whatever line input you have, whether that's a line-in or mic jack on your PC's sound card, the built-in jack on your Mac, or perhaps, in special cases we'll get to in a minute, a digital input.

A Mac's sound inputs and outputs are integrated into its hardware, so if you're a Mac user, you won't need to know much about sound cards at all. However, if your Mac is an early PowerPC model or any 680x0-based Quadra, Performa, or PowerBook, the one thing you'll need to know about your sound is that it won't help you with CD-making because it's mono-only. If you want to record CDs from analog sources, and your Mac is sound-strapped in this way, it's time to give up all that early '90s nostalgia and buy a new machine. Odds are just about anything else you want to do—such as acquire MP3s online— will benefit from the upgrade too.

On the other hand, if you're using a USB-equipped iMac, iBook, or Power Macintosh G4, your inputs are sound and you're powerless to tamper with them anyway, but you may want to stick around for a second because we're going to touch on USB sound devices at the end of this section.

And Mac users won't need to purchase additional USB devices, at all: The built-in line inputs are sufficient for the kinds of procedures this book will walk you through. But we hope many of you will want, after reading this book, to embark on more sophisticated CD burning adventures, and at this point you'll surely want to know about the kinds of equipment available for advanced digital audio projects.

Some PC users, like their Mac counterparts, will find that their sound inputs and outputs are built into their computers. Many times, all the chips you need for sound are grafted on your computer's motherboard, and all incoming and outgoing sound processes occur there, eliminating the need for an ISA or PCI sound card. Like the Mac's inputs and outputs, these sound jacks are fine for this book. Unlike a Mac user though, you will usually have the option of disabling your motherboard sound chips and sticking a new sound card into one of your available slots.

> *You can replace most PCs' sound cards with another of different quality (see **Figure 5.1**). Here's the thing though: The sound card that came with your computer, despite that it's probably really cheap, may be a good, solid card. We've witnessed a $15 Yamaha sound card rivaling the performance of a $100 SoundBlaster. Why this is we can only guess, although we imagine it has something to do with Yamaha scoring or making a set of really good chips on the ultracheap and deploying them on some equally cheap*

sound cards, never knowing that it is actually shipping a good, quality product. Because of this phenomenon, we insist you try what you have for a sound card first.

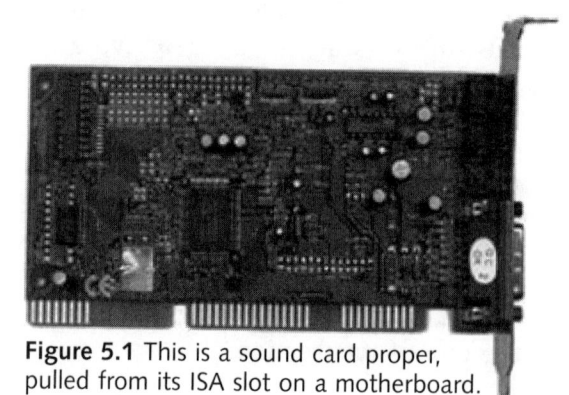

Figure 5.1 This is a sound card proper, pulled from its ISA slot on a motherboard.

If your music sounds bad when you record to your hard disk from a cassette deck or turntable but everything sounds good when these same components are used in your stereo system, the fault probably lies in your sound card, and it's time to consider buying a new one.

To save you a couple bucks, we'd suggest you begin by purchasing another analog card, that is, a card just like the one we've been talking about here, with nothing further than line-in, line-out, and mic jacks. This new sound card should feature one more thing, though. You should be able to upgrade it to digital, so that you have a little flexibility in the future. For instance, both Creative Labs' SoundBlaster Live! Value card ($100) and Turtle Beach's Montego II card ($70) are purely analog cards, and both will serve you well when you're digitizing records and tapes through their analog line-in jacks. But if it happens that one day you want to get even more high-tech in your capture of signals to your hard disk, these cards have connections where you can attach a digital tandem card via a small cable. These add-on cards are typically called daughter cards, just so you don't get confused when you're shopping. Quite easily and inexpensively—$34, to be exact—you can add a Hoontech SB DB-3 daughter card to your Sound Blaster Live! Value card (see **Figure 5.2**), and have a host of new digital in and out connections available to you. Same story with the Montego II card, but its digital daughter card costs a little more, just because it's not quite the standard that SoundBlaster cards are and not many people develop hardware around it.

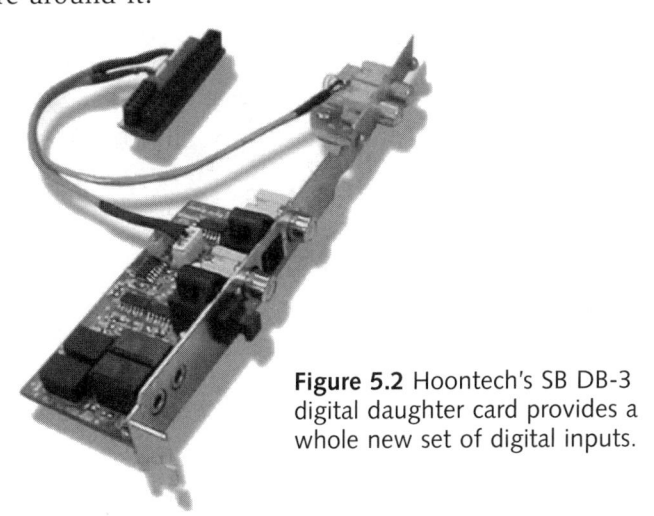

Figure 5.2 Hoontech's SB DB-3 digital daughter card provides a whole new set of digital inputs.

If you're hell-bent for digital to begin with, you can purchase digital sound cards (see **Figure 5.3**). All the reputable sound card manufacturers make these: Creative Labs (www.soundblaster.com) has its Sound Blaster Live! Platinum ($200), and Turtle Beach (www.turtlebeach.com) has its Montego II Plus ($150). Then there are professional digital sound cards, which will naturally set you back a great deal more (usually around $500). On the high end, people gravitate toward the Darla card from Echo Digital Audio (www.echoaudio.com)—perhaps because it's a relatively inexpensive professional-grade piece of equipment—and the CardDeluxe from Digital Audio Labs (www.digitalaudio.com). A good place to start when you're looking at professional digital audio equipment is www.tapeless.com.

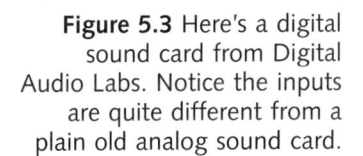

Figure 5.3 Here's a digital sound card from Digital Audio Labs. Notice the inputs are quite different from a plain old analog sound card.

If you do decide you want to use digital-in rather than the analog line-in on your sound card, you'll naturally want your analog signal digitized before it hits the digital-in on your sound card. When you use the analog line-in on your sound card, the incoming signal gets digitized on-board your sound card and is recorded from there to your hard disk. Some people are really uncomfortable with this, because analog line-in connections can be noisy just by their nature and the electronics on board the card might not be all that good at converting an analog signal to digital data.

We'll tell you that we're both pretty comfortable with the on-board A/D (analog-to-digital) conversion that occurs on most of today's analog sound cards, but some people will tell you that we're foolhardy if we don't perform A/D conversion outside of our computers, away from the sound card.

There are all kinds of ways to digitize an analog signal before it hits your sound card. Probably the most cost-effective is to use a DAT (digital audio tape) machine, since a lot of people are throwing them away or selling them off cheap. Simply record your analog signal to the DAT cassette and then record from the DAT cassette to your computer (see **Figure 5.4**). You can also buy machines called A/D converters, but you won't find many in a consumer price range. They typically have metal wings, the wings you screw onto a rack mount, so they cannot cost less than $400. For a look at some A/D converters, go over to www.tapeless.com, and check out its Hardware page.

Figure 5.4 A DAT machine.

If you choose to use a DAT machine, see to it that this DAT machine features defeatable SCMS. SCMS (serial copy management) is a protection scheme implemented in a lot of DATs that will allow you to make one digital copy of something but will disallow copies of that copy. Over a standard-issue S/PDIF (Sony/Philips Digital Interface Format) connection—the digital connection a lot of people use to connect DATs to sound cards—the SCMS component of a DAT sends additional information that gets written to whatever storage medium you're working with. That information essentially says to all who would ask, "You cannot copy me anymore, you ne'er-do-well." Most times, fortunately, you can turn SCMS off on your DAT. SCMS, too, only comes into play with S/PDIF connections, so if you have an AES/EBU (Audio Engineering Society/European Broadcast Union) digital connection—sort of the pro version of S/PDIF—on both your sound card and your DAT, you should connect that way to avoid SCMS concerns altogether.

One final item you can add to perform your A/D conversion for you—here it is, folks, the future, for both Macs and PCs—is a USB signal converter. These things plug straight into your machine's USB port, PC or Mac, and don't require a sound card. The latest and greatest of the USB signal converters is Egosys's Waveterminal U2A (see **Figure 5.5**), which you can see over at www.egosys.net. Despite periodic problems—the kinds of problems intrinsic to all new technologies—these USB signal converters are already pretty hot items. The Waveterminal U2A, at the time of this writing, is already on backorder at most outlets. We haven't gotten our hands on one of these just yet, so we can't really fill you in on its features, other than to say these things look cool and shall most likely come to rule the digital audio hardware scene.

Figure 5.5
Egosys's Waveterminal U2A. This is likely the future of digital audio hardware.

Phono preamplifiers

Say you jumped the gun a little and plugged your turntable directly into your line-in jack. You'd notice that no sound comes out of your speakers, and when you go to record, no levels are present. As you know, or could guess just by watching a turntable, an LP's grooves vibrate a stylus, and these vibrations become sound, immediately, right there. You can hear a record playing even if the volume on your speakers is all the way down, though only just barely, and only if you're standing right next to your turntable. The vibrations of the stylus then become electric signals in the head of the tone arm, and the electrical signals are passed along the tone arm, all the way on down to the tips of the RCA cables dangling from the rear of your turntable. The thing is, the vibrations in the stylus caused by the LP aren't powerful enough to be loud, and the ensuing electrical signals produced in the tone arm head are similarly weak. They must be amplified to become audible. That's the first thing a phono preamplifier does: It make audible the relatively weak electrical audio signal coming out of your turntable.

Now say for a minute you are able to hear the record playing over your computer's speakers, even though you're not using a phono preamp. You'll be astonished at the incredible lack of bass you're hearing, and you'll wince at the overwhelming treble. That's not what records sound like, right? Well, actually, it is, up until they hit a phono preamp (see **Figure 5.6**).

Figure 5.6 Here's Audio Research's LS8MKII Tube Preamp, just so you have an idea of what preamps look like.

The RIAA Curve, a quick digression

Wide grooves on a record slowly and lethargically vibrate the stylus, producing bass notes; narrow grooves agitate the stylus quickly, producing treble notes. The treble grooves are superimposed on the bass grooves to produce the whole vibration in the stylus that constitutes a typical song, bass and treble. To produce a true bass note, though, these bass grooves must be extremely wide, so wide that if a record were cut to produce true bass notes, you'd only be able to get about five minutes of song on a standard 33 RPM vinyl record.

About 50 years ago, some people devised a way to get bass out of narrower grooves without ultimately losing any fidelity. They figured if they could attenuate the bass in the original signal some, the groove cut onto a record would end up being relatively narrow. So, when a record is being cut—they are actually cut, with a machine called a lathe—a bass-reducing equalization curve is applied to the audio signal coming in to produce the cuts. You've probably performed the application of an equalization curve to an audio signal yourself, using your stereo's graphic equalizer. Maybe you have five little sliders on your graphic equalizer, maybe you have thirty. Imagine a curved line running through those little sliders, in whatever positions you've moved them to—connect-the-dots, if you will. That curved line is known as an equalization curve. The equalization curve applied to the audio signal reduces the strength of bass signals (see **Figure 5.7**), thus reducing the width of the grooves that are cut into the record.

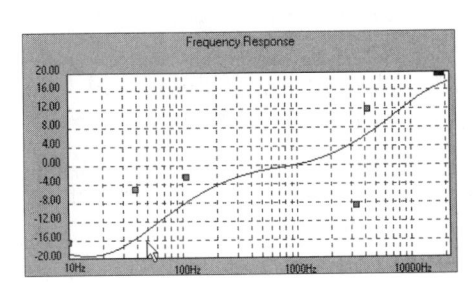

Figure 5.7 This is the equalization curve that the RIAA came up with to narrow the all-too-wide bass grooves, graphically represented by Diamond Cut Audio Restoration Tools. The pointer indicates the area in which bass signals are attenuated.

It was the RIAA (Recording Industry Association of America) that came up with this curve—yes, the very same RIAA that's coming down hard on the MP3 crowd today. Its equalization curve has been cutting narrow bass grooves since 1953, when it became the standard way of altering an audio signal that's to be cut to a record. Pretty much every song on every record since 1953 is equalized this way.

The mere fact of physical contact between a stylus and a record produces a lot of high-frequency noise—fingernails on a chalkboard, in essence. If those fingernails were playing music, though, and if those music signals were boosted high enough to drown out the screech, the screeching wouldn't cause us to cringe. So, to the end of drowning out the noise of contact (usually called surface noise), treble is enhanced in the equalization curve (see **Figure 5.8**), in the same way bass is attenuated.

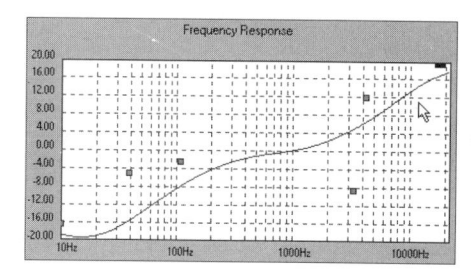

Figure 5.8 The curve again, only this time the pointer indicates the area in which treble signals are enhanced.

A phono preamp, in addition to amplifying incoming sound signals, applies the inverse of this equalization curve (called an RIAA Curve) to the audio signal coming in from the turntable. The phono preamp boosts the bass that was cut and cuts the treble (as well as the surface noise, those fingernails on a chalkboard) that was boosted during the cutting of the record (see **Figure 5.9**). In so doing, it brings the sound back to normal, finally yielding very high fidelity to the original audio signal. That's why you need a phono preamp for restoring as well as for listening to records. A stereo receiver will also work here, as its own phono in will amplify and apply an RIAA Curve to an incoming phonograph signal.

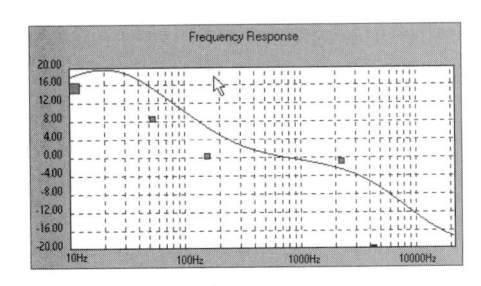

Figure 5.9 This is what a preamp applies to the signal coming from your turntable: the RIAA Curve.

The two preamp camps

There are two kinds of preamp: One that works using vacuum tubes and the other using electronic chips. The former is more expensive, sometimes exorbitantly so. Whether or not you know it, the second you select and purchase a preamp of either sort, you've walked onto a battlefield and declared allegiance to an army.

General Johnny Goldenears and his army demand that preamps use tubes, because, they say, a great deal of warmth and presence is added to their music, and they cannot live without that. Johnny Goldenears' army is tiny, but they're really well financed—so well financed that they can afford to hear better than the rest of us. "MP3 lacks sufficient dynamic range!" is their mewling war gurgle.

On the other side of this battlefield, footsoldiers Bob and Josh scoff at the notion that wealth endows individuals with superhuman hearing. As far as we've seen, the Johnny Goldenears phenomenon occurs only among the rich and is therefore suspicious. They say that they hear better and more than you, and your Mom, and Apple Pie, and the Flag combined. We do not believe them; we believe that this is one of those fictional narratives people like to feed themselves to feel good about who they are. We all deceive ourselves to feel good, sure, but decent people do not flaunt wealth, which is what Johnny Goldenears is doing when he says he hears better than you and consequently needs a tube amp to derive any listening pleasure from his records.

> If it happens you're working with a record or cylinder made before 1953 and you're using a preamp that applies an RIAA Curve, playing your record or cylinder will bass you to death. This is really easy to fix. In the digital audio editing software we'll be talking about in Chapter 7 you'll often have access to a graphic equalizer. In the graphic equalizer, apply the RIAA Curve to what you record, and all will be well. You're essentially reversing the RIAA Curve when you do this.

Your preamp choices are wide and varied, with prices ranging from $20 to $20,000. If you're looking for a decent starter kit for your PC, there's a great, inexpensive ($129) all-in-one package over at Diamond Cut Productions (www.diamondcut.com) that includes not only a phono preamp but also in our opinion the coolest digital audio editing/restoration software around, Diamond Cut Audio Restoration Tools. There's no comparable package for a Mac, but that's OK, because all that means is that you're set with the task of locating a decent preamp.

> *The only solid advice we have to offer Mac and PC users in selecting a preamp is that the digital audio editing software packages we discuss in Chapter 7 can make up for a lot of the bad things a preamp might do, so it's not necessary to spend a lot of money here. Remember, too, that a stereo receiver will work just fine in place of a preamp, so you may not want to buy a preamp at all.*

Stereo peripherals

If your stereo receiver has a line out and a turntable and cassette deck attached to it, all you'll need to do to be ready to record your analog material is run a Y cable (see Chapter 7) from that line-out to the line-in on your sound card or to the mic jack on a Mac (see **Figure 5.10**). That's it. As you'll also see in Chapter 7, though, that's not necessarily the best way to go about attaching your deck and turntable to your computer. When you do this, you run the risk of introducing strange and annoying electronic noise into your recordings. Not only that, who wants their computer in their living room? Out here, since we're on these infernal machines all day, we relegate our computers to our workspaces and don't want to see them after 5 o'clock or so. If we do see them, we tend to seize up in spectacular muscle spasms and call desperately to our loved ones for beer.

Figure 5.10 Here's the back of a stereo receiver.

We talk in detail about turntables in Chapter 7, and Chapter 8 offers a thorough treatment of cassette decks, so we'll delay our discussion of those items until then. Don't run out and spend any money on those things just yet; remember our mantra: What you have is probably good enough.

Additional CD-ROM drives

The only time you'll need a CD-ROM drive in addition to your CD-R drive is if you intend to copy CDs drive-to-drive. But, as we discuss in Chapter 9, "Copying CDs," copying an audio CD from a source drive—such as an CD-ROM or DVD-ROM drive—to your destination CD-R drive often results in either an unusable CD or horrid sound. All you need is a single CD-R drive; none of the projects in this book require any additional optical devices. In fact, if all you have is a CD-R drive, don't even consider getting a CD-ROM drive. You'd be throwing away money. Save up for a DVD-ROM drive instead: That way, you can watch movies and look at the Encarta Encyclopedia on your computer (we frankly haven't found any other uses for our DVD-ROM drives, but we've been told that we will someday).

Hard disks

Our hard disks are our best friends. You might find that sad, but just wait until you're done digitally polishing a dirty LP to a mirror sheen. Then you shall comprehend the tenderness and kindness of your hard disk too, and you shall forego any and all human relationships from that day forward, as we have.

Everything you rip and every bit of music you acquire from the Internet—records, tapes, CD tracks, MP3s—you'll store on your hard disk (see **Figure 5.11**). There, you'll manipulate your music, producing, ultimately, a better package, which again you'll save to your hard disk. Then, from your hard disk, you'll transfer your product to CD-R media, which you can then play in just about any modern CD player. As opposed to something like disc-to-disc copying, transferring data from your hard disk to CD-R media is reliable, and you're able to preview what exactly it is you'll be burning. Your hard disk furnishes you with a great deal of flexibility.

Figure 5.11 A hard disk that Bob popped open for examination.

It used to be that serious PC CD-R people, such as Bob, would insist on SCSI devices: SCSI burners, SCSI hard disks, SCSI everything. There may be some merit to this: SCSI is a really fast way to transfer data, and it's better able to keep up with the stringent data demands of a CD-R drive. Today, though, IDE hard disks and CD-R drives contend very well with the relatively sluggish IDE/ATAPI way of moving data and can often burn CDs as effectively as their SCSI counterparts. Consequently, IDE vs. SCSI isn't that big of an issue anymore. Bob still likes to blame everything on IDE though.

Knowing that CD-R media holds approximately 650 MB of data, it's good to keep at least that much space free on your hard disk. Shortly, you'll learn too that since standard digital audio data occupies about 10 MB of space per minute of song, and since that space can easily double once you set to splitting an album or tape side into tracks, you may want to think about keeping 2 gigabytes free on your hard disk or purchasing another 2-gigabyte hard disk. Two gigabytes cost very little these days: We're looking at a 2.1-gig hard disk right now over at www.pricewatch.com that will only run us $49 (see **Figure 5.12**).

BRAND	PRODUCT	DESCRIPTION	PRICE	DOMESTIC Ship/Handling	DATE/HR	DEALER	ST	PART#
Quantum	QM52160CY-A BF2160AT CY-SERIES	2.1GB BIGFOOT EIDE 3600RPM 12ms 128K CACHE 5.25LP-1 YEAR WARRANTY	$49	STARTS AT 8.00 VIA FED EX	4/4/00 1:23:55 PM CST	Computer Disk Service Inc. 888-499-4111 805-553-9099	CA	BF2160AT
Maxtor	72004AP	2.1GB EIDE 3.5	$58	Read This!	4/28/00 10:51:33 AM CST	Global Micro Inc. 800-595-8288 714-628-9400	CA	72004AP
Maxtor	82100A2	2.1GB EIDE 3.5	$58	Read This!	4/28/00 10:54:03 AM CST	Global Micro Inc. 800-595-8288 714-628-9400	CA	82100A2
Quantum	in stock QM32160ST-A 2.1GB EIDE Fireball Stratus, 5400RPM, Ultra DMA	OEM, 1-year warranty	$60	Starts at $9	4/27/00 7:38:10 PM CST	Team Excess 877-772-2900 619-280-1200 -- P.O.'s accepted Online Ordering	CA	-
Seagate	ST32110A 2.1GB	2.1GB 5400rpm EIDE	$60	Read This!	3/13/00 10:32:46 AM CST	Widgets, Inc 800-722-8798 310-457-2543	CA	-

Figure 5.12 Over at www.pricewatch.com, look at how cheap 2 gigs are!

Much like the classic Freudian Neurotic, a hard disk can appear fully functional but be entirely conflicted and scattered on the inside: It does what it needs to do as far as getting programs and files going, and displaying those to your monitor, but the information that constitutes the programs and files can be spread out all over the place, and this sometimes hinders smooth operation. Fortunately, your hard disk has the same kind of recourse the neurotic has: a hard disk can wash its hands as compulsively as its likes, and while that doesn't fix the core problem, it ameliorates the anxiety, and smooth operation can resume.

This hand-washing is known as defragmenting. Programs and files on a hard disk, over time, come apart: Erased data leaves a hole, and incoming and preserved data move in to fill these holes as they're able to fit. A lot of times, a whole data unit (a file or program) can't fit in this hole, so only part of it goes in, and the rest of it goes elsewhere. If that happens enough, you end up with dismembered data units, dispersed all over your hard disk. Defragmentation reunites these dismembered things, rearranging programs and files data in an ideal order or an order conducive to fast and hassle-free user operation anyway.

As you might imagine, more programs and more files lead to more fragmentation, and increasing degrees of fragmentation can really stymie the CD recording process, which demands unflinching data flow. So we suggest either you look into getting a new 2-gigabyte hard disk that you'll devote solely to audio files or you dedicate a 2-gigabyte partition on your existing hard disk to audio files. This has two advantages. First, there won't be any programs, and the kinds of things programs do, to interfere with proper data arrangement. Your audio files will be better able to keep their integrity. Second, when it comes time to defragment your audio disk, or the partition dedicated to audio, it won't take long to scour the drive. We recommend you defragment your audio disk often: Once after every five records or tapes you restore should do the trick (see **Figure 5.13**).

If the partition or drive is dedicated to audio, you can also just reformat it when things get messy. Many times that is quicker that defragmenting it. But be really careful: Choose the wrong drive here and everything is toast.

That's about it for pertinent hardware. Now you're going to learn to burn.

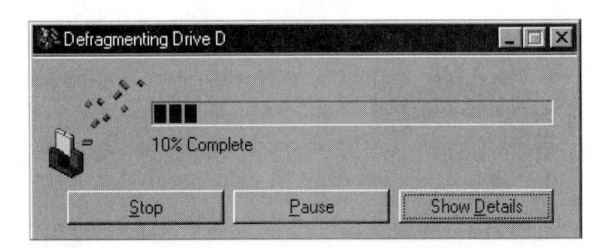

Figure 5.13 This is the Windows disk defragmenter utility.

Recording and Troubleshooting

Recording an audio CD is much like painting, which they say is 90 percent preparation and 10 percent actual painting. However much we may enjoy popping in a blank disc and watching it burn, that's barely a tenth of the process in some circumstances. But we don't want to dismiss that final 10 percent; our job is not over until the drive tray opens and presents us with a finished, working disc. No doubt we've blithely deceived you throughout the book and said the burn's a no-brainer—just push the record button and you're on your way, or something to that effect. Josh has been most cavalier about it, and he knows better. His first burns were all disasters, as were Bob's, albeit ten years ago, when disasters were easier to come by.

Recording's no bed of roses. We hope that all your recording endeavors go smoothly, from your first excited attempt to your last feeble mouse click from your deathbed. But believe us, it will not always go so smoothly. Things can and will go wrong, and so we want to give you some information about setting up your hardware and operating system so that things go as smoothly as possible. We shall also look at some of the causes of failure, mostly buffer underruns, and show you how to make the necessary changes to prevent the same errors from occurring in the future.

Let's look at both Windows and Mac OS to see what systems settings are conducive to trouble-free CD recording. Getting these settings right will prevent many of the problems that might bedevil you in your initial recording attempts.

Recording with Windows—It's a Wonder It Works at All

With Windows, as you might guess, many things can go wrong that have nothing to do with the recording process. That testy OS just crashes, and randomly, some would say. When Windows is running, a lot of things are going on behind the scenes. The goal, of course, with a multitasking operating system is to perform multiple tasks at once. Windows tries to do this, or pretends to do this, but unless you are running the much more robust Windows NT or Windows 2000, that's not really what's happening.

We know what you want to do: Start your burn and continue with other work on your computer. That powerful machine on your desk is not meant to only record CDs while you watch the progress bar and sit with your hands in you lap and your heart in your throat. But we must tell you, on your first couple of attempts, that is exactly what you must do. The goal is to preempt any disasters by making sure that everything—hardware, software, and media—is properly aligned and that your setup will indeed burn CDs successfully.

> *We'll even suggest at this point that you turn your screensaver off. In the right circumstances, triggering the screensaver can abort a burn. Besides screensavers, other background programs that are likely troublemakers are power saving options, disk utilities, and virus checkers.*

Let's start by looking at some basic Windows settings. These settings generally affect the data-transfer rates of your CD-ROM or DVD-ROM drive and CD recorder. Some of these settings influence overall system performance as well. If you go to the Control Panel and click System, Windows will bring up the System Properties window. Click the Device Manager tab there, and you will be presented with a list of attached peripherals. Find your CD-ROM drive or CD recorder and click the plus sign or double-click the CD-ROM icon to expand the category. Here you should see a list of all attached CD and DVD devices. Highlight a drive and click Properties or double-click the drive icon. You should see the dialog box that appears in **Figure 6.1**.

The General tab will show the device status. Make sure it says "The device is working properly." Next, click the Settings tab. Now we have three options that we want to check on: Disconnect, Sync data transfer, and Auto insert notification (see **Figures 6.2** and **6.3**).

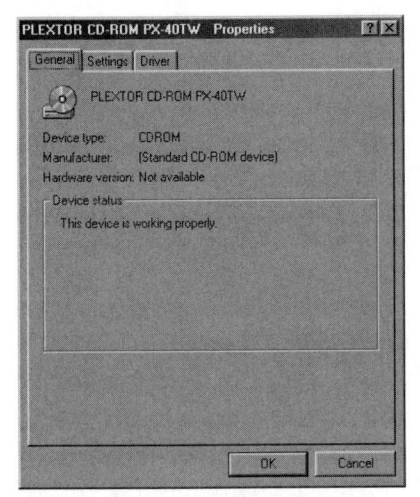

Figure 6.1 The General tab in your Windows Device Manager will show you the status of any drive attached to your system—something well-worth knowing before the burn kicks in.

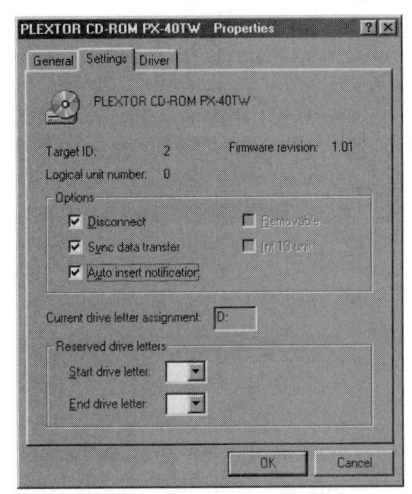

Figure 6.2 Also worth checking before recording is the Auto insert notification status in your Settings tab.

Auto Insert Notification

This feature assumes that every time you insert a disc that is capable of starting itself—an autorun disc, as it is called—you want that disc to start.

We want Auto Insert Notification, or AIN, to be set to off. If we are recording and we put a disc in the drive, we don't want it to automatically start and run whatever it feels like running because this will eat into the system resources that we need for the recording process itself. Additionally, with AIN on,

Windows scans, or polls, all the CD and DVD drives constantly to see if you've inserted a disc. We don't want Windows polling our recorder (or our CD-ROM or DVD-ROM drive if it is the source of the transfer) for new discs while we are recording our own disc. First, it is none of Windows' business what we are doing with our recorder or CD-ROM drive. Second, this polling uses some system resources and its propensity for asking our drive for information about itself while we are reading or recording can potentially disrupt the data flow and cause a buffer underrun. When you turn AIN on or off you need to reboot your system, so be prepared to restart after disabling this function.

Sync data transfer

This option lets you, in some cases, speed up your data transfers. What those cases are we are not exactly sure, because we get conflicting information when we research whether we should use this option. We don't give up easily, but in this case we have no specific recommendations to make, lest we steer you wrong and cause you great hardship. The best rule of thumb to follow with this check box is this: If your recorder or software manufacturer suggests that you turn it on, do so. If it suggests that you turn it off, do that. If it doesn't make a suggestion, turn it off. If you have problems recording, turn it on and try again. If you are still having problems, then the fault lies elsewhere. We hope that this definitive answer will please you, but we expect that it won't.

Disconnect

IDE recorders do not respond to the disconnect command, so you want to turn disconnect on for IDE recorders. SCSI recorders, however, understand disconnect through their controller cards, and so you should turn disconnect on in the controller BIOS. As for the check box, leave it off for a SCSI recorder, unless you have problems. As with Auto Insert Notification, if your recorder or software documentation requests a setting different than those we have talked about, follow the documentation.

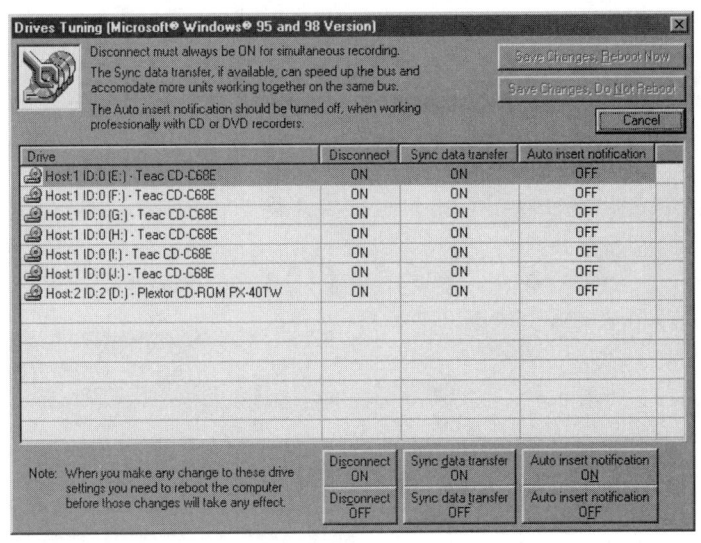

Figure 6.3 Prassi PrimoCD Pro allows you to change all these settings from within the program. Very convenient.

Microsoft's FindFast

When you install Microsoft Office, you get a program called FindFast. FindFast scans your hard drive for Office documents and indexes them for you. This is all very kind of Bill but not to our liking, because if FindFast starts during a recording session it may cause a buffer underrun. Go to the Control Panel and choose Add/Remove Programs. If FindFast is there, uninstall it, unless other operations that you use demand it. In that case, take your chances.

Read-ahead optimization

Using read-ahead optimization for your hard drive under Windows can be a cause of buffer underruns. Turning it off will have little effect on your system performance, so turn it off to be on the safe side or if you are having problems recording. To turn off read-ahead optimization, open the Systems Properties control panel (see **Figure 6.4**). Click the Performance tab on the right (see **Figure 6.5**). Then click File System under Advanced Settings at the lower left. You will see the screen pictured in **Figure 6.6**. Move the read ahead optimization slider all the way to the left to disable this feature. Click Apply. You will have to restart your computer for this change to take effect.

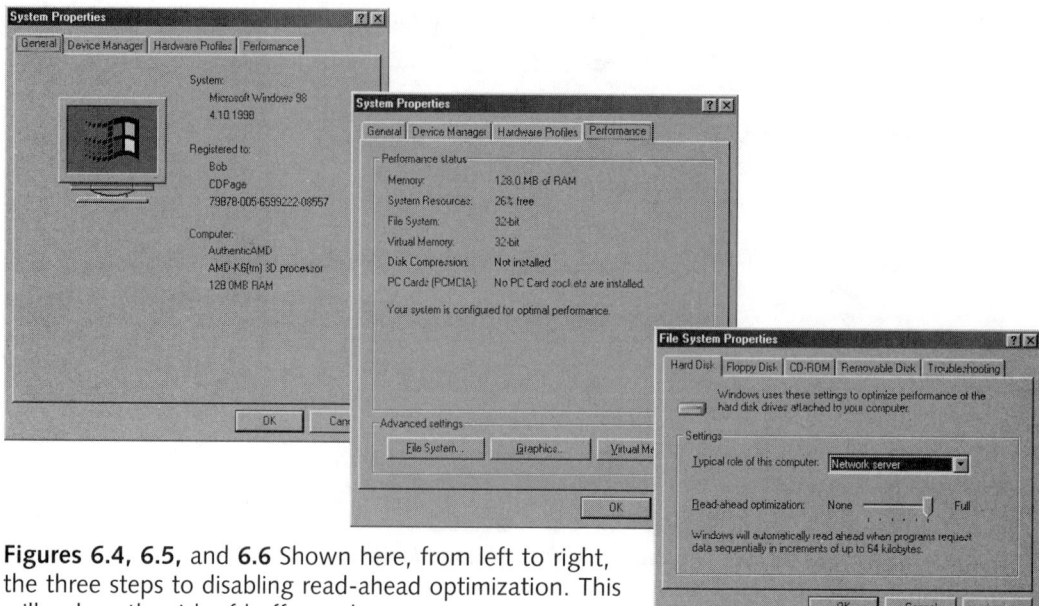

Figures 6.4, 6.5, and **6.6** Shown here, from left to right, the three steps to disabling read-ahead optimization. This will reduce the risk of buffer underruns.

IDE busmaster drivers

SCSI recorders and hard drives can move data quickly without taking up precious CPU time. They don't need to use any CPU processes to make data transfers across the bus. IDE recorders and hard drives, on the other hand, use CPU cycles to transfer data unless they get help from something called busmastering. A busmastering driver will allow IDE devices to transfer data independent of the CPU, freeing CPU cycles for other tasks and speeding up the data transfer rate to your recorder. To take advantage of busmastering, you must have a busmastering driver installed and the DMA (Direct Memory Access) box checked on your drives Settings dialog. Once the driver is installed, your settings screen will look like **Figure 6.7**. Note the addition of the DMA box on the lower-right side. Busmastering drivers should have come on the CD-ROM or floppy disk included with your computer. If you do not have those, you can download the drivers from your computer manufacturer's Web site. Follow the instructions in the readme file to install the busmastering drivers. You can also find many busmastering drivers at www.bmdrivers.com, www.windrivers.com, and www.driverguide.com.

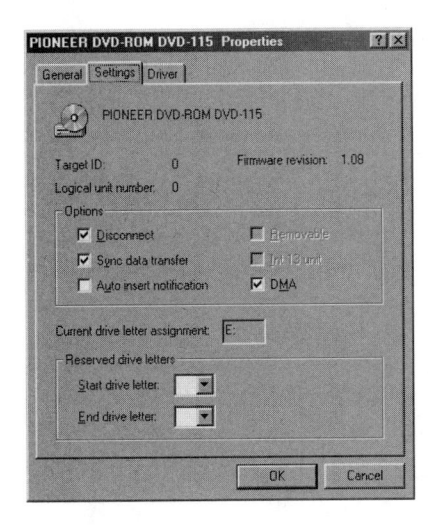

Figure 6.7 Here's what your settings menu will look like with a busmastering driver installed, which will enable your IDE recorder to transfer data without using CPU resources.

On the Mac, read-ahead caching is not part of the operating system, but some CD-ROM drivers may enable it. You will need to look at the driver software's user's manual to see if it is implemented and, if it is, how to disable it, assuming that you are having recording problems.

autoexec.bat and config.sys

These files are leftovers from Windows 3.1 and DOS. Except when you have some device that has no native support in Windows 95 and later versions, you don't need them or any of the real mode drivers that they contain. Take a look at these files and look for old drivers with the extension .SYS. If you are sure that they do not control a nonsupported device or special program, just delete them from the file. Better yet, erase autoexec.bat and config.sys altogether. Windows 95 and later versions don't need them.

Sure and Stable Mac Recording... and iMac Limitations

If you are going to do your recording on a Mac, we have good news and bad news for you. The good news is that the Mac OS is not so prone to the vagaries of the Windows OS. The bad news is that you have little recording software to choose from, although the software that is available is excellent. (See Chapter 3, "Audio Recording and Ripping Software," for more information on Mac recording software.) The other bad news concerns the first generation of iMacs, which have only two USB ports. The fastest drives available for USB recording are 4x units; in reality, we have found that iMacs have a hard time handling a 4x burn. Audio recording at an archaic 2x is about the best you can hope for, and even that results in occasional buffer underruns. Recording at 1x is underrun-proof, but it's a life-sapping process we wouldn't wish on anyone. It's not that the USB recorders for the iMac are bad—these are rock-solid IDE units in USB clothing that would work fine in other circumstances—rather, it's because of the paltry data transfer rate allowed by USB. It's a great technology for keyboards and mice but not so great for CD recording. On the other hand, a mid-'90s vintage 680x0 Mac, external SCSI-only, makes a great host unit for 4x recording, and recent iMacs equipped with FireWire, SCSI-only first-generation Power Mac G3s, and IDE and SCSI-ready Power Mac G4s make redoubtable burn partners.

Recommendations for IDE Recorders

Most Windows PCs have two IDE buses. Try to use the secondary bus and set the recorder to master without a slave, if you can. Another option, if you have too many IDE devices to do that, is to buy an additional IDE card and use it to control the recorder. Of course, theoretically, the IDE recorder can be a primary slave, a secondary master, or a secondary slave. We have just found that it works better if it is by itself on the bus as a master. But if yours works OK as a slave, or as a master controlling a slave device, don't worry about it. You will also want to go into your BIOS (usually by pressing the Delete key on startup) and disable UltraDMA for the secondary IDE controller.

Rules and Regulations for SCSI Recorders

If you have a SCSI CD recorder and a SCSI card that came with it and no other SCSI devices, the setup process is pretty simple and you can skip the remaining paragraphs in this section. Your SCSI card should be set with termination as Automatic or Enabled. Your recorder should have the termination set to On. Plug in the card, double-check termination on the recorder, according to your user's manual, and make sure that Parity is set to On for the recorder. Install the card and plug in the recorder and you should be ready to go. If you are adding a recorder to an existing SCSI card, be sure to read the rest of this section, unless you are already well-versed in the ways of SCSI.

SCSI recorders, whether on the PC or the Mac, have special rules you must follow to set them up and keep them working properly. The SCSI bus, sometimes called the SCSI chain, can generally handle as many as seven devices. These can include CD recorders, scanners, external hard drives, magneto-optical drives, and tape drives. Each peripheral attached to the SCSI card will have a unique SCSI ID number, from 0 through 7. The SCSI card is usually set to 7. Hard drives are set to 0 or 1. You can set your recorder to 2, 3, 4, 5, or 6, assuming no other device is using one of those IDs. You can set your recorder to 0 or 1, if you do not have any SCSI hard drives, but we recommend playing by the rules and leaving 0 and 1 open.

The next thing about SCSI is that it requires termination. You terminate SCSI by adding a terminating resistor to each end of the bus. As signals are sent back and forth across the bus, the terminating resistor picks up stray signals and suppresses them. So as not to suppress legitimate signals going to devices, the terminating resistors must not be on any device except those on each end of the bus. And the devices on each end of the bus must always be terminated. Sometimes you enable or disable termination with a resistor that plugs into the device and sometimes with a dip switch or a jumper on the drive. Some internal SCSI cables also have terminating resistors on them. These are useful if you have a SCSI device that makes no provision for termination. In that case, you will need to put that device on the end of the bus and use the special cable.

Check your SCSI chain and make sure that each device is set to a unique ID and that the last device on each end of the chain is terminated. Your SCSI card is the last device on one end if you are running no external SCSI drives. Most of today's SCSI cards handle termination automatically. But you need to go into the SCSI card BIOS and make sure that automatic termination is set to On. See your user's manual on how to do this. On Adaptec and Advansys cards, do this by pressing

CTRL + A on startup when you see the card initializing. Other brands of SCSI cards may use different schemes.

Another thing to remember about SCSI is that the total cabling on the bus cannot exceed 19.6 feet, counting both internal and external cabling and throwing in a couple feet just in case. For maximum cable lengths on Fast, Fast and Wide, and Ultra SCSI, see the Mac section later in this chapter.

> *Here's why you have to follow the SCSI rules exactly. If you have improper termination, conflicting SCSI IDs, or excessive cable length, sometimes everything will work fine. Sometimes, nothing will work. Sometimes, some devices will work and others will not. The scariest scenario (and this happens) is when everything seems to be working fine. It can continue this way for months and then one day you'll start having strange problems, some even that seem totally unrelated to the SCSI card or devices. Then those problems may go away and everything will work fine again. Then one day other problems come up. They stay or disappear. An improper SCSI bus can do just about anything—it's goofy, really goofy. And it is so tough to track down because the difficulties may come and go or may not show up for months. So get it right the first time, and double-check it every time you add or remove a device. There is almost nothing more difficult to troubleshoot than the ephemeral problems caused by an improperly set up SCSI bus.*

Now, if that hasn't made you run screaming in terror over to the IDE camp, let's look at a few more things we need to keep in mind when using a SCSI recorder.

We can set a lot of options on the SCSI card itself. For CD recording, we want to check the following list to make sure we avoid any problems. Get into your SCSI card's BIOS and check these settings. If you have other SCSI devices that need these options, don't change the option. If you just have a recorder or your other devices don't require these features, just set them as follows:

- Synchronous negotiation: Disable (Enable for 10x and faster recorders)
- Maximum sync transfer rate: As slow as possible (Higher for 10x and faster recorders)

- Disconnection: Enable
- Plug & Play SCAM support: Disable
- BIOS support for bootable CD-ROM: Disable
- BIOS support for INT13 devices: Disable
- Support removable media as fixed disk: Enable

Check that you are using the most current ASPI (Advanced SCSI Programmer's Interface) drivers for your SCSI card. Go to the manufacturer's Web site and download the latest if you are not. The same goes for the firmware in your recorder, but with one caveat. If everything is working OK, leave the firmware (Recorder BIOS) alone. Most of today's recorders have a flash BIOS that you can upgrade through software. If your recorder seems troublesome, you might want to download the latest version and update the BIOS. Just remember this: Follow the manufacturer's instructions exactly. If you misstep, the recorder can become useless and you will have to send it in for a replacement BIOS.

SCSI on the Mac

Mac SCSI devices, like PC SCSI devices, must be turned on when you start the computer and left on when the computer is running. Remember that each SCSI device must have its own ID number. Macintosh computers with a SCSI bus have seven SCSI ID numbers; the computer itself is set to ID 7. Internal hard drives are set to ID 1 and CD-ROM drives are usually set to ID 3. A Wide SCSI adapter can have 15 SCSI IDs, but the card will require an ID for itself. You must terminate the device on each end of the SCSI bus or attach a terminating resistor.

> *What are all these confusing SCSI names—which include SCSI, Fast SCSI, and Ultra SCSI? The various flavors differ primarily in how much data each can move at one time and how fast each can transfer data. For example, plain old SCSI can carry 8 bits of data at a transfer rate of 5 MBps, Fast and Wide SCSI can handle 16 bits of data at speeds of 20 MBps, and Ultra SCSI can pass 16 bits at a time at 40 MBps.*

The total length of SCSI cabling cannot exceed 6 meters or 19.6 feet. Fast SCSI and Fast and Wide SCSI limit the overall cable length to half that. Ultra SCSI is limited to 3 meters if you have one to four SCSI devices and to 1.5 meters or 4.9 feet if you have four to eight devices.

Troubleshooting Recording Problems—Causes of Buffer Underrun

Here are some things that can interfere with the proper operation of your CD recorder and CD recording software and cause buffer underruns:

- Cause: Source devices that do bursts transfers
  Solution: Disable the device

- Cause: Incorrect SCSI controller settings
  Solution: Set according to the instructions in this chapter

- Cause: SCSI termination problem
  Solution: Check termination

- Cause: You are using a compressed hard disk
  Solution: Don't do it

- Cause: Thermal recalibration (only on very old hard drives)
  Solution: Buy a new hard drive

- Cause: Your hard drive is very fragmented
  Solution: Use the Windows Defragment utility or various Mac defragment utilities to clean up your hard drive

- Cause: There is insufficient space in your temporary directory
  Solution: Make more room by erasing unneeded files

- Cause: Bad hard drive
  Solution: Run hard drive diagnostics or replace hard drive

- Cause: Bad CD recorder
  Solution: Have it checked by the manufacturer for proper operation

- Cause: Badly written software
  Solution: Use something else

- Cause: Your CD-ROM drive is spinning down
  Solution: Turn off any power saving features in Windows and in your computer BIOS

- Cause: Recording from network drives
  Solution: Don't do it, or if you must, record at 3 A.M., or kick everyone else off the network

- Cause: Trying to record system files or open files
  Solution: Don't do it

- Cause: Source CD is scratched, dirty, or damaged
  Solution: Clean or replace disc

- Cause: Blank CD is scratched, dirty, or damaged
  Solution: Clean or replace disc

- Cause: Bad recording media
  Solution: Use a different piece of media

- Cause: Insufficient system buffer
  Solution: In the system.ini file in the C:\Windows directory, set the vcache to MinFileCache = 512 and MaxFileCache = 4096. If you have more than 16 MB of RAM, you can set it to 25 percent of your RAM capacity. Just don't set it higher than 16 MB (see **Figure 6.8**).

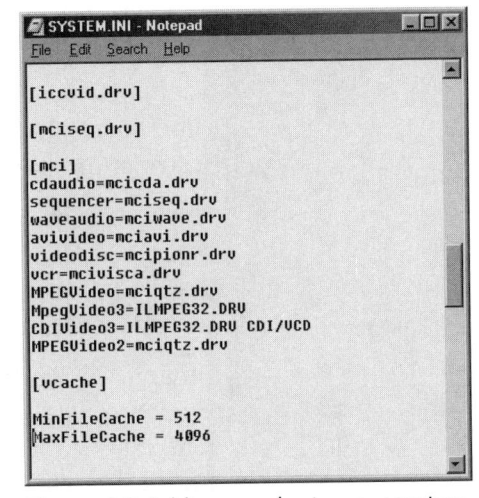

Figure 6.8 Adding vcache to your system buffer may prevent buffer underruns.

What if nothing works? Then you should call the technical support line for your recorder and software and hope that you can get a live voice within an hour or so. Really, tech support ranges from excellent to nonexistent. However, a few Web sites can help you, through their own information or tutorials or through forums where some people will try to solve your problem and some people will be rude to you. Depends on the day of the week and the mood of the participants, it seems. Try the following sites if you can't stand the tech support hold time:

- www.cdrcentral.com
- www.cdrinfo.com
- www.cdfreaks.com

The following newsgroups may also be helpful:

- alt.comp.peripherals.cdr
- alt.comp.peripherals.cdr.mac
- comp.publish.cdrom.hardware
- comp.publish.cdrom.multimedia
- comp.publish.cdrom.software

And there is a lot of general and specific information on CD-R and CD-RW at: www.fadden.com/cdrfaq/

CD-R Media

CD-R media is now manufactured by the millions each year, and there are lots of manufacturers, dye types, coating types, reflective materials, and printable and not-so-printable surfaces. With all these discs available, chances are that you will at some time or another come across some media that does not seem to work in your recorder.

Theoretically, all media should work well in all recorders. In reality, that is not always the case. A good place to start is to use the media brands recommended by your CD recorder manufacturer. Most manufacturers will recommend their own, of course.

Buying CD-R media in bulk, such as in hundred packs, can be economical, with blank discs selling frequently for less than a dollar each. Major media names such as TDK, Taiyo Yuden, Kodak, Maxell, Verbatim, Mitsui, and Ricoh deliver quality media pretty consistently. There are, of course, many unbranded, unmarked, or no-name media available on the market, and some is top quality, some less so. If you buy the cheapest media you can find and it works well for you, there is no reason to change or to pay more. Problems with media will likely manifest themselves in slow seek times, discs that take a long time to be recognized by the drive, discs that can be read in some drives and not in others, and just poor sound when you play them. Just remember that you usually cannot go wrong buying brand name media. (Check out Chapter 3 for a description of CD Identifier, a program that identifies media by brand, for ways to identify premium media in cheaper, debranded form.)

When handling both blank and recorded media, treat each piece, even if it is blank, as if it is a very expensive import CD. Pretend you paid $30 for it. Pretend you bought it from one of the Big Five record labels off their soon-to-be-up Web sites where they are going to sell tracks for $4 each. Pretend it has twenty of those tracks on it. There, you have an $80 disc that you paid a buck for. Ten years ago you would have paid $80 for a blank. The point is, CD-R discs must be treated with care. They can take a lot of abuse and still record and play, but the more carefully you handle your media, the better luck you will have recording it and the better will be the finished product. Dust, scratches, fingerprints, peanut butter, beer, and other foreign materials all will contribute to a botched recording session or a poor-sounding disc. Use the following rules when handling CD-R media.

- Label the media before recording. Open the jewel case, do not remove the disc, label it with a permanent marker, let it dry for about 5 seconds, and close the jewel case cover. If you are using paper labels, print and put them on before recording. If you label the disc after recording and the application of the label ruins the disc, you have just wasted all of your recording time.
- When you are taking the disc out of its case, hold it by its edges while pressing the center button in the jewel case so the disc releases cleanly. Then place it carefully in the recorder tray. Close the tray immediately. If the disc is not correctly seated in the tray and jams the tray when closed, check the disc for physical damage.
- When recording is finished, remove the disc should from the tray immediately and place it back in the jewel case, unless you are going to listen to it right away.
- Closely examine any discs you inadvertently drop or otherwise mishandle before you record.
- Never leave discs, recorded or unrecorded, in direct sunlight.
- If a disc does get dirty, just wash it with warm water and mild soap, using your fingers, and pat it dry with a towel. Then let it sit for a few minutes to finish drying. Put it in your drive wet and you can imagine what centrifugal force will do!

Using Your Computer While Recording

After you get the hang of making a disc, it is not a very good allocation of resources to use the powerful machine on your desk to burn CDs but not perform any other task for the fear of a buffer underrun. A reasonably fast Pentium-class machine with 32 MB of RAM, properly set up, can record at reasonable speeds at the same time that you perform other tasks. Two caveats: The other tasks must not access the drive or recorder being used as source and destination, and if you are recording from the hard disk, you should not perform disk-intensive activity while the recording is going on. But surfing the net and word processing while recording are proper ancillary activities and should not cause problems on most fast machines. All in all, your burn speed, your recorder interface, your CPU speed, amount of RAM, hard disk condition, and most important, what other programs you are running will determine whether you must watch with hands firmly in lap or move on to other tasks.

Highway 61 Restored

7

If you've been replacing all your favorite LPs with their CD equivalents, stop now.

Believe it or not, your digital remastering of Dylan's *Highway 61 Revisited* will categorically be better than the one available at your local CD store. You alone have the best grasp on what sounds good to your ears; consequently, you're better than the best audio engineer when it comes to digitally restoring your favorite LP for your personal use. Even if "Like a Rolling Stone" is worn to a barely audible nub (as it should be, if you ask us) and "Desolation Row" is marred with a huge scratch, you and your software will be able to pull out a better digital track than any record company could, simply because you're doing all the pulling. Subjectivity has that particular advantage over acoustic science. (One caveat, though: Some subjectivities have been known to offend the neighbors, so sometimes it is best to keep one's subjectivity to oneself.)

The beginning of the CD era marked a transition for record industry back catalogs. Record companies began to consider what back titles were likely to sell with the new medium. That old blues record you picked up secondhand may not have been deemed worthy of CD release, as the major players set out to codify a new music canon. Anyone with a vast record collection amassed over many years knows a certain distinctiveness was lost in the transition to CDs. Here's your chance to get it back, to preserve the amalgam of musical artifacts that informed the likes of *Highway 61*. You can't save the world from the myopia of the recording industry, but you can save yourself.

But if you intend to publish your results, this isn't the chapter—or book—for you. Many—and we're not kidding when we say *many*—legal considerations arise when you're duplicating copyrighted material. We'll touch on some of these issues in Chapter 14, "Legal Issues: a Quick Overview," but it's neither intended to be a guide on how to thwart those who protect and own copyrights nor designed to show you how to publicize and profit from your digital remasteries. The legal issues aren't the only considerations either. Audiences ain't real easy to please (although some will say a pleased audience is the badge of mediocrity), and vinyl restoration can become a complicated procedure, way beyond the scope of this book. It's an art, as intricate as car repair, but like car repair, there's a simple conceptual framework anyone can wrap his head around. We'll leave the weird styli, arcane preamplifiers, and blue amberol for you to discover elsewhere. For now we'll just toss you some spark plugs and an oil filter and show you what to do with them.

Making Connections

Having heard us detail the procedure of unifying your modern home stereo and your computer with that one simple connection in Chapter 5, you might get to wondering why this chapter contains so many new connections, cables, and pieces of equipment. We have several reasons for that. First, some ugly and noisy wiring issues arise from connecting your computer and stereo in that fashion, especially with ground loops. The combined thirty-odd power cords of your home entertainment center, your printer, your scanner, your fax, and your computer have to go someplace, and we hope they won't all be in the same outlet—that's kind of dangerous—but by having them in different outlets, you're probably going to get a ground loop, which might add angry noise to your recordings. Second, we're pretty sure not all of you wish to lug your entire home entertainment system over to your CPU—in fact, neither of us wants to acknowledge the existence of a computer when we're trying to relax with some tunes, let alone see one lurking in proximity. Third, and most important, this new set of connections, we hope, will be illustrative of several of the finer points of home recording, especially on the level of various pieces of equipment. If you're *safely* unified and are not finding cruddy 60-cycle hum in your recordings, then by all means, forego the new connections.

Otherwise...

Stuff You Need on the Outside

Surely, you've seen a turntable before—you're going to need one of those for this endeavor. If your turntable vanished alongside your fondue pot, don't lose heart. We've seen a couple mass music format changes, and a lot of people, following the trends, replaced their nice, old turntables with dual tape decks and more recently with CD players and changers. If you stick your head into any thrift store, odds are you'll find a pretty nice—if old—turntable for 20 or so bucks (see **Figure 7.1**). If thrift doesn't suit you, you can still get new turntables—in fact, with the renewed interest in "the warmth of vinyl" and the bizarre "DJ" phenomenon (getting a check for hauling one's record collection around the country and playing it for people strikes us as cheating in some sense), the turntable is making a vengeful comeback. Prices range in the standard stereo equipment fashion, fifty to ten million dollars, and every price in between. For those restoring 78s, you can pick up an all-in-one type turntable (one that will play 78s, 45s, and 33 RPM LPs) for around 300 bones, or you can email the guys at The Edison Shop (edisonshop@enter.net) who'll inexpensively make an all-in-one turntable for you out of the standard one you've got.

Figure 7.1 Just in case you haven't seen one, here's what a turntable looks like.

There are two basic categories of turntable: belt drive and direct drive. Belt-driven units use elastic belts that are calibrated for different speeds and adjusted internally (or, occasionally, manually) like bicycle gears. Depending on frequency of use, belts will eventually wear out and require replacing, which can prove challenging (aligning model numbers and such for the perfect fit). However, with a good, well-treated turntable that you use primarily for audio restoration rather than everyday listening, the belt may not get stretched out of spec for years, if ever. However, many aficionados swear by direct-drive turntables for just this reason, although the direct-drive models you're most likely to see in stereo stores these days will be high-priced professional turntables designed for DJs. You'll end up paying extra for sync-stopping and the like, which you really don't need. So if a salesman foists a direct-drive über alles rap on you, don't be suckered in. A midrange belt-drive player should serve your purposes just fine.

You'll also need a preamplifier between your turntable and your PC. You don't need to get a superexpensive one, but this is one of those instances where you won't regret shelling out a few extra dollars. Although it's true that today's software can compensate for many of the faults a preamp might have, working around a shoddy preamp can get on your nerves, and you increase the chance of degradation every time you alter a track with your software. It's always better to get a good sound going in, and for this, a reasonably good preamp is requisite.

A recommended course of action: Use the preamp you've got, and then, if you're still not hearing a track you can shape into satisfying sound, upgrade your preamp. In place of a preamp, you can use a stereo receiver's input (see **Figure 7.2**), and grab your signal from the device's line output (most often designated "tape out").

High-quality RCA cables never hurt, but again, don't break your bank buying them. All told, you'll need two pairs of RCA cables. One of the two pairs should be four feet, long enough to run between your preamp/turntable rig and your computer. A gasp of terror may go up here: Some will argue that audio signals deteriorate along the lines, and that more line can only mean more deterioration. Our reason for a particularly long cable is that computer monitors regularly fire off a lot of electromagnetic noise, and if that noise gets too close to the cartridge of your turntable, it'll happily attach itself to your recording. This stubborn noise is usually worse than any degradation a long cable might cause.

The other cable, as you've probably guessed, runs from the turntable to the preamp, so know that distance if you have to buy one. Many turntables, however, come with an RCA cable built in—if your turntable has one, you can forego the shorter RCA cable.

> *Another cabling option is to get a long RCA Y cable—also called a stereo patch cable—instead of the long RCA cable (see **Figure 7.3**). These cables are always nice to have around, but you'll find limited choices as far as quality is concerned, simply because there's no real market for them yet. Many people insist on high-quality RCA cables for their racks; only a few insist on high-quality Y cables. This may change, as the computer moves from the den to the living room, but for now, Y cable comes in fewer flavors than RCA cable.*

Figure 7.2 This is the rear of a stereo receiver—you may find it looks something like the rear of your preamplifier, at least in that there are several RCA jacks. If you're using this receiver as your preamp, you'll want the line from your turntable to run to phono in and the line to your computer to run from tape rec.

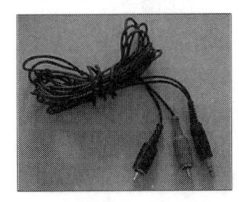

Figure 7.3 This is a Y cable. The end with the two RCA plugs (left) will run to your preamp, and the stereo-mini end (right) will run to your line in, whether that's a line in on your soundcard or a Mic jack on your iMac.

If you go the long RCA cable route, you'll probably need to attach an RCA-to-stereo-mini adapter. The input and output plugs of your computer will most likely be stereo-mini. If they're not stereo-mini, you've probably got a nice sound card or a fancy USB Wave Terminal, and you already know how to run cable from this to that. When you shoot down to Radio Shack or any professional audio store, you may encounter two separate piles of this adapter. They look exactly the same except for one small feature: If you hold up an adapter from each pile, you'll notice one adapter has a single colored ring around the metal shaft and the other has two colored rings around the metal shaft (see **Figure 7.4**). The one with two rings is the stereo-mini—the other is a mono connection.

Figure 7.4 Notice the two rings around the shaft of this stereo-mini plug. Those two rings delineate two channels, the right and left channels that constitute stereo. A plug like this but with only one ring around the shaft delineates only one channel, hence mono.

While you're out, consider replacing your turntable's stylus. Many people just plain forget to do this from time to time. You might be surprised by how clean a sound a virgin stylus elicits from an LP, particularly a high-quality stylus. These can get costly, of course, and you may not want to spend a lot given that you won't be using your turntable often, now that you've got all these beautiful digital reproductions. Nonetheless, to make a beautiful digital reproduction... well, we're sure you get the drift by now.

Because magnetic storage is so cheap, think about picking up another hard disk, one that you'll dedicate to storing the album sides you rip. Two gigabytes is usually more than sufficient, and a 2-gig hard disk won't set you back more than 50 bucks these days. Since we suggest that you defragment the drive that will contain your audio material before each ripping session, you'll come to appreciate having this small and discrete space to defragment. An alternative, of course, is to dedicate a partition of your existing hard disk to audio material—this is fine too, but taking a shot in the dark here, all your partitions are probably full of stuff you need and subsequently cannot accommodate a brand new slew of stuff. But either way is fine.

To ensure good, solid final tracks for the burn, and to avoid being threatened with violence, you should pick up a pair of studio headphones. It's much, much easier to concentrate on your tracks with headphones; isolating yourself from the noise and flaws of the world makes amending the noise and flaws of your tracks a lot easier. You're going to want to listen to your tracks in both environments—with and without headphones—for flavor and comparison, but when you get down to the dirty business of editing and restoration, you'll probably want to be listening at a semihigh level (be careful with your ears though!), and semihigh levels piped beyond your own hearing might get you shot or divorced—this is yet another time headphones come in handy.

Now, bring all this stuff near your computer…

Connecting your stuff

First, power down and then unplug everything—computer, monitor, printer, all of it—we'll plug it back in shortly, in a particular way. Second, just so you know, we're going to be working in an environment where feedback squeals are possible—albeit remotely. Feedback squeals, something we've all unfortunately heard and may have suffered bodily damage from, occur when an input device receives its own signal, so any time you've got an input device (such as a microphone) and a related output device (speakers, for example) working near each other, proceed with some caution. Please be careful: These squeals can cause everything from tinnitus to permanent hearing loss.

This isn't the most space-efficient project you'll ever undertake. You're going to need to clear room for your turntable and a preamplifier near your computer, about four feet away from your monitor (as we mentioned, renegade electromagnetic radiation from computer monitors has been known to add supertenacious noise to a recording, and that's the last thing you need if you've got a mauled record on your hands).

Plug your turntable into your preamp's phono-in jack. Then, if appropriate (most times it is), run your turntable's ground wire to your preamp's chassis someplace—often, there's an area on preamps designated Phono Ground, where connecting is simply a matter of loosening and tightening a screw around your turntable's ground line. That done, run that long cable, whether it's an RCA or a Y cable, from the preamp's line-out to your computer's line-in or mic jack. The RCA end plugs into the preamp and the stereo-mini end (or the end with an adapter) runs to your computer's line-in or mic jack. On an iMac, for instance, you'll plug the stereo-mini end into the jack that has the representation of a microphone etched next to it. On a PC, your line-in and/or mic jacks will be on your sound card.

> **Yet more stuff to consider**
> You can also place a graphic equalizer between the preamp and the sound card. It's not necessary for several reasons, not the least of which is you'll be able to equalize within your software. But if you feel that by doing this you'll get a better track going in, then by all means put one there.

Additionally, your sound card may feature digital I/O, in the form of S/PDIF (short for Sony/Philips Digital Interface Format) or optical connections or even both. You may have digital inputs and outputs built into the card (a $600 DAL card, for instance), or you may have a tandem card (such as Hoontech's $40 SB-DB3 that works with your SoundBlaster Live!). If this is the case, you have the option of doing your A-D (analog-to-digital) conversion outside your computer using an external A-D converter. These units start at around $300. Given the impressive quality of A-D conversion that occurs onboard many of today's analog I/O sound cards—that is, the sound card we're discussing here, the one with the line-in and mic inputs—it's difficult for some people to justify that expense.

Your PC's sound card may offer you a choice. Most of today's models feature both a mic port and a line-in port. Plugging into either of these will do the trick, but there is debate over which is the better choice. It's true that mic inputs tend to have, relatively speaking, high gain and a flat frequency response, both of which are desirable here, but it's also true that having an equalized preamp running into your mic might cause a few sonic problems—you're essentially running an amplifier to another amplifier when you do this—so the line-in may be the way to go. Fortunately, this ain't politics—you can try both ways within the space of fifteen minutes and see which one suits you.

Grab that power strip and plug your essential equipment into it: your turntable, preamp, CPU, monitor, and PC multimedia speakers, if those are powered (most likely they are). You can also plug in your other peripherals, such as your printer, but we'd suggest you don't—fewer fires mean fewer sparks. Do your dangedest to keep any sources of electromagnetic emission away from your turntable.

Plug your power strip into the wall, and then power up. That's it, you're now connected. But that's the easy part.

Stuff You Need on the Inside

The software that came with your CD-R drive may prepare your LPs for a burn, but you can do better. The popular mass-market packages are catching up, but you probably will always be able to find better packages. Figure this, when you're shelling out dough for software: The most expensive software package we'll discuss will run you 400 bones. (Remember, particularly with cool software, that expensive *does not* mean *best*.) That same $400 will purchase about 27 music CDs at Corpco Inc. Music Store, CDs mastered by someone else's hands and mass produced—inferior CDs! If you burn 27 digital copies you made of 27 LPs—superior-quality CDs, for the people by the people, mind you—that software package will have paid for itself. And that's just the most expensive package; the package we'll be recommending heartily and with mirth goes for less than $100.

If you are a Mac user, your choices are, at the moment, comparatively limited. Mac used to rule over the digital audio editing scene with an iron fist, but there was that recent time when Mac's popularity waned, which led to the decline and fall of its leadership in audio restoration. What we' suggest you do if you're using a Mac is go over to Arboretum Systems' Web site (www.arboretum.com) and peruse their wares. Arboretum offers tons of great software for the Mac, including Ray Gun (see **Figure 7.6**), but the one we'd have you scope out most thoroughly is Hyperprism ($299). You can download a free demo of Hyperprism at www.arboretum.com (see **Figure 7.5**). Not only does the company make quality software but it has also got Brian Eno's stamp of approval—you can't beat that.

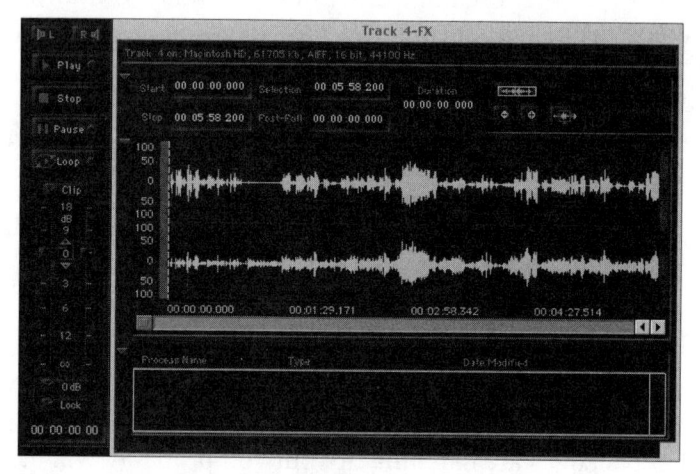

Figure 7.5 Arboretum Systems' Hyperprism.

If you are using a Windows machine, your software choices are much broader. let's take a quick peek at some of the packages out there:

Ray Gun, Arboretum Systems ($99)

Ray Gun is bare bones, yes, but good bones, the kind of past-preserving bones you'd see in a museum—the Lucy of the audio restoration arena. Though Ray Gun can function as a plug-in to many of the popular audio restoration tools, it works exceptionally well on its own, and you can't beat it for its price and sheer simplicity.

Figure 7.6 Arboretum Systems' Ray Gun.

On an subtle Seattle-gray background, you're presented with about seven controls, one of which won't work so well in the United States, no matter what you do. But even with this minimal set of tools, you can produce excellent results—we accomplished some of our best restorations with Ray Gun, all by itself. We don't know what algos whir behind that plain and tall interface, but man, they must be something else.

Here's what you get, as far as restoration options go, in Ray Gun: One effective and handy noise reduction filter that deals with general noise, such as tape hiss and broadband stuff; one equally effective and handy pop filter that flattens impulse noise such as clicks; one rumble filter that cleans mechanical noise (usually from the turntable itself); one 60-Hz hum filter; and one 50-Hz hum filter. You'll also find a slider-bar called Output, which may be considered essentially a gain control—that is, your sample gets louder when you move the control up and softer when you move the control down.

That's it, but that's plenty. In fact, those functions form the foundation of the total project of audio restoration. All configurable options and capabilities in other, more-complicated, audio restoration programs ultimately answer to denoising, declicking, derumbling, and de-60-Hz humming a digital audio sample (or de-50-Hz humming if you live in Europe—these hums come from the way we're wired, coupled with the process of making a digital audio sample with electric machinery). It's just the more you pay, the more ways you have to denoise.

Pristine Sounds Pro, Alien Connections ($200)

Most restoration and editing programs and even Windows Sound Recorder offer you a sonic picture. These sonic pictures are handy: Seeing the waveform you've recorded helps a great deal in the restoration process, because you'll often be able to see sonic disturbances in these representations as well as see the lack of disturbance, for comparison. It doesn't take long to get your eye and your ear working in unison when treating your digital recordings. You'll hear the niggling pop, zoom in on your sonic picture to the general area of the disturbance, actually see it, and then mend it until it pleases your ear and your eye. You'll find, too, that your eye can sometimes even compensate for your aural deficiencies—great moments in perception to be sure, a kind of poetic synesthesia.

Pristine Sounds Pro (see **Figure 7.7**) offers this function through something it calls a Frequency Space Editor. With this utility, you paint your modifications with different kinds and sizes of brushes. Your canvas is a sonograph, where one axis is time and the other is frequency. With one of the four brushes—denoise, declick, amplify, and mute—you can paint away disturbances, or anything else, as broadly or precisely as you choose. You can adjust the brush size for time and frequency, so you can cover as much of either dimension as you wish. This is the height of precision editing.

Another notable feature is the Sound System Profiler: It's a little test you take with the program to determine what sonic faults, if any, your sound hardware has. The program takes this data and compensates for these faults in real-time.

Pristine Sounds also contains the full range of standard noise reduction filters, enhancement filters (reverb for dead tracks, for example), two kinds of graphic equalizers, and even an all-in-one vinyl restoration tool. Much like Ray Gun, Pristine Sounds applies three standard vinyl restoration filters simultaneously (derumble, declick, and denoise) and offers an optional Room Ambience filter (very cool thing—you can define physical space and the resulting acoustics with it). You may, too, with the tool's Preview mode, hear the effects of what you're doing to your track as you're doing it.

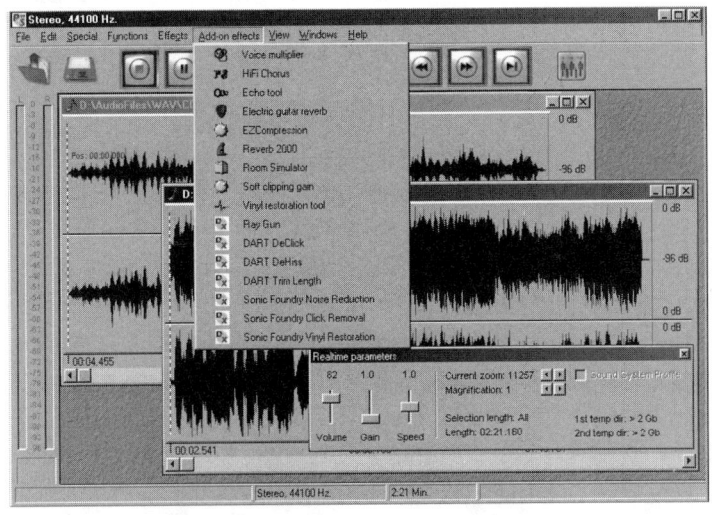

Figure 7.7 Alien Connections' Pristine Sounds.

CoolEdit Pro, Syntrillium Software ($399)

Pick up CoolEdit Pro and you'll never need another audio tool as long as you live. CoolEdit does everything: It even has something called a Brainwave Synchronizer that, the company says, is designed to alter your sample such that when you listen to it through headphones, your brain will begin pumping out large amounts of certain frequencies, and you will, in consequence, relax. We tried it, figuring any sample would work just by the nature of what the tool purports to do, but no dice, not with G.G. Allin anyway. CoolEdit also generates DTMF tones, so you can dial your phone with it, too.

We can't do this program justice in the short space of this chapter—the cost-to-functionality ratio is extremely tilted to the functionality side, the extras are endless, the interface is the most pleasing and navigable of all wave editors we've seen, and on and on. Forced to choose just a couple things to underscore, we picked two: the utter malleability of the thousand restoration and enhancement tools and filters the software puts at your disposal, and the fact that that malleability is almost always represented graphically. For example, CoolEdit's Click/Pop/Crackle Eliminator not only features 20 fully adjustable options—such as major disturbance detection, sensitivity settings, and rejection settings—but also represents these settings to you graphically within the filter interface (see **Figure 7.8**). You can count on things like that throughout the program.

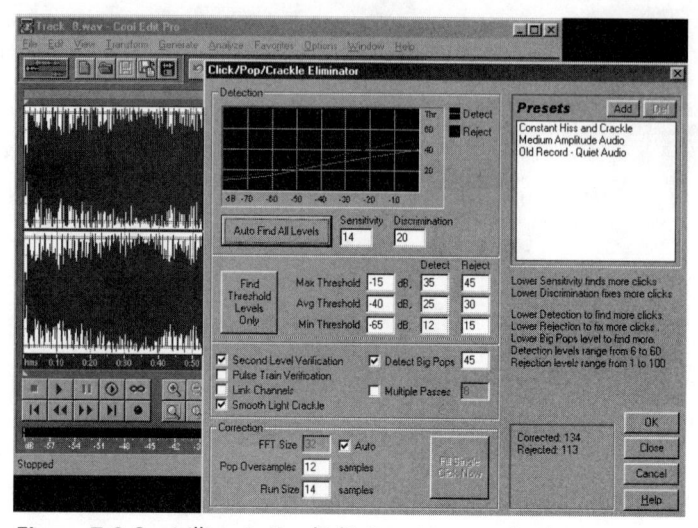

Figure 7.8 Syntrillium's CoolEdit Pro. Here's a look at CoolEdit's Click/Pop/Crackle Eliminator.

The structure of the program sort of guides your restoration project: You're encouraged, just by the way the program is built, to gradually hone your alterations until you arrive at a track you're happy with. Case in point: CoolEdit's graphic equalizer. When you launch the application, you'll first see a simple ten-band equalizer (represented graphically, see **Figure 7.9**) that you're able to manipulate as you listen to your sample. Once you've arrived at a good sound, you may move, by clicking a tab toward the top of the window, into a twenty-band equalizer to perform finer adjustments—your settings from the ten-band equalizer are preserved here, so you've only got another ten bands to manipulate. Finally you can move into a thirty-band equalizer, for even finer adjustments—again, your settings from the twenty-band are preserved.

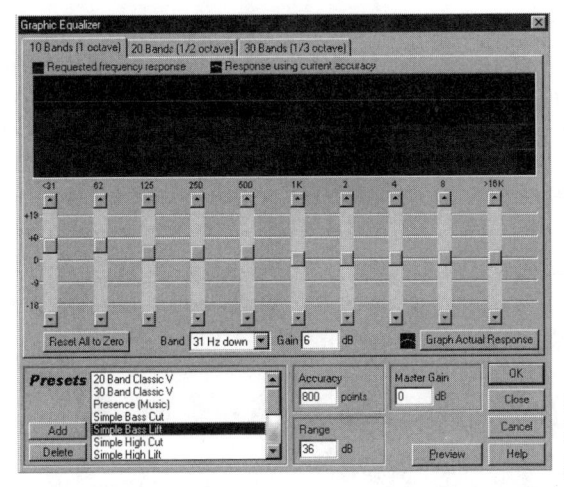

Figure 7.9
Here's CoolEdit's graphic equalizer.

> **On the bubble**
>
> Two more programs are worth checking out. First, the legendary Dart Pro 98 (Dartech, $299), an excellent, reasonably priced package built for audio restoration. Dart incorporates a CD recording function too. It's a fantastic all-in-one for all analog-to-CD projects. Second is Sonic Foundry's somewhat overpriced Noise Reduction ($349), a Direct-X plug-in that works within many programs, including most of the ones we've discussed. What it lacks in visual stimulation and configurability it makes up for in results: Used in tandem with Sonic Foundry's ultrapowerful audio editing program SoundForge ($499), Noise Reduction is unstoppable. Very cool applications.

Diamond Cut Audio Restoration Tools, Diamond Cut Productions ($99)

Our choice for the coolest software around is Diamond Cut Productions' Diamond Cut audio restoration tools (see **Figure 7.10**). Diamond Cut is worth the $100 for its user's manual alone. Well, maybe not, but if you're looking for comprehensive documentation and tutorials on the subject of vinyl restoration and a program that can effect every single one of the necessary restoration procedures—and some besides—Diamond Cut is the thing to get. It's a jovial product with lethally serious and astonishing technical applications—always an appealing combination. Although Diamond Cut is capable of any audio restoration job—cassettes, telephone recordings, whatever—it's built almost exclusively for vinyl, ancient (or *olde,* as the company puts it) to modern. It has that edge on every other program we've discussed and is the one we recommend you get.

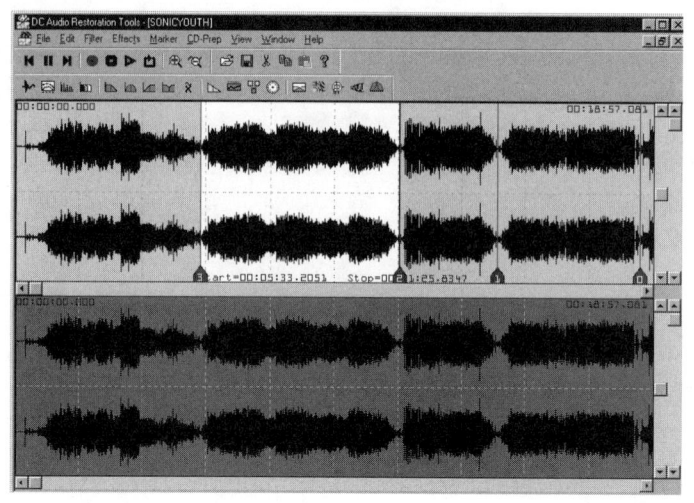

Figure 7.10 Our choice for the coolest digital audio editing software around, Diamond Cut Productions' Diamond Cut Audio Restoration Tools.

We'll also use this package to illustrate vinyl restoration. Most packages we discuss have similar features, so watch how we do things and then apply that to whichever package you choose, even on the Mac. Hyperprism for the Mac matches Diamond Cut filter for filter, and then some.

Initially, the names of the noise filters might freak you out a bit (declick becomes the Impulse Noise filter, dehum becomes the Notch filter, and so on), but the user's manual and help files carefully explain each filter.

Finally, there's a CD-Prep area—this is the goal, after all—containing all the necessary preburn adjustments: track-splitting, gain normalization, and even a Quantize option that'll move your track markers, wherever you've put them, to the closest multiple of 2352 bytes (size of an audio CD sector) for glitchless indexing, as the company calls it.

Let's burn.

Scrub before surgery

Before all else, clean your vinyl. The most convenient way to do this is to grab a jug of distilled water and a chamois and carefully wipe your record down. Alternatively, you can use devices designed specifically for cleaning records—vacuums and such—and places in your town will professionally clean your vinyl for you. If you go the water/chamois route (which should be sufficient for all but the most grungy records), play your record once—the stylus often dislodges stubborn dirt from the grooves that the chamois can't get to—and then wipe it down again. Now you should have a pretty clean record. You should also have heard your record playing on your computer's speakers. If you didn't, check your connections. If that's not the problem, fear not, it's probably your operating system's audio settings, which we'll get to directly after your record is clean and functional.

If your vinyl is warped, you can do a couple things. The first is not for the faint of heart: Preheat your oven to 125 degrees F. Then go to the hardware store and grab two panes of glass, big enough to sandwich an entire record between. Bring those home and place your warped record between those panes and cook the sandwich for five minutes—don't leave it, stay with it—and remember that you're cooking a record. You don't want this dish overdone. Bring it out and let the sandwich cool awhile, a couple hours usually does it.

If that scares you, and it should a little, there's another way. This method will fix problems caused by scratches and warping and is generally safe for use on all records. Grab the loose change from your pocket, and make sure you have one of each coin—penny, nickel, dime, and quarter. Place a dime on top of the tone arm's head (the thing that houses your stylus), and then play the record. If the dime doesn't help the stylus track properly, move on to the penny, and so on, all the way up to the quarter. You want the least weight possible, as this technique will eventually devour your record, and more weight will accelerate the process. Since we're only doing this trick once per skipping record, your tunes should be safe. If it happens that a quarter is called for, but the record, while not skipping, is rumbling something fierce, don't fret: You can get that rumble out with a software filter.

Recording

Once you get your shiny clean record in perfect functioning order, you're going to make a quick adjustment in your operating system's audio controls. In Windows, pop open your audio controls from the taskbar by double-clicking the loudspeaker icon in your System Tray. In the Options menu, select Properties. In the window that appears, select the radio box next to Recording, and click OK. In this recording window (see **Figure 7.11**), find whichever port you went into, whether it was the mic or line-in port, check the box marked Select below it, and move the volume slider above the box you checked up really high, almost to the top. Return to Properties in the Options menu, and select the radio box next to Playback. Between the volume bars of both Line-In (or Mic, if you plugged your preamp in there) and Play Control in this window, and the volume control of your PC's speaker's, achieve a comfortable listening level for yourself, and start playing your record.

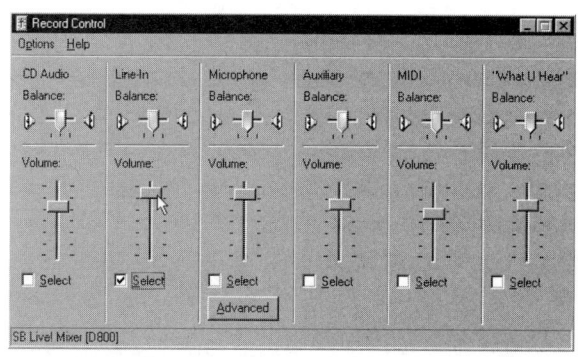

Figure 7.11 These are the adjustable Record Control settings. Right here, we're in the Recording Control window, where we've selected Line-In as our input and have moved the slider close to the top.

Vibrating and jostled turntables don't produce very good sound, for obvious reasons, so don't turn your speakers up so loud that they affect your turntable's stability. In fact, some people will tell you to turn your speakers off altogether.

Configuring your Mac's audio controls is just about the same story. From the Apple menu, select Control Panels, and from the Control Panels submenu, select Sound. A window should have appeared (see **Figure 7.12**), and off in the left you should see a column of options: you'll definitely see at least Alert Sounds, Speaker Setup, Input, and Output. Select Input.

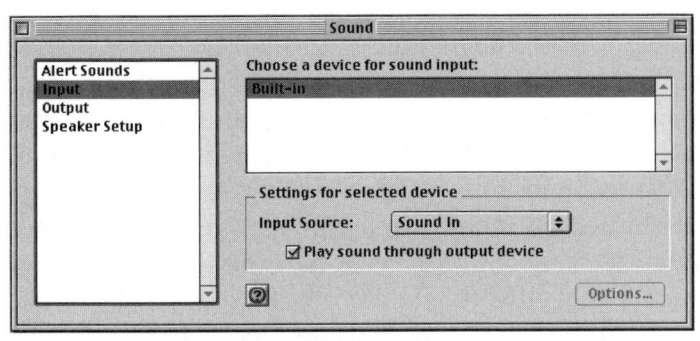

Figure 7.12 Here's the Mac's Sound Input window. We've selected Built-in as our input device and Sound In as our input source and checked the box next to Play sound through output device so we can hear what we're doing.

Now, off to the right, you'll see a field labeled Choose a device for sound input; we're selecting Built-in from the options listed below, as we're working with an iMac and we've run our cable from the preamp to the mic jack. Moving down now to the Settings for selected device, we've chosen as our Input Source Sound In and checked the box next to Play sound through output device because we want to hear our record through our iMac's speakers (otherwise, we'll have no idea what we're doing).

Just to make sure you're not muted, and to make sure your speakers are indeed your output device, select Output in the left-hand column of options. From the new options, we're again selecting Built-in from the Choose a device for sound output because that's the only option we have. You might want to adjust the volume slightly upward by sliding the Volume control to the right. Leave the Mute box unchecked. Now you're all set, you can close that window at your leisure.

If after all this you're still not hearing your album over your computer's speakers, something has gone terribly wrong. If you're working on a PC, you may need to reinstall or upgrade

THE LITTLE AUDIO CD BOOK

your sound card's drivers, which is ultimately no big deal. Go to the manufacturer's Web site and download and install the latest drivers for your model, or call the company's tech support line. Those people have a rough job, so be nice and have documentation of your problem readily available.

A Mac user probably isn't having any problems right now. If you are, it probably isn't your Mac causing them. That's one good thing about total integration: it's really easy to get everything to harmonize. Run through your audio settings once more, confirming that you've properly selected your input device, maybe even try other input devices for the sake of experiment. Then check your connections, and make sure your preamp is plugged in and turned on (don't be embarrassed if you forgot to plug it in, we do that constantly, especially on the weekends when we're relaxing). If you're still not hearing anything, we're not sure what to tell you, unless we're there looking at your rig, then we'll tell you something, even if we don't know what's going on. We have professional images to preserve.

Now fire up your software. All audio restoration software will feature a record function, and it's usually easy to find (most times, it's a superpronounced red button in the program's icon bar). In Diamond Cut, you can initiate the recording function by hitting the big red record button or by selecting Record File from the Edit menu. Picking either of those will summon the Record File window, where you're presented with a number of options (see **Figure 7.13**). Select 44.10 kHz for a sample rate (that's the sample rate stipulated by the Red Book, the document that lays out the CD Digital Audio Standard) and the channels you like (mono or stereo).

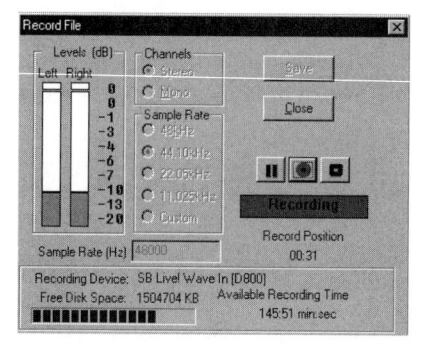

Figure 7.13 Now we're in Diamond Cut's Record File window. The peak level meters are remaining below 0dB, so we're in good shape.

122

7: Highway 61 Restored

One more irritation before we start: Find what you believe will be the loudest passage on your album and play it. Keep a close eye on the level meters to make sure they're high but not so high as to fill in the small rectangles above the 0dB mark. Those rectangles, if they happen to turn red, indicate that clipping has occurred, and consequently your recording will be distorted at peak moments (see **Figure 7.14**). Bad scene, but keep recording. We're going to fix that right now.

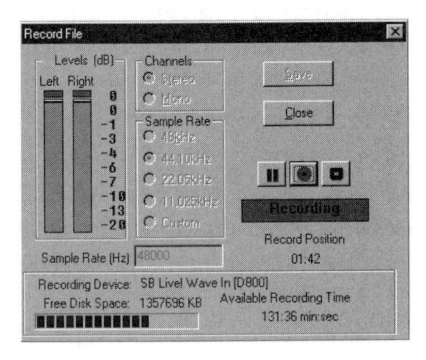

Figure 7.14 Ack! Clipping! See how those rectangles above the peak level meters are filled solid red, er, filled in with a color, probably gray? That means we're going to have a distorted track.

Since we're on a PC here, we're going to return to our Audio Controls (double-click the loudspeaker icon in your System Tray) and once again select Properties from the Options menu. Select the radio box next to Recording, and click OK, just like we did before. The Record Control window should appear, superimposed on Diamond Cut. Move it over a bit, so you can see your peak levels in Diamond Cut's Record File window (see **Figure 7.15**). Now, whichever slider bar (Mic or Line-In) you moved up before should be brought down some; you'll notice the peak levels in Diamond Cut's Record File window moving up and down in unison with the slider bar.

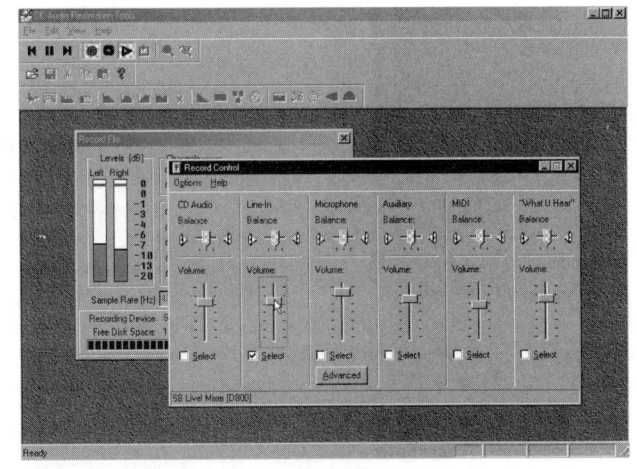

Figure 7.15 We've remedied the clipping problem by adjusting the Line-In slider bar in Record Control.

123

Move the slider bar in the Record Control window just high enough to prevent clipping. Close Record Control, and close Diamond Cut's Record File window. When you're asked here if you want to discard the file you just recorded, click the Yes button. Now open Record File in Diamond Cut again, either by way of the big red button on the task bar or by selecting Record File from the File Menu, exactly as before.

In Diamond Cut's Record File window, hit record and then play your album. Do it in that order for two reasons: It's easy enough to pull the extraneous silence out later with a familiar Cut command, and the *silence* that precedes the first track often contains a snapshot of the general noise found throughout the album. Given that this *silence* is supposed to be silent, you can snip it and apply noise reduction filters to it until it is indeed silent and then proceed from there to apply those same filters with the same settings to the rest of the recording. Exercise caution when doing this, as you may have overdone the filtration process to achieve silence, and the tunes will suffer the consequences. If you did overdo it with the filtering, you can always undo the filtering and try again.

When the record has finished playing, hit stop. Name the file, and save it. Now you can either record the other side of the album, creating two large .wav files in the directory you've specified or you can begin restoring side one. Space on your disk will probably dictate how you proceed.

Restoration

Here's where things get complicated. The noise reduction filters you'll be using are often open to configuration, and it can be difficult to know just what configurations to stipulate. You've got something we don't, however: You've got your ears, and those, for the moment, are a better guide than anything we could lay before you. More good news: Most audio restoration software allow you to preview results before you apply the filter and to adjust parameters on-the-fly. And yet more good news: Anything disturbing to your ear will also most likely be disturbing to a filter, and you'll be notified. Experiment liberally with the filters, and please yourself, above all else. After you've restored two or three albums, you'll find that you've gotten pretty good at it—or at least pretty good at turning out something you're happy with.

We'll just look at the common noises and their respective filters a bit to give you an idea of what they can do and what havoc they can wreak when you're not careful. After that, you're on your own, as it should be.

If you're restoring your records for sentimental purposes, it may sometimes be better just to rip them out and burn them straight, as is, without any further tampering.

The high-pass, or rumble, filter

A lot of times, turntable mechanics will introduce low frequency noise into a recording—this is generally referred to as rumble, as that's what it sounds like. The good thing about removing rumble is it's localized at those low frequencies—sometimes so low that no other information besides rumble could exist there—and can be easily spotted by a high-pass filter, also referred to as a rumble filter. Of course, when you're working at these low frequencies, you're getting close to the bass instruments—keep your eye out for those and you should be fine. The Diamond Cut Highpass Filter (see **Figure 7.16**) has options for setting Frequency and Frequency Slope (as well as your Preview option, so you can hear what you're doing). It's best to keep the Frequency setting really, really low: Your best bet is to begin at the 10 Hz setting and move the slider slowly upward until you're satisfied with the results. When you're happy, apply the filter. This will cut—or weaken beyond audibility—everything below the frequency you finally arrived at.

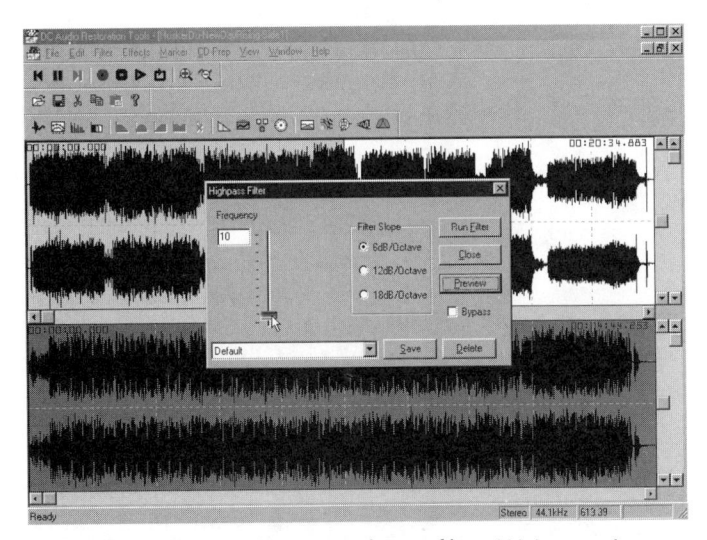

Figure 7.16 Diamond Cut's Highpass filter. We're moving the slider slowly up from 10 Hz here.

Explaining Frequency Slope takes a great long while, so we're going to leave that out; we'll simply let you hear what adjusting that parameter does to a sample—when you're doing this experiment, get the Frequency slider up a ways just so you can hear what's happening beneath it.

The declick, or impulse noise, filter

Clicks and pops jar everything: your ear if you're listening and your eye if you're looking at your waveform. They're distinct because they occur loudly, quickly, and unpredictably, but a lot of things can occur loudly, quickly, and unpredictably in music, and that's where problems arise. These filters can also create problems because when they remove a click or pop, they sometimes leave an approximation of what they imagine would be there if the click weren't, which can lead to weird, small, ugly things all over the place.

Because of those potential hazards, a lot of people choose never to use this filter and instead fix the click by hand. You have many ways to do this, but they all involve locating the disturbance in your waveform—that "picture" of your track—and then zooming in and selecting it for edit. If the noise is short enough, you can cut it out entirely and perhaps never miss that particular segment. You could also simply mute it—your ear, or your brain rather, will close that tiny gap for you by imagining something to put there (a process similar to the one that makes several stills passing by in rapid succession appear to move—as in film or animation). Some software packages will allow you to generate your own sound to paste over the click, and as we mentioned, others will automatically generate what they think would sound OK there (Diamond Cut's Interpolate function does a pretty good job of this).

But if you've got scores of clicks and pops and don't particularly feel like going in after each one of them, declicking might work for you. Diamond Cut's Impulse Noise filter looks a little complicated, but you'll be using only two of the three sliders at any given time. (If you're restoring vinyl, you'll use the Size and Tracking sliders, and with anything else you'll use the Size and Threshold sliders.) You'll also see several preset configurations that serve as starting points—pick the preset you

7: HIGHWAY 61 RESTORED

feel is most applicable to your situation (see **Figure 7.17**). Now you get to walk the tightrope.

Let's use vinyl as our case study here. Check the Vinyl LP box, and select the preset LP DeClick Start Point. Now move the Tracking slider up so that when you hit the Preview button (do that now), you can hear all the clicks and pops you heard earlier. Slowly move the Tracking slider down until you're happy with what you hear. Hit the Run Filter button, and you'll get a readout of how many clicks per second are happening and how many are being removed and replaced (see **Figure 7.18**). If it looks about right, let the filter run; otherwise, start over with different settings.

Figure 7.17 This is Diamond Cut's Impulse Noise filter, known in other programs as a declick filter. We're set for Vinyl here, but Diamond Cut also provides presets for things such as Early Shellac records and Acetate recordings.

Figure 7.18 Oops, we moved the threshold slider too far down, and now all kinds of stuff (see pointer) is being mistaken for clicks and consequently being removed, including good solid areas of song.

127

The Size setting determines in how many samples a suspect click must be found to be convicted of being a click and subsequently removed. So, if your clicks are sudden, adjust that slider down, and if your clicks are of the longer pop variety, move the slider up. Hit the Preview button again. Move the Threshold slider up again, then slowly down, as before. Eventually, you may end up with a satisfactory declicking job.

Median filter

The Median filter takes care of crackle: The incessant clicking and popping, somewhat akin to a campfire, that you hear time to time on an old record. Some people advocate crackle. (There's one cool recent instance of crackle actually being added to a track: Liz Fraser's cut on Massive Attack's *Mezzanine*.) If you're not happy with the crackle on your recording, run the Median filter.

In Diamond Cut, the Median filter is a simple one-slider affair. Since crackle tends to be somewhat consistent throughout a record, as opposed to clicks and pops, you'll have a pretty good idea of what a Median filter applied to the whole track will sound like from a small sample (see **Figure 7.19**). As always, hit the Preview button and this time move the slider up from 0 as you listen. When happiness is achieved, run the filter.

Figure 7.19
Crackle has both advocates and detractors. For the detractors, there is the Median filter or, as it is known elsewhere, the decrackle filter.

Dehiss, denoise filter

Remember that lead-in silence you snipped off and saved? If it's a hissy item (you'll hear that hiss referred to as tape hiss even if it's that distinct hiss of vinyl LPs), you may wish to run a dehiss, denoise, or similarly named filter over it until you're convinced this sample that is supposed to be silent is in fact silent (see **Figure 7.20**). Again, as with all filters, use just enough force to get the sample where you want it; otherwise, you risk choking your track to death. If it's available to you, use the utility in these filters that captures the removed noise. You can then listen to these captives and make sure the filter pulled out only noise and hiss and not any of your music. This is one filter you'll have to experiment liberally with; we can't offer too many tips that won't become obvious during your experimentations anyway.

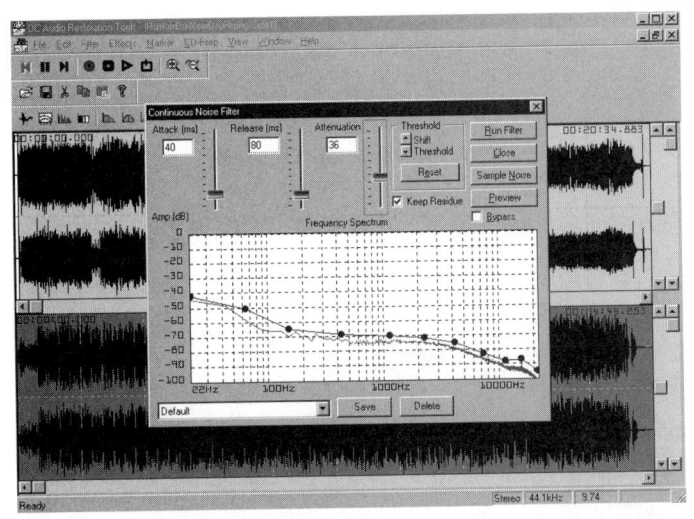

Figure 7.20 Diamond Cut features two kind of denoise filters, a dynamic noise filter and a continuous noise filter. Here's the Continuous Noise filter, which is excellent for ridding a track of tape hiss. Yes, tape hiss is used to describe LP hiss too.

Dehum, debuzz, notch filter

Sometimes you'll notice a distinct hum in the tracks you have copied. Hum can come from just about anywhere: nearby power lines and transformers, household appliances, you name it. If it's electrical and close to your computer, it's a suspect.

> *The most notorious source of hum is a ground loop in your equipment. To avoid these, see to it that all of your equipment is plugged into the same power strip. If you're still getting hum, turn off all but the most essential electrical items in your vicinity and don't be blow-drying your hair while you're restoring records.*

One cool advantage you have over recording studios here is that hum happens mostly in professional-grade equipment, and you may never encounter it. Unfortunately, that very same professional-grade equipment can introduce hum into the original live recording—this hum, of course, isn't your fault at all, but it'll be there no matter what you do, at least during the recording phase.

Since hum is at a specific frequency (60 Hz in America; 50 Hz in Europe), software can easily locate it and get rid of it (see **Figure 7.21**). Usually these filters ask that you give a frequency—if the hum is your equipment's fault, tell it 60 Hz if you're in the States and 50Hz if you're in Europe, or if the hum is the recording studio's fault, tell it 60 Hz if it was mastered in the States…you get the idea. That done, run the filter.

Figure 7.21 Diamond Cut's Notch filter.

Reverb

If your recording sounds dead in the water, and it's not a result of overapplication of filters (if that's the case, go back and undo your filters, and have another stab), try adding reverb (see **Figure 7.22**). Most software offers a reverberation filter, and it always helps when a track requires a little life.

Equalizers

If you got a good track going in, or if you added equalization outside the computer using a graphic equalizer, you'll never need to touch the equalizers most software packages feature. Nonetheless, they can be fun to play with at the tail-end of a project. The results do sometimes surprise you (see **Figure 7.23**).

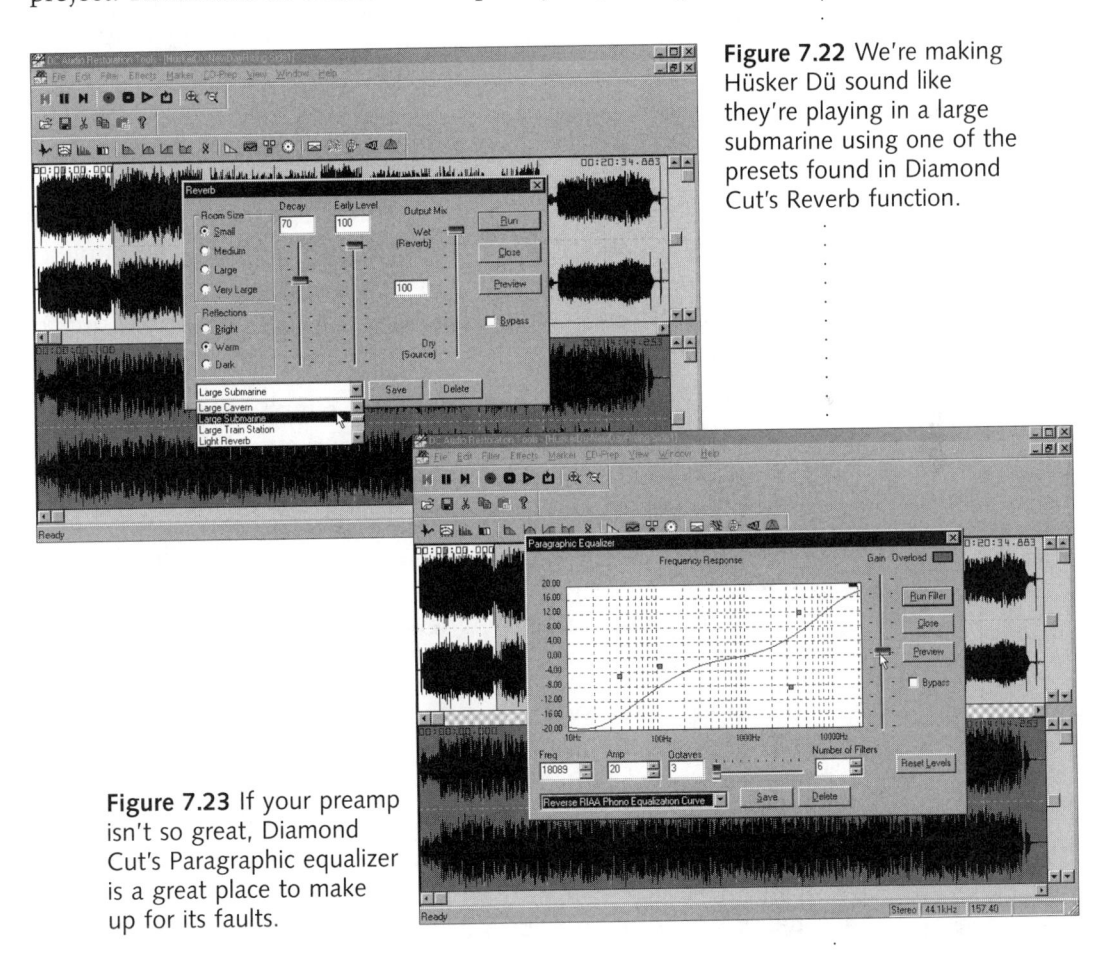

Figure 7.22 We're making Hüsker Dü sound like they're playing in a large submarine using one of the presets found in Diamond Cut's Reverb function.

Figure 7.23 If your preamp isn't so great, Diamond Cut's Paragraphic equalizer is a great place to make up for its faults.

Preparing for the Burn

Just a few more things before we finish this project. The first is splitting into suitable tracks the huge recorded file that results from your restoration efforts. Most programs have a feature called Track Splitter, Detect Silence, or something similar that will go through your file and place markers at any silence and then sometimes proceed to carve your file, at each marker, into the smaller files that becomes your tracks. Many times, however, recordings aren't divided at all: for example, Corelli's *Concerto Grosso* and the Dead Milkmen's *Beelzebubba* each contain areas of distinct musical movement, but the music in these areas is continuous, with no silence to indicate the movement has changed. Then you've got guys such as John Cage who actually implement silence as part of their work; if you hit Cage's *Four Walls* with an automatic track splitter, you'd end up with about 10,000 tracks, when it really has only about 15 "scenes" over two "acts." It is often best to manually split your tracks. This is easily accomplished and will take less time than running a silence detector. Be aware, though, that if you choose to retain the source file (that's the big file you just copied, your digitized album side) when you're making all these smaller files, you're effectively doubling the hard disk space your music will take up.

In Diamond Cut, you split your tracks simply by placing markers wherever you'd like one track to end and another to begin (right-click the waveform where appropriate and then select Add a Marker from the menu that pops up (see **Figure 7.24**). Then from the CD Prep menu select Chop File Into Pieces. That done, you'll have all your tracks ready to queue for a burn in the same directory where you placed your original file. Easy enough.

Finally, listen to your tracks, just to make sure all is well and to your taste. Handy tip for Windows users: You can right-click any audio file to get to the Properties area. In that window, you'll see a tab called Preview—get in there and hit the play button. You'll never have to wait for a player to load up again. At this stage, it's nice, too, to bring friends and loved ones in to listen to your stuff. Remind them, of course, that you're looking for opinions on structure, not your taste in bands. You may have to go back over everything once a consensus opinion in reached, but you'll find it may be worth it.

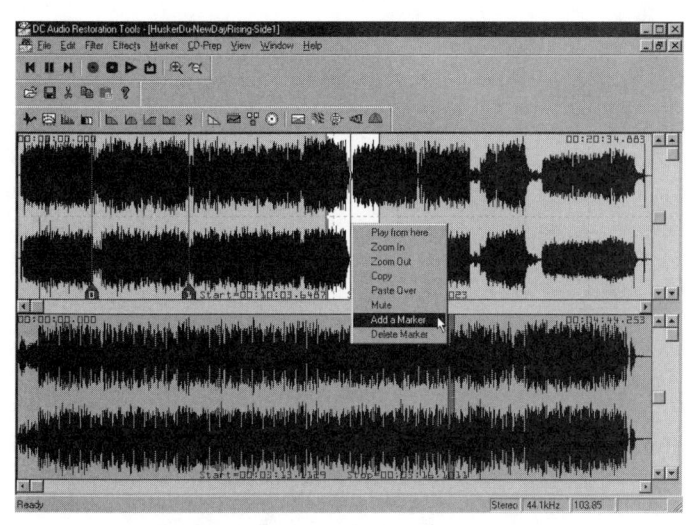

Figure 7.24 Placing a track marker on your waveform is just a matter of click and select in Diamond Cut. The lines marked 0 and 1 indicate markers we've already placed.

The Burn

Recording your restored audio will be a standard-issue burn: no special steps will be required at this point.

Shut down your audio restoration software and other open programs. Turn off the screen saver and any power management features (those things that shut your monitor down after a period of inactivity). Fire up your burning software. Queue up your tracks in any order you like, tell your software you're making an audio CD, and burn your CD. Now you should have the best digital remastery of anything ever in your hands. Nice job!

Restoring and Recording Cassette Tapes

Unlike a record, all those cords, connections, and electrons flying all over the place along with your own trepidation don't really come into play when you're recording a cassette tape to CD. Cassette decks aren't nearly as complex as record players when you're hooking them up: You might laugh a little when you see how easy it is to run a cable between ins and outs. Tapes also endure wear and storage a little better than records do. You won't have to clean your tape, then play it, then clean it again as we did with our records. Finally, tapes don't usually house the panoply of noises that records do. Except under extraordinary circumstances, you won't have to wrangle with clicks or pops or crackle when you're restoring an audio signal from a tape. You'll most often want to be rid of only a single kind of noise, so you'll have to apply only one type of filter. If you understand how to restore a record, even in a rudimentary way, you won't have any problems here, getting your tape to CD.

To connect a cassette deck to your computer, run the very same cable we talked about in Chapter 7 from your deck's line-out jacks to the line-in jack on your sound card or the mic port, just as you did before. Tapes, unlike records, don't require any special equalization or amplification outside of the playback device itself—that is, your deck—so you don't need to involve a preamp here. If you like, you can again run a line from your receiver's tape out to your line-in, so long as you have a tape deck connected to your receiver.

Unplug and Plug In

Once again, we'll have you power everything down and unplug them from your power strip. Take your cable—whether you decided on a Y-cable or an RCA cable with a stereo-mini adapter at one end—and plug the RCA ends into your deck's line-out jack. Plug the stereo-mini end of the cable into your line input jacks, whether that's a mic or a line-in jack on your sound card. Now gather all your power cords—monitor, CPU, tape deck, powered speakers—and plug them into the single power strip in the single wall outlet. We're doing this, as you know, to avoid adding the noise of electricity to your recordings, these ground loops we discussed in Chapter 7. Don't blow dry your hair either or make toast—at least until you're done recording to your hard disk, OK?

> *Like turntables, tape decks can be had on the cheap now, likewise because CD has come to reign over the music distribution scene. Be warned, though, that if you buy a used deck, there may be some serious wear and tear on the tape heads that are used to read the tape. New heads for a used deck can get expensive and are not as easy to install as something like a stylus on a record player. It might be better here, if you don't have one, just to buy a new, but cheap, tape deck—a single tray is all you need for what we're doing and your software can make up for a lot of the deficiencies a deck might have. Remember, too, if you have a deck, use that one first, then upgrade if you're dissatisfied with the results.*

It's been our experience that head-cleaning kits—those little cassettelike things you can buy at audio or record stores or even grocery stores that scour the innards of your deck instead of playing music—don't usually result in an appreciable sound improvement. But since they may actually work for you, and since they run about $3 each, it couldn't hurt to pick one up and use it on your deck.

To be on the safe side, we'll have you keep your deck pretty far away from your computer monitor, just as we had you keep your record player away. As with most record players, tape decks work by way of magnetism, and the stray electromagnetic emissions from your monitor might add noise to your recording.

Now you're connected.

Recording

Recording a tape to your hard disk is almost the same procedure as getting a record to your hard disk, except that you'll be pressing a play button on your tape deck instead of starting a record player and that you may have to adjust the recording level in your operating system again. (In just a second, we'll get to one other striking oddity unique to cassette decks—it's no big deal at all, just something to be aware of.) Let's run quickly through the recording procedure outlined in Chapter 7, "Highway 61 Revisited," and we'll point out the idiosyncrasies of tape decks and the medium itself along the way.

Let's return to our operating system's audio controls, just to make sure everything is in order. On a PC, double-click the loudspeaker icon in your system tray. In the window that comes up, called Play Control, select Properties from the Options menu. In the Properties window, select the radio box next to Recording and then click the OK button at the bottom of the window. The Properties window will vanish, and you'll have a new set of audio controls in a new window, the Record Control window. Here, you'll select your line input by checking a box next to the word Select beneath whichever line input you plugged into. In **Figure 8.1**, we've selected Line-In as our line input. You'll then set your recording level by adjusting up and down the slider bar just above the Select box, remembering that you want as high a level possible here without clipping, as we discussed in Chapter 7. You'll see in **Figure 8.1** that we've set ours close to the top. You can now close the Record Control window. If it happens that during recording that your levels aren't high enough or that your levels are too high and you're clipping, return here and adjust the slider bar accordingly.

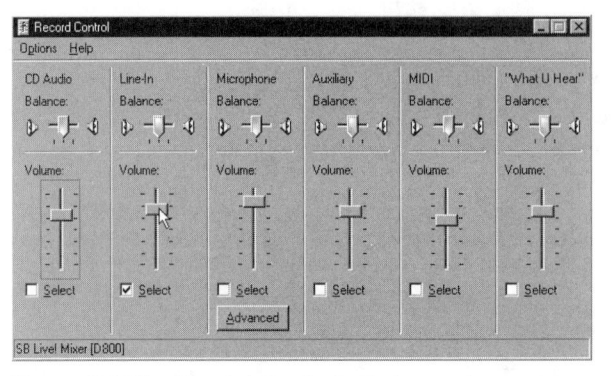

Figure 8.1 The Record Control window, where we've selected Line-In and are adjusting the recording level by sliding the bar upward (see pointer).

On the Mac, you access your audio controls through the Apple menu at the top-left corner of the screen. From the Apple menu, select Control Panels, and then from the Control Panels submenu choose Sound. In the control panel that pops up, select Input from the left-hand column of options. In the Choose a device for sound input field, select Built-in—or whatever else you may have plugged into. From the Input source pop-up menu select Sound In. Check the box next to Play sound through output device. Now close that window; you're good to go.

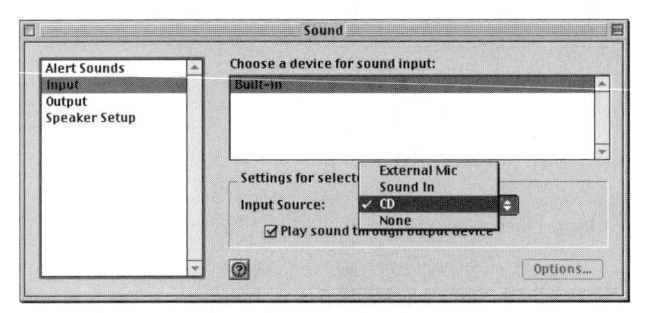

Figure 8.2 The Mac's Sound control panel.

Now play a tape in your tape deck. Surely you've played a tape before, so we don't really need to go through getting a tape from your collection, pressing Eject on your deck, putting said tape in the tray, closing the tray, and pressing some Play button or other. After you've pressed Play and passed the initial silence that follows, you should hear your tape play over your computer's speakers. If you're not hearing anything, we'll refer you to the recording section of Chapter 7 where we discuss your operating system's audio controls in a little more detail and offer a couple of troubleshooting tips.

While you're listening to your tape over your computer's speakers, go have a look at your deck. You might find that you have a switch or dial or something that will turn on and off Dolby Noise Reduction, or NR for short; you may even find you have a couple selections there at your NR dial—B, C, or Off, usually. Whether you choose to apply Dolby NR at the deck is completely up to you and your ear. Try it out, see what you think. You'll probably notice that the Off position renders the sharpest sound but at the cost of added hissing noise, called, appropriately, "tape hiss."

> *What the RIAA Curve is to a record, Dolby NR is to a tape. The idea behind the two methods of noise reduction is precisely the same: Enhance the treble to drown high-frequency noise out. So before an audio signal hits a tape, the treble is enhanced using a Dolby encoder; then, during playback, if you switch Dolby NR on, the treble is attenuated, along with the already drowned hiss.*

Since in just one moment we'll be doing pretty much the same thing Dolby Noise Reduction does—that is, we'll be dehissing what we record to our hard disk using a dehiss filter (we generally don't apply any noise reduction at the tape deck)—we disable Dolby NR and deal with the ensuing tape hiss later. Our digital audio editing software can sometimes be more discriminating than Dolby NR in what noise it reduces, so we like to have a straight hissing track to work with.

> *If the track you record from your tape ends up too crisp, you can always bring the treble end down using your digital audio editing software's graphic equalizer, which we discuss in Chapter 7 and Chapter 11, "Compilation Discs."*

139

Stop and rewind your tape now; we're just about ready to record. Launch your digital audio editing software—we're going to use Diamond Cut on a PC again here to illustrate the recording process, as it is an excellent product and usefully representative of digital audio editors everywhere, PC or Mac. We open the Record File window by pressing the red Record button on the task bar up top. Once there, we select the Stereo radio box and 44.10 kHz for our sampling rate, just like we did before when we were recording a record. With that done, we're all set, so we hit the Record button in the Record File window and start playing our tape.

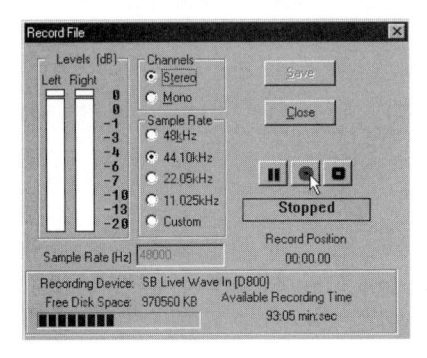

Figure 8.3 The Record File window in Diamond Cut. Here, we're about to record the side of our tape.

It is important that you begin recording in the software before you begin playing your tape. From the silence at the beginning of a tape, many digital audio editors, including Diamond Cut, will take a general snapshot of the hiss and refer to that snapshot when deciding what's hiss and what isn't in applying its dehiss filter to a song. Certainly, you can take a hiss snapshot from the silence between songs, if you like, but you'll find you have more silence to work with at the beginning of a tape. Often, too, more silence means more accurate hiss averaging.

When the tape side is done playing, stop recording in your software. In Diamond Cut, you do this by simply pressing the Stop button in the Record File window. You then press the Save button, which summons a typical Save File window. Name it, save it, that's it. Now you should have Side A or Side B or whatever side you recorded saved onto your hard disk for editing. Once you're done saving your file, Diamond Cut will build the waveform that is your tape side and display it for you (see **Figure 8.4**). Now let's fix this thing up.

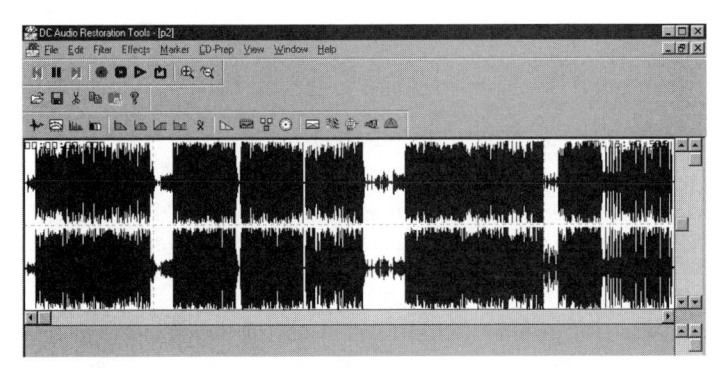

Figure 8.4 The waveform Diamond Cut built for us after we saved our tape side to our hard disk.

Taking a Noiseprint

We're going to give Diamond Cut's dehiss filter an idea of what the hiss on our recording is like now, so that it can efficiently remove it. We start by selecting the beginning of our recording, directly before the first song starts, where it's supposed to be silent but instead is hissing at us.

In Diamond Cut, as in most digital audio editors, you select a segment of a waveform by left-clicking the waveform and dragging your pointer over the segment of the waveform you wish to highlight. You'll find, once you've made your selection, you can hone it further by running your pointer over one boundary of your selection, left-clicking and holding again, and dragging the boundary in whichever direction you like (see **Figure 8.5**).

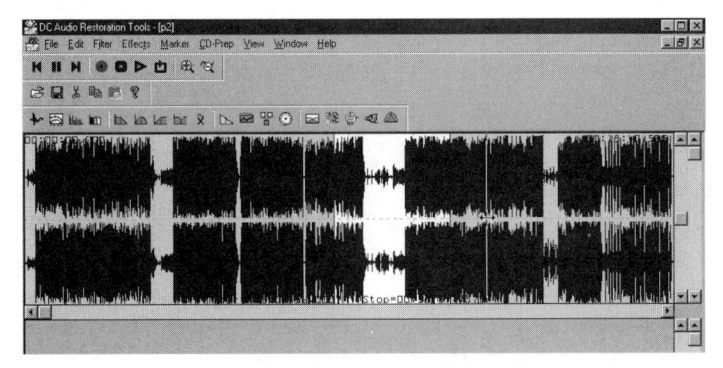

Figure 8.5 We're dragging the rightmost boundary of our selection off to the right a little (see double-headed arrow about two-thirds over), to sharpen our selection.

THE LITTLE AUDIO CD BOOK

> *If you're not seeing your whole waveform, get into Preferences from the Edit Menu. In the Preferences window, in the bottom-left corner, you'll see a field called Display Length Limit. In that field, type how many megabytes of song you'd like to see displayed as a waveform, remembering that 1 minute of song equals 10 MB of hard disk space. We've typed 2000 there, which is the size of the hard disk we've dedicated to audio.*

In **Figure 8.6**, we've selected the beginning of our waveform. If we press the play button in our task bar right now, we'll play our selection instead of the whole waveform. Now we're going to zoom in on the segment we highlighted by clicking the Magnifying Glass with the plus sign in it up on the task bar.

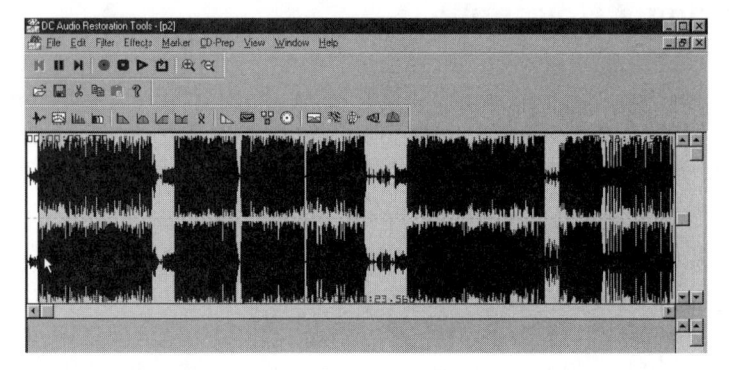

Figure 8.6 The beginning of our waveform is highlighted (see pointer at left).

After zooming in on this area, we'll be able to see a really good representation of the "silence" (in truth, it's really hissy and not silent, but it's supposed to be silent—you get our drift) before the first song. It's represented as that long flat line right before the spiky recording levels (see **Figure 8.7**). To make sure this representation of silence is accurate, we're going to select the line and then press Play on the task bar to listen to our selection. You mustn't select anything more than silence. If you do happen to select something other than silence, such as part of a song, the filter will consider that to be part of the noise it will cut. As you might imagine, it's no good for a filter to run around cutting out chunks of music.

142

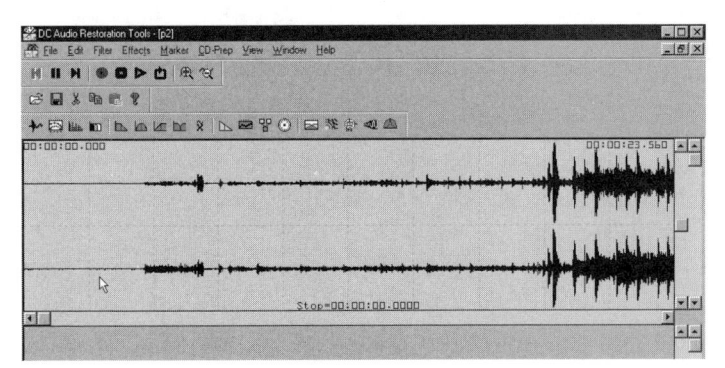

Figure 8.7 The flat line directly above the pointer represents silence, sort of (it's not really silent but it's supposed to be).

Dehiss filters go by many names, Continuous Noise Filter being one of them. You may find in your digital audio editor that your dehiss filter is called Noise Reduction Filter, DeNoiser, or even DeHiss Filter. They all do just about the same thing: Eliminate continuous broadband noise, concentrating particularly on the high end of the frequency spectrum where hiss is most pronounced.

Once we're certain we've selected an area of silence, we launch Diamond Cut's dehiss filter by selecting Continuous Noise from the Filter menu. In the Continuous Noise Filter window, click the Sample Noise button in the upper-right corner. You'll notice, after the filter processes your silence—you'll get a Progress Meter right after you've clicked the Sample Noise button—that a graph appears in the middle of the window (see **Figure 8.8**).

This graph's *y* axis represents amplitude, or how relatively loud something is, and its *x* axis represents frequency. Now notice the two lines in the graph. The upper line, which in color is blue, is the action of the filter—that is, it's the line below which noise will be attenuated or cut when the Continuous Noise filter is run. The lower line, which is red, signifies the noise itself.

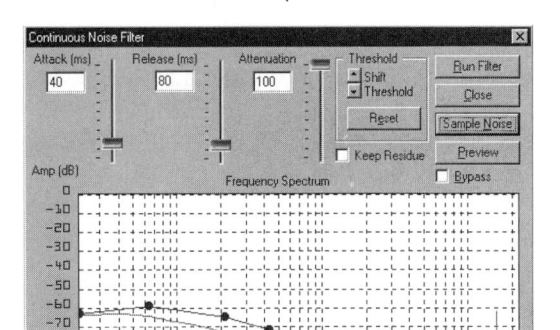

Figure 8.8 We're in Diamond Cut's Continuous Noise Filter window now, where it's drawn up a graph for us.

143

See how the lower line in **Figure 8.9**—the noise line—gets thick and concentrated up in the high frequencies, off to the right in this graph? That's the sibilant, hissing part of hiss we want to be rid of. You'll see, too, from this graph, that hiss is located at a relatively low amplitude. On the amplitude y axis, 0 represents something like gain overload—clipping, you remember—so our noise line, relative to that, is pretty quiet, hovering between -60 and -90dB across the frequency spectrum. So what we have here is an excellent graphic description of hiss: It's a high-frequency, low-amplitude noise, at least on a tape.

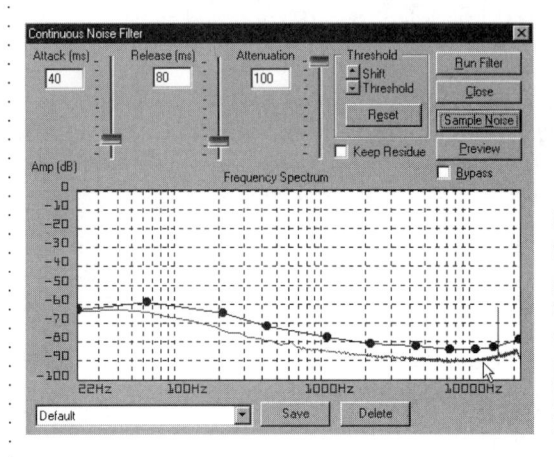

Figure 8.9 Notice the lower line in the graph, representing the noise Diamond Cut located. The pointer is showing the high frequencies, the hissy part of tape hiss.

Since hiss is relatively quiet, you can just cut it—even in the middle of a song—and be done with it. That's the good part about hiss: It's hard to hear unless everything around it is equally or less quiet, and high-amplitude music signals drown it out. That's the idea behind a dehiss filter: It cuts or weakens everything below a certain amplitude, leaving the song ultimately unaffected.

The upper line, then, represents the amplitude below which signals get cut (see **Figure 8.10**). The Continuous Noise filter automatically draws this line for you, at about 10dB above your hiss, and the filter will proceed to weaken or cut everything below that amplitude when you set it on a song. If you move the upper line up—which we'll do in a second, it's totally adjustable—more stuff will be cut, maybe even your song if you move it high enough. If you lower it, more stuff will be allowed to pass, including hiss. It's a fine line, you see, and you can make finer adjustments to it. We'll get to that momentarily.

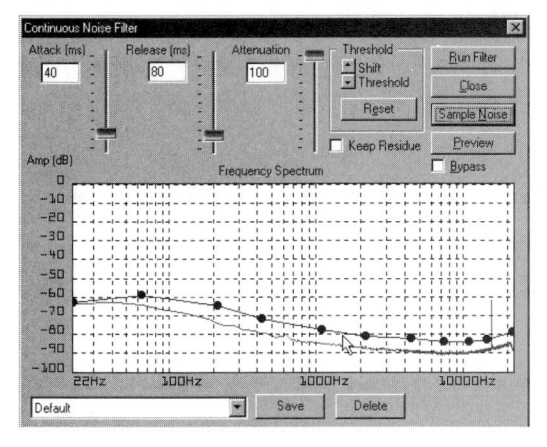

Figure 8.10
The pointer here indicates the upper threshold line, below which noise will be attenuated or cut altogether.

We're going to save our upper line as a preset now by clicking the Save button at the bottom of the Continuous Noise filter. Name your preset in the window that pops up, and save it by clicking OK (see **Figure 8.11**). When we proceed to dehiss our tracks, we'll summon our preset dehiss curve from the drop-down menu right next to the Save button.

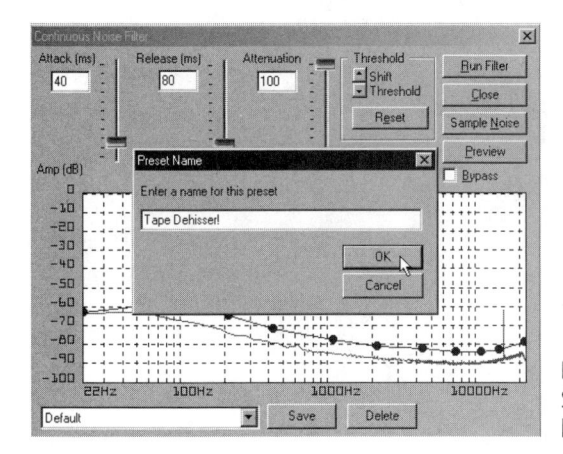

Figure 8.11
Saving the threshold line as a preset.

Track Splitting

As you'll see in a moment, based on the structure of the song you're filtering, you can make a couple adjustments in most dehissing filters. Because of that, it's better to work with only one track at a time when applying the Continuous Noise filter.

We'll tell you here, once again, it's better to split your tracks yourself instead of using an automatic track-splitting, or detect-silence, utility. Often a single song will contain some silence and then resume; fake endings such as the one in the Contours' "Do You Love Me?" are among the coolest moments on record. If it you hit a song like this with an automatic track splitter, you'll end up with two tracks, which probably wasn't what the artist had in mind. In addition, splitting your tracks yourself is often much easier than using a detect-silence tool.

You can easily see, in your waveform, where songs come to an end: The representation of your recording levels drop sharply and suddenly (see **Figure 8.12**). We're going to select one of these areas where a song ends and another begins, and we're going to zoom in on it. Once there, we'll drop a track marker directly and precisely between songs.

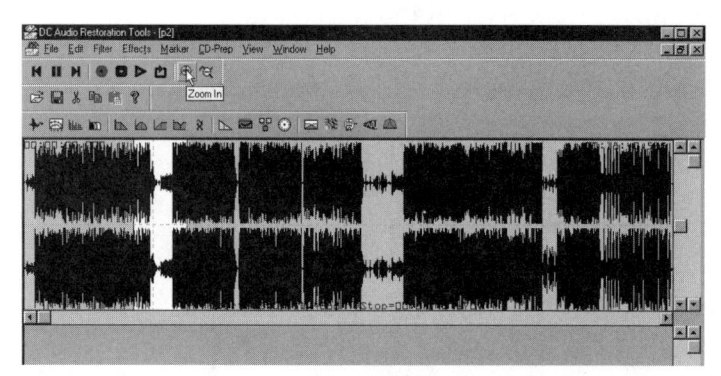

Figure 8.12 Here we've selected the frontier between songs and are preparing to zoom in on it.

A fade-out lingers in the early part of our selection, so we're going to have to mouse over the left boundary of our selection and move it toward the right. After enough adjustments like this, we eventually arrive at the dead-end of the first song and place a marker there. You place a marker, you remember, by right-clicking the waveform and selecting Add a Marker from the menu that pops up (see **Figure 8.13**). If your marker doesn't land precisely where you want it, left-click it and drag it wherever you want it.

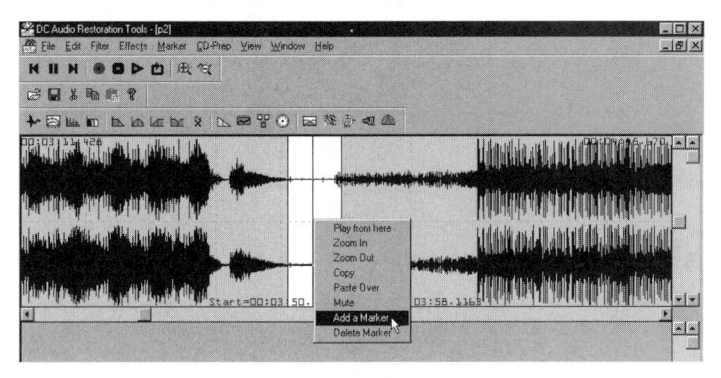

Figure 8.13 Now we've zoomed in, and we're dropping a track marker.

Once we've placed all of our markers, we select Chop file into pieces from the CD-Prep menu (see **Figure 8.14**). It does what it says it's going to do: It chops our big tape side into the seven songs that constitute that side. We elected to preserve our original file because we might mess up when we're restoring it and have to begin again, and because we have room on our hard disk to do that. We now have our uninterrupted tape side *and* the seven delineated songs on our hard disk, doubling the size of the original recording.

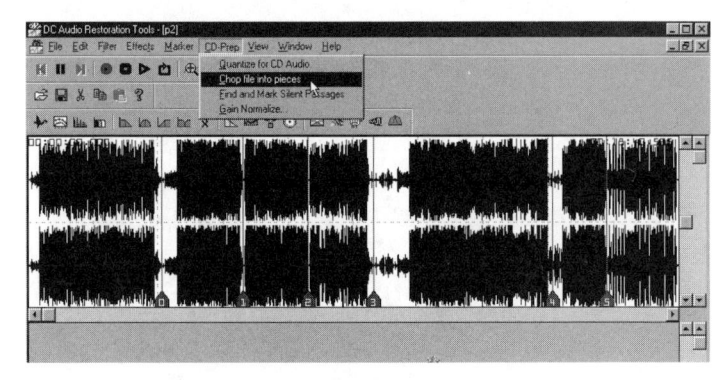

Figure 8.14 Chopping a file into pieces.

Since Diamond Cut doesn't know what tape we ripped, it named the tracks something like p2_01.wav, p2_02.wav, and so on. What we're going to do now is listen to each—they've been layered on top of one another automatically—and resave them under their proper names. You rename and save a file in Diamond Cut by selecting Save Source As from the File menu, which brings up a standard Save As window. Rename your file, save it, and close it. Listen to your next one, repeat the process. Do that until you're back at your original waveform, save that, and close it. You should have a clean workspace.

Dehissing

Now we turn the job over to your ears. From here forward, there's little we can tell you that your ears and a little experimentation won't. In that we know what these adjustments in the Continuous Noise filter do, theoretically speaking, we can offer some guidance, but you're mostly on your own now.

Open one of your tracks, whichever you like, by selecting Open Source from the File menu. Diamond Cut will build your waveform for you now and display it. Select the whole waveform by double-clicking it. Once again, open the Continuous Noise filter by selecting it from the Filter menu. Call your preset dehiss curve forth by selecting it from the drop-down menu next to the Save button (see **Figure 8.15**).

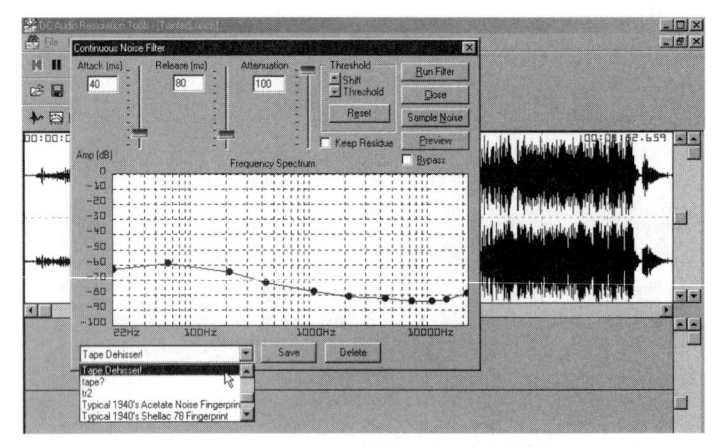

Figure 8.15 Summoning our saved preset dehiss curve.

The same graph we saw just a second ago will appear as it did before (see **Figure 8.16**), only this time, the upper threshold line is the only thing present in the graph—the lower line representing your noise is gone, and that's just fine. Remember that this upper line was based on the lower line, this general noise picture, so the lower line is there in spirit.

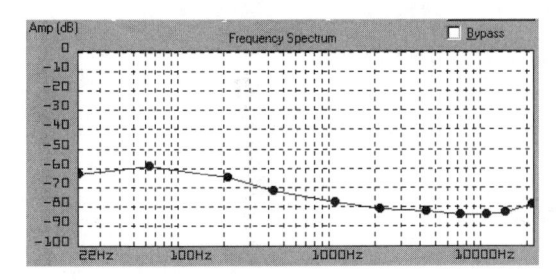

Figure 8.16 The graph we saw just a moment ago appears again, sans noise line.

After you've practiced a little with this filter, you can make fine adjustments around the lower line during the noiseprint phase of this project.

Now, so that you can hear your adjustments as you perform them, click the Preview button off to the right side of the Continuous Noise filter window. You'll hear your track now, as it will play once you apply the Continuous Noise filter. If you're working with a loud song, or an area within a song that's relatively loud, you won't hear any filtration happening because the audio signals coming through are above the upper line in terms of amplitude and passing straight through the filter, unaltered. At quiet moments, however, such as an intro or an outro, you'll be able to hear the effects of your filter: The hiss is being cut, as it falls below your upper line in terms of amplitude.

Because the effects of this filter are only pronounced during quiet moments, find a relatively quiet area within your waveform and select it (see **Figure 8.17**), just as we selected the introductory silence of this tape a second ago. Drag the Continuous Noise filter window out of the way to get to your waveform, if you need to. Return to the Continuous Noise filter window—drag it back up, if you have to—and click Preview again. Now, when your selection plays, the effect of the filter will be audible. Leave your selection playing by way of Preview; don't stop it. We're going to mess around a little now.

THE LITTLE AUDIO CD BOOK

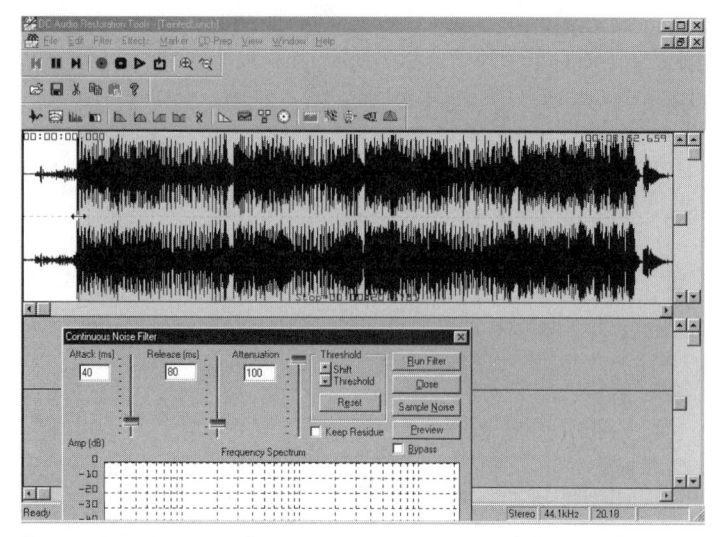

Figure 8.17 We're selecting a quiet portion of this track (see two-headed arrow) so that we may hear what effect the Continuous Noise filter produces.

So you can hear what happens, we'll head on up to the Threshold part of the Continuous Noise filter window. Next to the words "Shift Threshold," you'll find a pair of arrows, one pointing up and one pointing down. Clicking the down arrow moves your threshold line downward, and that's reflected in the graph (see **Figure 8.18**). When you do this, you'll hear your selection become progressively more hissy, because you're lowering the amplitude threshold, allowing hiss and other noise in the lower amplitudes to pass.

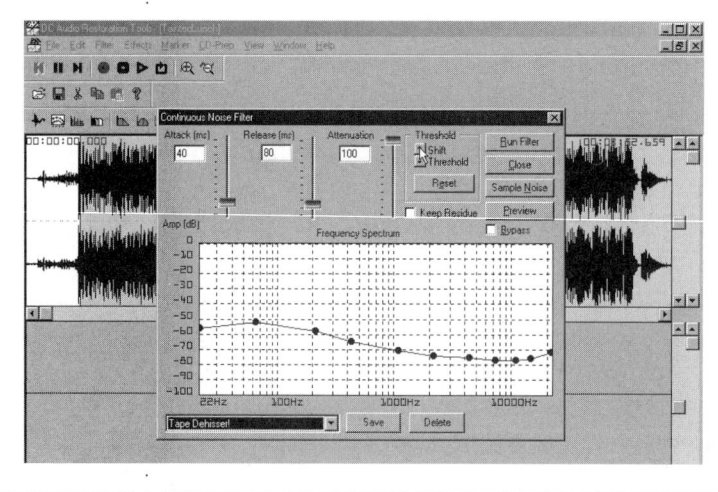

Figure 8.18 We're adjusting our whole threshold line here (see pointer).

Clicking the up arrow next to Shift Threshold moves your amplitude threshold up and cuts more powerful signals—if you move it up high enough, the filter will cut your whole track and you'll end with silence.

If you like, you can also alter your upper threshold line by clicking and dragging the small points found along it. In **Figure 8.19**, we've adjusted the line so that the low-frequency, low-amplitude noise goes straight through the filter and the hissing at the high frequencies is cut.

Directly beneath the Shift Threshold arrows you'll see a little box next to the words "Keep Residue." When you check that box, as we've done in **Figure 8.20**, you'll hear what's being cut. This is handy to check from time to time to ensure that the filter is extirpating only hiss and not your song.

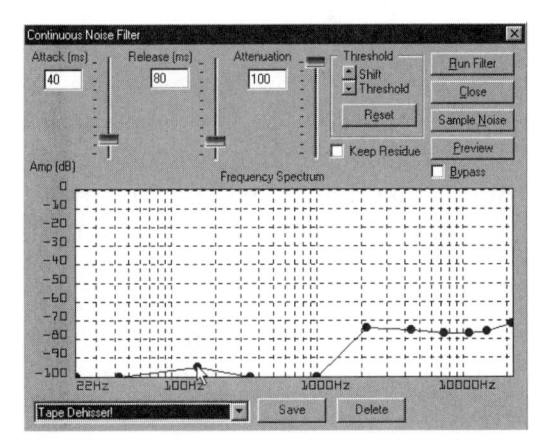

Figure 8.19 We've adjusted our threshold line here such that only high-frequency noise gets cut.

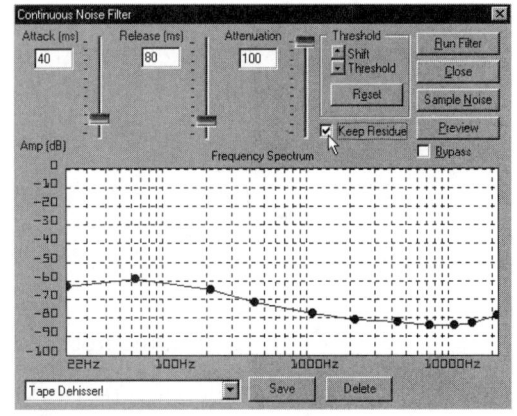

Figure 8.20 Checking the Keep Residue box from time to time helps guide your dehissing project.

To the left of the Shift Threshold arrows is an Attenuation control. Attenuation here refers to how seriously the Continuous Noise filter will weaken the noise below your upper line. Sliding that bar all the way up tells the filter to cut any sound below your upper threshold line, and sliding it all the way down tells the filter to do nothing to the sound below your upper line. If you can stand a little hiss, we'd advise you to slide this bar somewhere in between 0 and 100 (see **Figure 8.21**). You can cause some weird things to happen when you eliminate sound below your threshold line, and you might end up with some digital bleeps and blips in the quieter moments of your track.

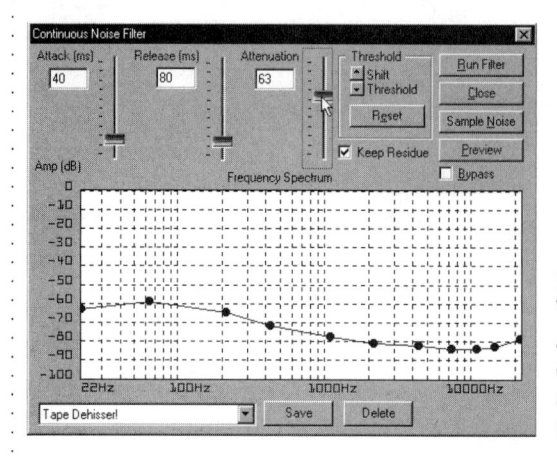

Figure 8.21
We're sliding our Attenuation control down a little here to avoid strange blip noises.

At the far left of the Continuous Noise filter window you'll see two adjustable sliders, Attack and Release. The terms *attack* and *release* are traditionally associated with dynamics processors, such as compressors. Attack time refers, in processor-speak, to how fast an effect gets applied to an incoming audio signal, and release time refers to how long the effect is applied to a signal. In the Continuous Noise filter we're working with, attack and release are kind of the same thing, analogous anyway: The filter has to know when to go in and clean something it suspects as noise—attack it—and it has to know how long it should filter this thing it attacked before it lets go.

When we're working with a cassette tape, we set the attack time to around 40 ms, or milliseconds, and the release time to about 80 milliseconds—that usually does the trick. But, if it sounds like the filter is slacking, that is, not going in fast enough after our hiss, we bring the attack time down some; alternately, if it sounds like the filter's got a hair trigger, we bring the slider up some. If after adjusting the attack time we hear periodic warbling and whooshes, we bring the release time down some by sliding that bar down (see **Figure 8.22**). You'll be able to hear these things, just as we do, and you'll be able to adjust accordingly.

8: RESTORING AND RECORDING CASSETTE TAPES

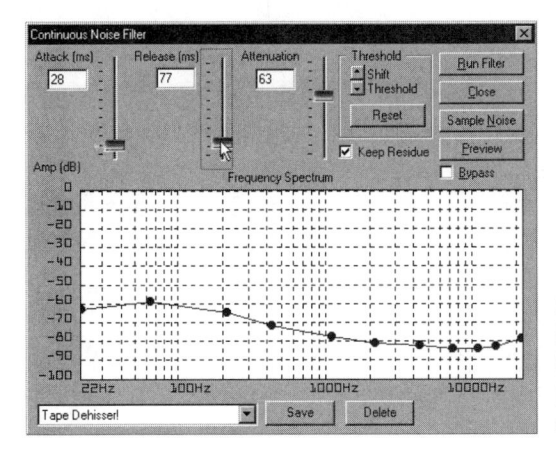

Figure 8.22 We don't like the whoosh we're hearing, so we're bringing the Release slider down some.

Once you're finished with your fine adjustments, drag the Continuous Noise filter out of the way and select your whole waveform by double-clicking it. Drag your Continuous Noise filter window back up, and preview your whole track, with the adjustments you've made. If it sounds good to you, run the filter by clicking the Run Filter button in the upper-right corner of the window (see **Figure 8.23**). If you're not happy with what you hear, adjust some more, and keep adjusting until you're happy. Then run the filter.

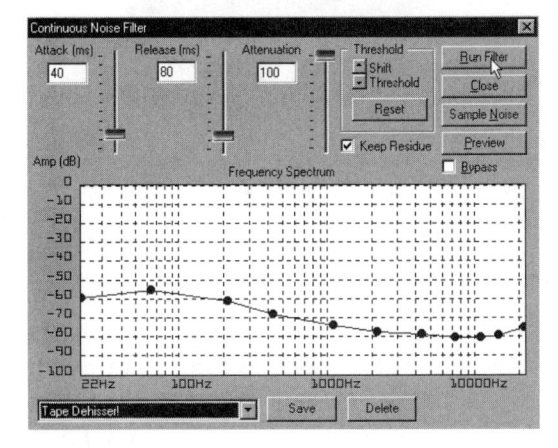

Figure 8.23 Running the filter.

Once you've run the filter, your track will come out dehissed and will be saved to the Destination area, directly beneath your original (see **Figure 8.24**). Double-click the destination to select your dehissed track, and play it, by pressing the Play button in the task bar. If you're still happy (you probably are, since you just listened to it a second ago using the Continuous Noise filter's Preview function and found happiness), select Make Destination the source from the File menu. This will do exactly that: It moves the dehissed file into the Source area. Now you can save it again by selecting Save Source as from the File menu—save your file as whatever you like. You're done with that track.

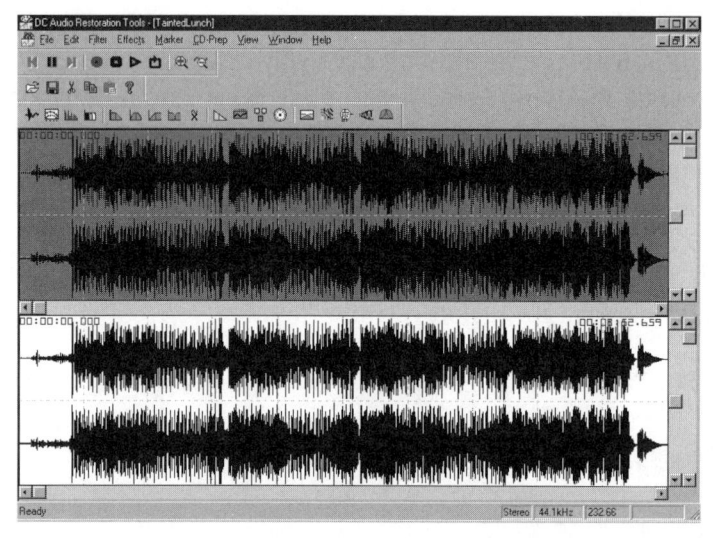

Figure 8.24 Your dehissed file arrives finally in the Destination area (the waveform at the bottom), right below your hissy source (the waveform at the top).

Now you're ready to move on to the next track. Repeat the procedures we just described with all of the tracks you wish to burn to CD. Then rip the other side of your tape, carve it up, call up your preset dehiss threshold line, dehiss again. Soon enough, your tape's ready to be burned.

Right before you go to CD, you'll probably want to clip the silence at the beginning of the first track of each side and at the end of the final track of each side. You do this by selecting the silence, as we've been doing, and selecting Cut from the Edit menu (see **Figure 8.25**). No big deal at all.

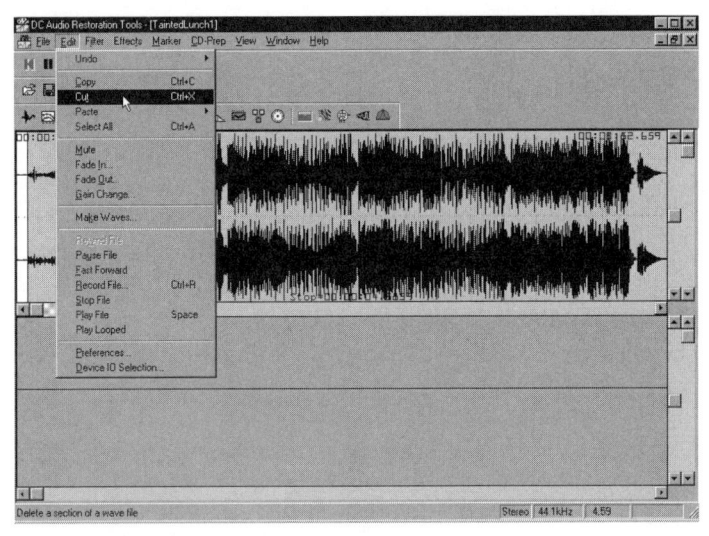

Figure 8.25 We're clipping the silence off the beginning of the first song of Side B of our tape here.

The Burn

Save whatever you may have open, and exit Diamond Cut. Open your favorite CD-R software, tell it you want to make an audio CD, queue up your tracks, and burn them. That's it. Bob likes to get real complex here during the burn. Before he burns anything, he goes to Kentucky Fried Chicken and gets a deluxe bucket, which he proceeds to eat, saving the bones. Then he drives home, approaches his computer chanting something about "Finger Lickin' Good," and he shakes his bucket of chicken bones at his CD-R drive. Josh just hits Burn, frolics outside for ten minutes, and then returns to see if it worked. Try both ways, see which way you prefer. Some folks, we've heard, go watch TV during the burn process—you can try that too.

Copying CDs

One of the remarkable facets of human consciousness, at least at this historical moment, is that it tends to resist change like it's the devil himself. We get used to things, grow comfortable with them, and cling to them with peculiar force. It's probably that same force we use when clinging to sanity—or life even. Our universe crumbles a bit when the liquor store runs out of our particular poison. Even if we end up with a better-quality six-pack, we'll still be bummed, simply because it's not what we're accustomed to. We'll wager, too, that we could get at least one analog guy—that guy who prefers his LPs to their CD equivalents—to confess that he likes his LPs not because they sound better but rather because that vinyl sound is what he's used to, and music on vinyl constitutes his vision of what music should sound like.

To preserve the comfortable order, we're sometimes tempted to apply old notions and familiar means to new situations, but it's often a mistake to do so. Being that many of us are children of the dual-tape deck, we might imagine that copying a CD is pretty much the same thing as duping a tape. Put the source here, put the blank there, hit record, and soon enough, you've got a viable copy. Today's CD-R software can certainly emulate that procedure. Most CD-R software packages feature a copy capability and some utility or other that rips from the source drive and records to the blank in your CD-R drive with the touch of one digital record button. Using a copy feature, however, is not the best way to duplicate an audio CD. In fact, it ranks among the most precarious. Now, when we say "precarious," we don't mean that you'll end up with a poor copy each time you trek down one of these treacherous recording paths. We mean that some ways are much less reliable than others. A good rule of thumb, when faced with a choice between audio CD recording procedures, is that if a procedure doesn't involve your ear, try not to have anything to do with it.

This chapter will detail both the good ways and the questionable ways to duplicate an audio CD. The former because, well, we want you to have a good copy, and the latter because they illuminate problems you'll encounter in all of your audio recording endeavors. Once again, we're going to be duplicating copyrighted material, and we'd have you exercise the appropriate discretion.

The Ubiquitous but Sometimes Nefarious Copy Utility

Most of today's CD recording software packages feature a copy utility. There's usually nothing extravagant about them: Many times all you get are two fields, where you select source and destination drives, and the option of involving your hard disk in the copy procedure or writing directly from one drive to another, generally known as copying on-the-fly (see **Figure 9.1**). And naturally, you'll also find some permutation of the traditional big red Record button, if not an actual big, red Record button. Children of the dual-tape deck can see where this is going already, right?

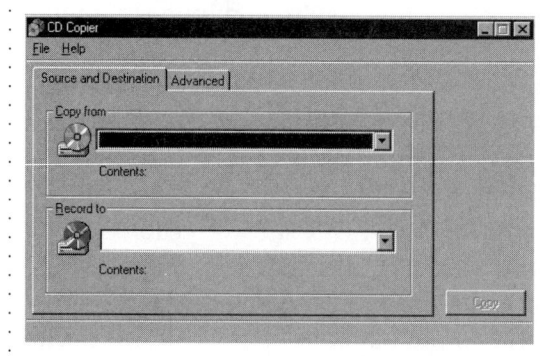

Figure 9.1
The simplicity of copy utilities belies the complexity of getting audio data from a source CD to CD-R media. This copy utility is part of Adaptec's Easy CD Creator package.

You guessed it: If you have a CD-ROM drive (or DVD-ROM drive or anything that is capable of reading CDs) and a CD-R drive, you can put whatever CD you wish to copy into that CD-ROM drive and a piece of blank media into your CD-R drive and you're half way to a dupe. But not necessarily a good dupe, at all—it could even be extraordinarily ugly. To proceed from this danger to the next danger of copying a CD using a copy utility, you'll need to perform Digital Audio Extraction (DAE, or as we like to say, ripping), which is more complicated than simply copying a file from a CD-ROM drive to a hard drive. After all, we're not copying files, we're copying tracks—true, as we've said before, digital audio data is in some respects like any other data. The complications come in how audio data is arranged on a disc and the limited directory information that tells a reader where that data is (see the sidebar "Why is extracting so exacting?"). The CD-ROM drive containing your source disc must be DAE-capable, a talent less common than we might imagine from these powerful machines of ours. If your source drive is not DAE-capable, your results could be disastrous.

After making sure our hardware is equipped to rip, we'll fire up the software and get down to business. We select a Hitachi DVD-ROM drive for our source and a Plextor CD-RW drive as a destination, and we're loaded for bear. Opening up Prassi's Primo CD, we choose Disc-to-Disc Copy from the File > New Job menu. You'll notice, incidentally, the big red Record button in the Direct Copy Job window. Now, within that same window, the one with the Record button, you'll see toward the bottom-left-hand corner a box that, when checked, will make a temporary image on the Hard Disk and copy from there. If you are going to do a drive-to-drive copy, we suggest you check that box or a comparable box that you should find at this point in whatever software you use.

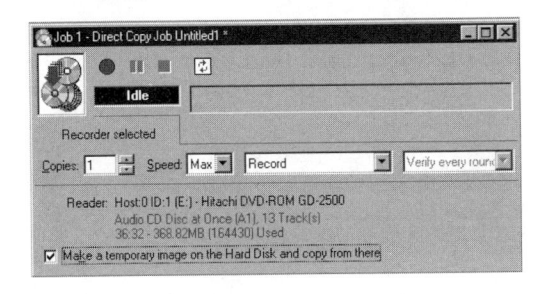

Figure 9.2 Prassi's disc-copy function should look familiar to anyone who has used a disc-copy utility. We've checked the box in the lower-left-hand corner.

Why is extracting so exacting?

Given that the first CD-ROM drives weren't much more than modified audio CD players, you'd guess that CD-ROM drives would be really comfortable dealing with audio data, whether it's playback or extraction to the storage medium of your choice. That's not the case. The Red Book, the standard document that contains the published specification for Compact Disc-Digital Audio, stipulates an elegant way of writing audio data to CD, but readers of this data—stereo units, CD-ROM drives, what have you—don't need to be all that precise in the way they read.

To play an audio CD, all a CD player needs to do is get its laser somewhere near the beginning of a track, in that area of silence that precedes it. This approach is fine for playback, but for a CD-ROM drive to extract an audio track accurately and duplicate it on a hard drive in useful form, more precision is required. The reason for this is inherent in the differences between CD-Audio and CD-ROM. CD-Audio is designed for a specific purpose: linear, track-by-track playback on CD players. Because all audio discs share a simple structure that is not common to all CD-ROMs, an audio disc contains less information to describe the organization of its contents than a CD-ROM, which may contain any kind of data used on a computer.

An audio disc's table of contents (TOC), much like a book's, is a good general resource for knowing what's where but won't always lead you to the right spot. Although this book's table of contents may tell you on what page the chapter "Copying CDs" begins, that doesn't tell you where the part about audio extraction is. Likewise, the TOC on an audio CD tells the CD reader about where the song starts, but unlike a CD-ROM with data on it, it does not tell it exactly where it starts.

Audio discs were designed to be read sequentially, in real time, with the digital data converted to an analog signal that would be played through a stereo's speakers. There was no need to have data on the disc to pinpoint the exact location of the beginning of a song. That extra data containing an exact starting address for each song takes up space that could otherwise be used for storing more music. The 2,048 bytes of user data in each 2,352-byte CD-ROM sector can be accessed exactly because the header information in each sector contains the precise address of the data block.

An audio block, on the other hand, contains 2,352 bytes in each physical block and all of these bytes are used for audio data. No header exists; there is no information in the block that allows for the exact positioning of the read head over a specific block.

If you don't check that box, the procedure will move much more quickly but you'll risk encountering weird stuff such as buffer underruns and buffer overflows, and ultimately, because of those things, coasters. Copying discs without employing your hard disk is referred to as copying on-the-fly, and it's frowned on by almost everyone who has copied audio discs this way and reaped the occasionally horrid results. To get a good on-the-fly copy, data from the source disc will have to be read more quickly than it's being written but not too much more quickly.

We'd use a stonemason's analogy here, but Josh finds stonemasonry repugnant, so instead, we shall make use of a cake decorator's analogy. You have a nice blank cake before you, and in your hands, you're holding that bag that squirts icing. Using that bag, you intend to write the name of your friend and good wishes on a cake. If you're too gentle, you won't have any icing to delineate anything, the cake will remain blank, and William shall never know that you care about him. If you run out of icing, you'll have to find a way to seamlessly finish "Birthd" with "ay" or else lose the entire meaning. And if you press too hard, "William" will become "Wubbn." Data, like icing, must move steadily with the queue, in its dictated position, all in the face of a volcano erupting centimeters away.

If data isn't arriving fast enough to keep up with the recorder, it's all over. CD recording requires a constant flow of data, so a recorder keeps a reservoir of data for itself—a buffer—so that little flow interruptions, diversions, and occasional jostling that occur in typical data transfer don't mess everything up. The recorder can then proceed writing data from the buffer, which will gradually fill itself up again. Sometimes, though, interruptions in the data stream are so severe that the buffer empties out, the data flow stops, and recording grinds to a halt. Coaster! This is called buffer underrun and can happen for several reasons, often because your source drive reads too slowly and cannot keep up with the writing process.

An audio disc can have an unreadable area on it, resulting from a scratch or dirt or because the CD itself was poorly pressed. During playback, the unreadable areas, called errors, don't really pose a problem: CD players by nature go back and take another stab and are usually able to read the data they couldn't read the first time. That's called error correction. Readers normally don't correct for errors during on-the-fly copying because that takes time they don't really have here. When a reader encounters errors during an on-the-fly copy, it may stop offering data altogether, the software won't attempt to compensate, and you'll get a buffer underrun. Alternately, many CD recording programs—or even the drives themselves in some cases—will throw up their arms in exasperation at this error and pass on whatever they feel like making up that day to placate the recorder. What they pass on ain't Barry Manilow, or maybe it is. Other software will send a string of 0s (essentially digital silence) to the recorder until it starts receiving decent data again.

Too much data may arrive in the CD-ROM's memory cache during an on-the-fly copy, which happens when the ROM drive is reading the audio disc faster than the data is being asked for by your software and the recorder. Since the CD-ROM drive has to be on its toes, it might start forgetting older data to handle new data, the data being read. That's buffer overflow. Your software might inquire after this forgotten information, as it hasn't been written yet, and the CD-ROM drive only kind of remembers where it was due to the imprecise nature of digital audio. So, imprecisely, it reads and passes on imprecise information. Although you probably won't blow the disc entirely, you'll get some very unpleasant noise.

Fortunately, you can overcome most of those problems by checking that small box that tells your software to extract the data to your hard disk first and then proceed with the burn. Primo CD, and many of today's other software packages, will create what's known as an image, a kind of utopian data layout, on your hard disk and then take that layout and burn it to CD.

The cool thing about hard disks is that, unlike CD-R drives, they can deal with interruptions. So, the process of extracting data to a hard disk and burning an image to CD is much more reliable than the on-the-fly process, and you're much less likely to get a coaster. Time ceases to be a concern here for your software and your source drive: Your software won't have to answer to a recorder just yet, and the demands your software makes on your source drive won't be so stringent. Most important, there's time to get data right during the transfer to hard disk—the CD-ROM drive can have another go at the data if it needs to when it encounters an error. Everything relaxes a bit, you know, like when the boss leaves to go play golf, or whatever it is they do when they're not exploiting the masses.

Another bonus: When you burn an image, most programs give you the opportunity to save that image. This enables you to make multiple copies from that image, so you'll never have to bother extracting your disc again. Bear in mind, though, that these image files occupy a lot of hard disk space (even more than 650 MB for a full disc), so keep an eye on your resources if you've got a bunch of images laying around.

Unusual CDs, and some problems

Every once in awhile, you'll come across a CD that transgresses the 74-minute rule laid out by the Red Book standard. This will confuse some programs, and they won't proceed. Other programs will go ahead with the burn, as they're privy to a secret: The 74-minute rule isn't hard and fast at all. Ordinary media can sometimes be burned out to 76 minutes—Bob even got out to 77:02, a true Chuck Yeager. To get out that far, however, his CD-R drive had to support what's called overburn, which simply means his drive, when accompanied by the proper software, can burn out past 74 minutes. So, with a combination of a drive that's capable of overburn and software that won't shy away from pushing the envelope, you can dupe all 78 generous minutes of Michael Jackson's *History* CD.

There exists, too, 80-minute media. When you are looking for it (a good place to check when you're looking for media of all types is www.octave.com), you'll notice that the CD-R software manufacturers that cannot figure out how to work with 80 minutes will admonish you that you're doing something very dangerous here, you're going outside of the spec, you hooligan. Then the people who are able to contend with 80-minute media boast that their software can handle even 80-minute media! As with overburn, you'll need capable software and a capable drive to use 80-minute media.

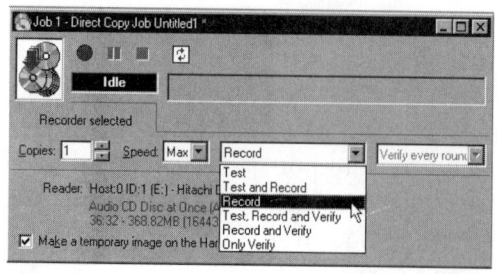

Figure 9.3 Filling in the fields. Our decision to simply record—rather than test and record—is yet another hazard of duplicating audio CDs with a disc-copy tool. A failed test would abort the process and save us a piece of media.

So let's proceed. The box has a check, right, so now we need to make another couple decisions (see **Figure 9.3**). First, since we're being safe here, we can tell our recorder to record at maximum speed in the Speed field. If we were doing an on-the-fly copy, we might have to take our recorder speed all the way on down to 1x, depending on how quickly our CD-ROM drive is capable of extracting audio (remember that our source drive must extract faster than the data is being written but not too much faster). We'll also tell our software how many copies of the source CD we want—we just want one today, but you're totally welcome to make more than that. Finally, we're given the option of testing, recording, or verifying or just about any combination of the three. Test will run the copy procedure without actually writing anything to CD-R and will report back any problems encountered. Record will simply go ahead with the burn. Verify will scan the CD resulting from the burn and report any problems. Both of us are in a hurry to get to the bar today, so we're simply going to record by selecting Record, all by itself, from the Record drop-down menu.

Push the big red button.

Depending on the extraction speed of your source drive, and the speed of your recorder, you'll be waiting ten minutes to an hour, but eventually you'll have a copy. Listening to that copy, you may find it stinks. The possible reasons for its stinkiness are numerous and extraordinarily difficult to pinpoint, but know this: That's not the first time that that's happened, and that's why we do things differently around here. And we do them with only one drive.

How Bob and Josh Copy CDs

We didn't listen to the tracks that hit the hard disk before we burned them to disc, so if our copy stinks, we don't know if the problem arose from the extraction process or the recording process. Not only that, every single song on that CD is on its duplicate. What if we don't particularly like some of those songs? We're stuck there, too. And if we don't particularly like the job the studio did in producing and engineering this artist's work—why is that bass so muffled?—we didn't have an opportunity to adjust for the perceived faults using our digital audio editing software. So this copy utility, ultraprone to error already, has also deprived us of any flexibility. That's why we extract to hard disk, listen to the tracks, and *then* burn them. That solves everything—almost, anyway.

We can say with pretty good certainty that if you have a CD-R drive, you have a digital audio extraction tool, a "ripper." In the extremely unlikely case you don't, or if you don't like the one you already have, there are herds of rippers roaming the Internet, many freeware or shareware. The ones that cost you, too, won't cost you more than $30. Before you go out and purchase a ripper though, play with the ones you have, and see what you think. If you happened to get into MP3, you'll probably find a ripper built into your favorite MP3 software. Then, of course, you'll have one built into your CD recording software. For instance, if you're a Mac user, you probably have Adaptec's Toast 3.x on your machine someplace. Toast's ripper is found in the Goodies folder in Toast Audio Extractor, where you'll simply select a source CD drive and then select files on the hard disk for a destination, and you're done. The more recent Toast 4.0 adds a utility called CD Spin Doctor (see **Figure 9.4**), which has been included with the Deluxe Edition of Adaptec's Easy CD Creator—the software that ships with most PC recorders—for years. CD Spin Doctor also provides some rudimentary editing and restoration capabilities.

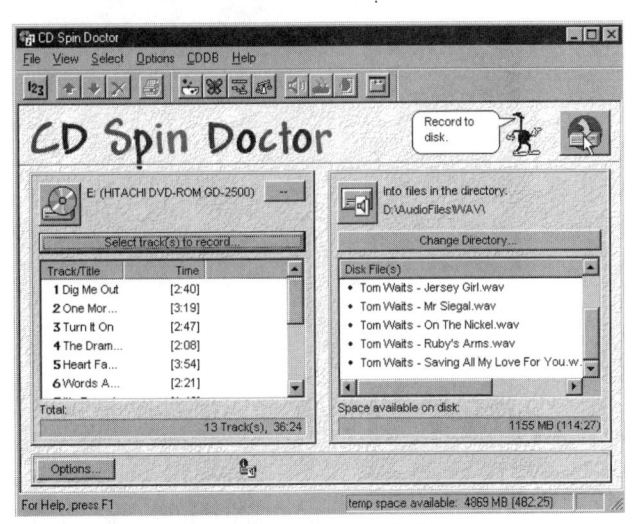

Figure 9.4 The Windows version of CD Spin Doctor, with an audio CD as a source and a hard disk as a destination. Notice the big red—well, just big—record button under the pointer.

Some recorder bundles only include a limited version of CD Creator, which doesn't include Spin Doctor. Not to worry—you can also do audio extraction in the main window simply by selecting the tracks you want and clicking "Extract" in the top panel.

AudioCatalyst

AudioCatalyst, from Xing Technology (www.xingtech.com), is an excellent choice for Mac and PC users and costs only $29.95. It's billed primarily as MP3 encoding software and serves very well in that capacity—in fact, many swear that the Xing MP3 encoding engine is hands down the best thing around for making MP3s—but AudioCatalyst really shines as just a plain old ripper. AudioCatalyst is actually two programs consolidated into one. The killer Xing MP3 encoding engine is coupled with a capable digital audio extraction tool called Audiograbber, created by überprogrammer Jackie Franck. Between those two powerful applications, AudioCatalyst could be the most formidable ripper/encoder combination on the scene today (see **Figure 9.5**) although Bob thinks Audiograbber is just as good.

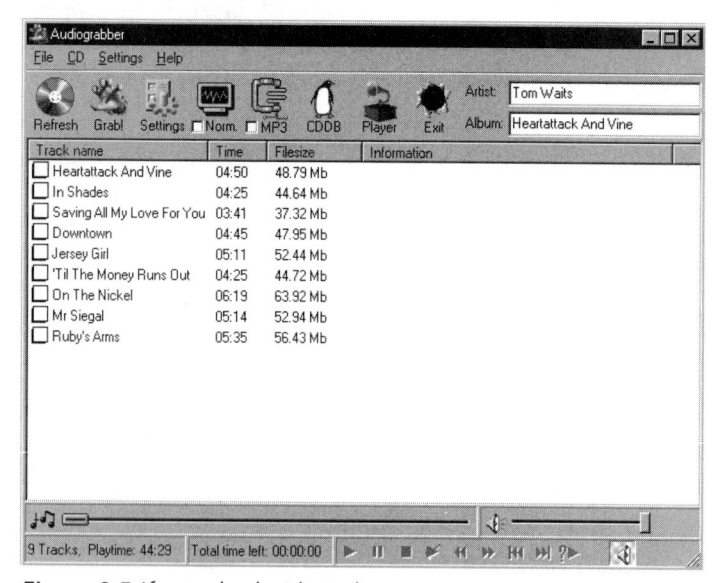

Figure 9.5 If you do decide to buy a ripper, you can't go wrong with AudioCatalyst or Audiograbber.

Before we do anything with Audiograbber, it's always good to defragment the hard disk you will store your tracks on, if you haven't done that in awhile (weekly is Josh's policy, but that's meticulous, and he is widely mocked for it). Also, make sure you have enough space on your disk to accommodate a bunch of tracks. Then it's time to open your ripper. We're going to use the Windows version of Audiograbber, as it has a bunch of neat stuff that illustrates the potential of ripping software, it features a few things that illuminate the complexity of digital audio extraction, and for extracting it looks and functions about the same as the Mac and Windows versions of AudioCatalyst.

> *For Windows users, you can purchase Audiograbber all by itself, with no added MP3 encoding capability, for $25, over at www.audiograbber.com. It's easy enough, too, to add an external encoder to Audiograbber. Just poke around the site, and you will find links to the assortment of encoders. We like the Lame encoder, but use whatever you find works well.*

> *Audiograbber and AudioCatalyst are examples of powerful and sophisticated audio extraction programs. If all the options and such scare you, just remember that lot of other rippers don't have to be configured at all. Some are even as simple as just clicking the track to initiate the rip. So, if Audiograbber intimidates you, use the one built into your recording program or go over to the Sonic Spot site (www.sonicspot.com) and get a simpler ripper. Sonic Spot has probably the most extensive and well-organized collection of audio tools that you will find on the Web.*

> *If you're using the Mac version of AudioCatalyst, you have a lot fewer options, so it's a little easier to set up, as are most things Mac. If you do have problems getting a good rip with another software, Audiograbber or AudioCatalyst may very well end up being your salvation, and some of these sophisticated things will become just plain good to know.*

Let's head straight into Settings, where we'll configure a couple of things (see **Figure 9.6**). (Get to the Settings window by hitting the Settings button—the image of gears—on the taskbar.) At the top of the Settings window, you'll see the field where you designate the destination directory for the files you'll be ripping—in our case, we've designated D:\Audio Files\WAV, "D:" being a hard disk we've dedicated solely to audio files.

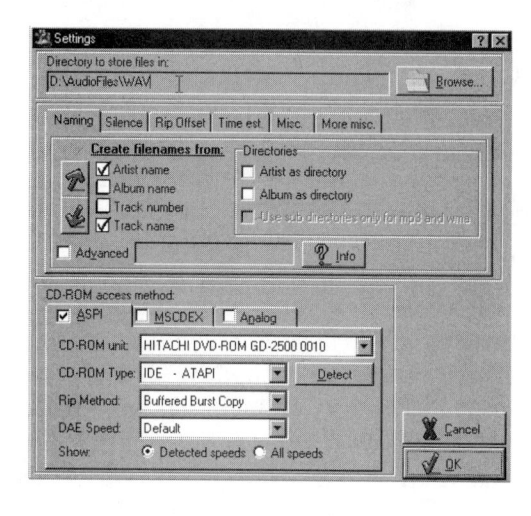

Figure 9.6
Audiograbber's Settings window. Our cursor is over the field where you designate a recipient directory for your tracks. We typed; you can browse.

Below this field, you'll find the first series of tabs we'll be thumbing through to configure the program: Naming, Silence, Rip Offset, and others. If you happen to have an audio CD in your source drive, you may have noticed that somehow this program knows everything about the CD you've placed in that drive and has displayed the names of the tracks on your source CD out in the main window. Audiograbber automatically gathers some abstract information about your CD and submits that information to the CD Database (or CDDB; www.cddb.com). CDDB then returns to Audiograbber the names of the album, artist, and tracks, all of which Audiograbber displays for you. What the Naming tab does, then, is allow you to choose how your tracks will be named when they become files, using the information gathered from CDDB.

For example, we're ripping Tom Waits' *Heartattack and Vine* today, and CDDB has this CD on file, so track names, album name, and artist name are all displayed in Audiograbber. Under the Naming tab, we've checked the boxes next to Artist name and Track name, so when we rip track 5, "Jersey Girl," we'll end up with a file called "Tom Waits_Jersey Girl.wav." Convenient, huh?

Whether you select anything under the next tab, Silence, will depend on how you intend to burn the files you rip. There's always a goodly hunk of silence at the beginning and end of each CD track because the reading head of a CD player lands sort of over there when it has to find a track, and as long as it lands in silence, indexing appears pretty seamless to the listener.

When you go to burn these tracks you've ripped, your software may give you a choice: Will you burn disc-at-once or track-at-once?

Some recorders and recording software support only track-at-once recording, which means the recorder writes a preliminary table of contents at the beginning of the disc, writes a track, returns to the table of contents, updates it with new track information, writes another track, and repeats the process until it has completed the writing job. Track-at-once is advantageous for several reasons, most related to flexibility in computer data recording; its only real benefit in audio recording is for users who don't have sufficient hard drive space to store all the audio tracks they want to burn at one time: It allows them to store (or stage) one track, record it, clear it off the hard drive, and repeat until they fill and close the disc. The disadvantage of track-at-once recording for audio is it doesn't allow you to control the length of silences between tracks. When the writer later stops to rewrite the TOC and await more data, it encodes some detritus on the disc in the coming and going (in data block size, equivalent to "two seconds" of recorded data) that an audio CD player or CD-ROM reads as silence. If your recorder or software does limit you to track-at-once, you'll want to clip the silence at the beginning and end of a track because you'll gain enough silence just by the nature of the way you're burning that you'll have noticeable gaps in the resulting disc if you don't.

If, on the other hand, you're going to burn disc-at-once, you'll probably want to leave the silence (see **Figure 9.7**). The laser never stops writing during a disc-at-once burn, so if you want silence, silence should be part of the data stream, that string of 0s we talked about. (Recent versions of Toast and Easy CD Creator allow you to choose 0, .5, 1, or 2 seconds of silence between tracks once you've created your track list. Default is half a second.) Regardless of whether you choose track-at-once or disc-at-once (unless you have a small hard drive and are using the stage-purge method), the process will appear identical to you: Prepare your tracks, make your track list, and choose record and the recorder will burn them as a single job.

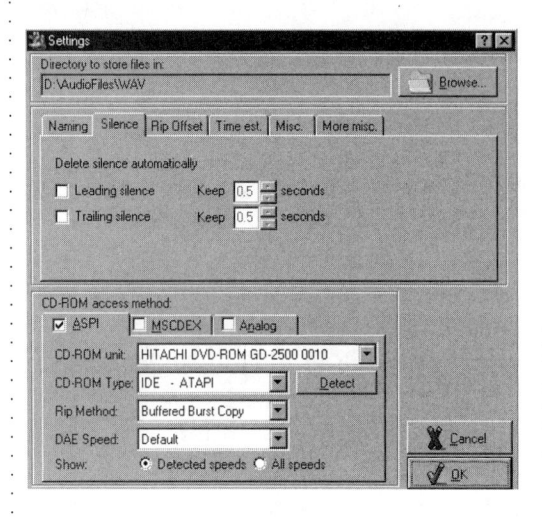

Figure 9.7 Whether you keep any silence will depend on how you intend to burn your disc. We'll be burning disc-at-once, so we'll keep the silence.

You'll most likely never have to mess with any of the settings under the Rip Offset tab. Some drives, you remember, aren't really fluent in the ways of digital audio and can't effectively find the "sort of over there" beginning of an audio track. Rip Offset corrects for that by seeing to it that the read head falls somewhere in the silence, after a few numeric adjustments in those fields. But, if you've got a pretty current CD-ROM, DVD-ROM, or CD-R drive, you'll never have to touch that stuff.

> *An interesting setting here, one that you may want to mess with, is the Partial Rip feature. It takes samples from songs, of whatever size you dictate and from wherever you dictate.*

You can't really configure anything on the Time est. tab. It displays information, specifically how fast a sample is typically normalized on your computer and how fast any track is typically ripped by your drive. You won't miss much if you ignore everything there.

The options on the final two tabs—Misc. and, tee hee, More misc.—are mostly self-explanatory. The only two things that might confuse you are whether to check the boxes next to Continue even if synchronization fails and Don't calculate checksum during the rip process. Synchronization refers here to the way Audiograbber deals with the imprecision of digital audio (see **Figure 9.8**).

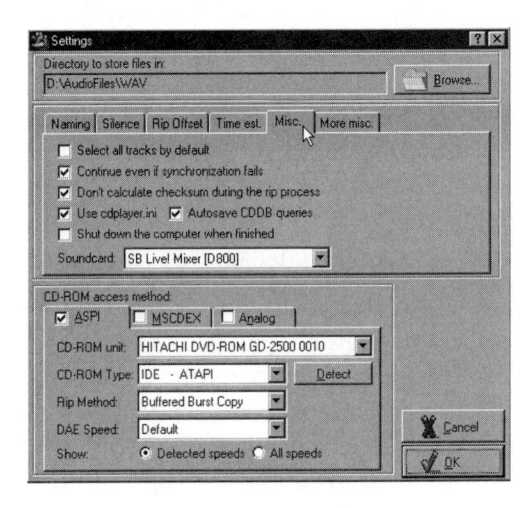

Figure 9.8 The Misc. tab contains a couple ambiguous items, the Checksum thing and the Synchronization thing. We usually check both boxes.

When a reader goes out to look for specific areas of audio data, it's not always immediately apparent specifically where that data will be found, given the relative imprecision in how audio tracks are constructed. So, if for whatever reason a reader needs to go back to audio data to get something, something has to guide the reader to a reasonably precise area or it will audibly ruin the track. That is, the audio data has to be synchronous or it sounds bad. So, synchronization as you'll come across it in Audiograbber is just whatever means is implemented to make everything jibe.

You will most often see synchronization referred to as *jitter correction*—in fact, the word *synchronization* used in this context is unique to Audiograbber. Some CD-ROM drives, you remember, may not be so hot at extracting audio data, just because there's not enough information present on an audio CD to get this particular CD-ROM's reading head to exact areas within songs—this is known as *jitter*. Software must the compensate for jitter by comparing data on an audio CD to other data on that CD and using those results to guide a read head to a precise location within a track. Because CD-ROM technology has been honed to the point where even audio tracks can be read and extracted with tremendous precision, jitter isn't the concern it once was.

We tend to like to continue even if jitter correction, or synchronization, fails just because if it does fail, the results may not be all that catastrophic, and if we find the results are catastrophic during our preburn listening, we'll just have another stab at ripping the track. As far as checksums go, you don't need to calculate one. You use checksums to compare one file against another for digital precision. We feel if a file sounds good, that's close enough—we don't really have the time or inclination to run around comparing checksums.

Below that first array of tabs, you'll find the CD-ROM access method tabs: ASPI, MSCDEX, and Analog. This is just a checkpoint to make sure the software knows how your computer is talking to your CD-ROM drive. The utility PCs and Macs use to talk with CD-ROM drives is called a driver. You'll commonly hear these referred to as ASPI drivers, because in almost all cases under Windows that's the driver that's in use. Unless something extraordinary is going on, all you'll need here is the ASPI tab. If you're running an old system, you may have to switch from the default ASPI to MSCDEX, which goes back to old MS-DOS systems.

Macs are more rigid in construction than PCs, so the question doesn't come up. In 99 percent of cases, under Windows just make sure this tab is set to ASPI and forget about it thereafter.

The first thing you'll see, running down the fields, are your available drives—we've selected our CD-R drive as the source. Pick whatever drive you've inserted the source disc in. The next field is just a statement of fact: It tells you what kind of interface you've got—IDE - ATAPI or SCSI.

Now things get kind of complicated: In the next field, you must choose your rip method from the drop-down menu. We've never had Buffered Burst Copy do us any wrong on the myriad drives we've used Audiograbber with, but you could have problems, at least theoretically.

When using Buffered Burst Copy, Audiograbber asks for a few seconds of data, writes the data to your hard disk, and then asks for another few seconds. A problem might arise when your reader is a really fast one or you've designated a really fast read speed. If Audiograbber can't keep up with your reader, that means your reader is going to have to slow down or even stop. So Audiograbber may ask for a few seconds of data, and the reader has to come back with, uh, now where did I put those particular few seconds, it's over there somewhere...we all know how that ends up. We personally have never encountered this, but you may. If you do bump into problems, try Dynamic Synch Width—this method involves that synchronization buffer that makes everything jibe (see **Figure 9.9**).

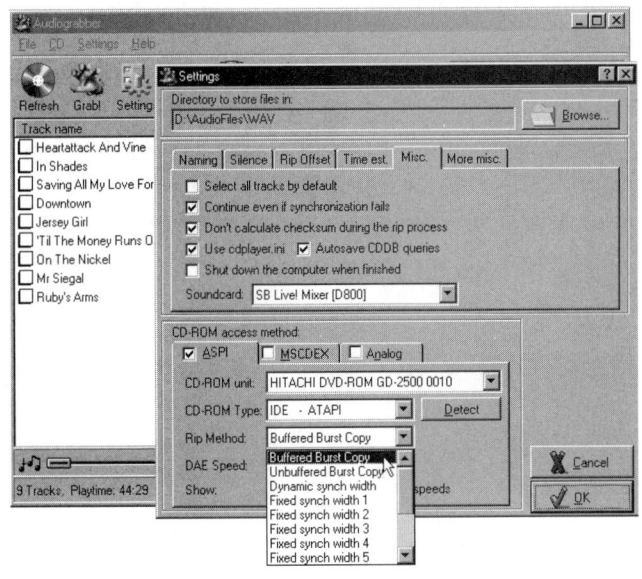

Figure 9.9 Rip Method's drop-down menu looks pretty intricate, but you'll usually only have to try Buffered Burst Copy or Dynamic synch width before you get a good rip.

Finally, tell Audiograbber how quickly you want to rip by way of the DAE Speed drop-down menu. Beneath DAE Speed, you'll see Detected Speeds and All Speeds radio buttons—press the Detected Speeds button there. Audiograbber will then automatically detect the digital audio extraction speeds your drive is capable of.

Then return to the DAE Speed drop-down menu. It may indeed be the case that your 32x drive can extract audio only at 10x, but that's OK. 10x is still really fast—so fast, in fact, that those theoretical buffer problems may become reality. We suggest you select Default from the DAE Speed drop-down menu, which should be the fastest DAE speed your drive can handle. Then, if you've already tried ripping using Dynamic Synch Width at Default Speed and are still not satisfied with the results on your hard disk, take your DAE Speed down a notch.

Now it's time to rip. Close the Settings window, and if you haven't already, place an audio CD in the drive you selected in Settings. If your track names don't appear in the main window, hit the Refresh button at the top-left corner of the taskbar. If they still don't show up, From the CD drop-down menu, select Get from CDDB. If after all that, the track names still aren't showing up, check your connection to the Internet: You must be connected for Audiograbber to contact CDDB. Now, place a check mark next to every track you wish to rip. Since *Heartattack and Vine* is one of those thoroughly good CDs, we've selected all of its tracks (see **Figure 9.10**). Now push Grab, that big scary hand on the task bar, which will initiate the rip.

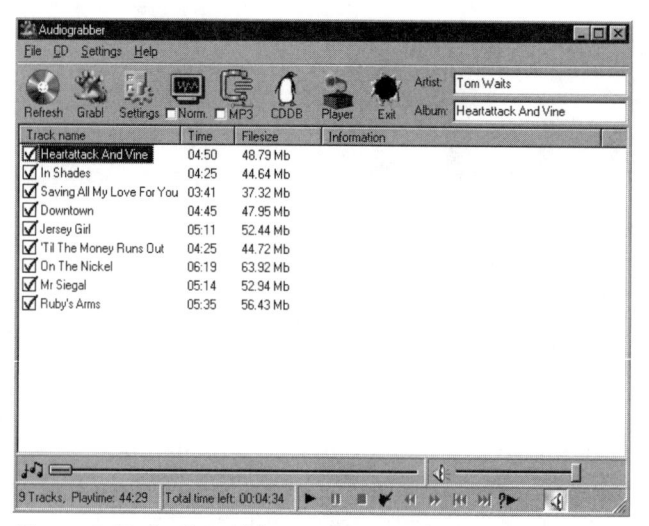

Figure 9.10 Audiograbber's main window, where we've placed a check next to every track we intend to rip—all tracks, in this particular instance.

A progress window should now pop up. There's nothing here you have to pay much attention to, although you might be alarmed by the Possible speed problems readout in the upper-right corner of the window (see **Figure 9.11**). These "problems" are the theoretical problems we just discussed in relation to the Buffered Burst Copy method of ripping, so *Possible* is the key word here.

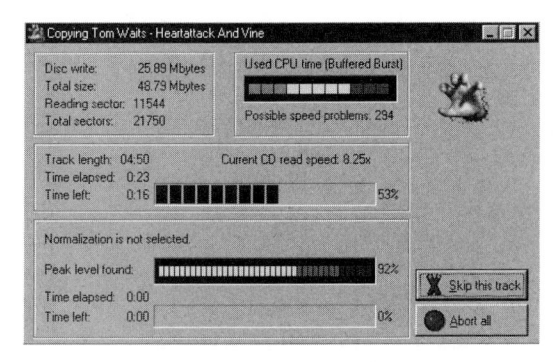

Figure 9.11 Audiograbber's progress window. Notice the Possible speed problems readout near the top right. Quite a few problems there, right? Listening to this track on our hard disk, however, we find we cannot tell a difference from the one on the source CD.

Five minutes later—we ripped at 10x—we have a directory containing all the tracks of *Heartattack and Vine*. Using that right-click-the-file > Properties > Preview thing we've been doing, we're going to listen to all of the tracks to make sure they sound OK. If we come across one that doesn't sound right, we'll discard it and have another try, knowing that the fault lays squarely on the extraction process. That's something you can't do during disc-to-disc copying and is yet another reason to extract, listen, and then burn. We've found that all nine tracks came out fine, so we're going to gear up for the burn.

> Bob is sometimes too impatient to listen to every track, so a lot of times he just burns the CD. During times of weakness, he just copies on-the-fly. Then he listens to them and if he finds an error, he just pitches the disc. Josh hates to see media wasted and has learned infinite patience from his studies in Tibet, so he listens to tracks all the way through. So when Bob's discs come out OK, Josh, despite his Buddhistic composure, is a bit jealous but figures it's just luck. When Bob's discs are bad, though, Josh gets the last laugh, and he laughs the laugh of 1,000 demons feasting on the soul of a damned wretch.

The Burn

The only thing to mention here is that we left both the leading and trailing silences on the tracks, so we're going to do a disc-at-once burn. A reminder: Not all drives support disc-at-once (nor do some older software tools, such as Toast 3.0 on the Mac), so be sure to check your drive—your software will usually tell you—before you decide to leave leading and trailing silences tacked on to your tracks.

Queue 'em up and burn, using whatever CD recording software you like. Just so you know, this particular copy of *Heartattack and Vine* will be going into Josh's car, so the next time he gets jacked, he won't be out the fifteen bucks it costs to replace his store-bought copy. Better than a car alarm, we tell you, these CD-R drives. Cheaper too.

Recording MP3s to CD

What is this *MP3* that it should oust *sex* as the No. 1 Internet search term? Must be something, huh?

Bird's blowing confetti, but you don't hear him blow, dig? That's MP3 in a nutshell: The MP3 encoding process rids a track of biologically unnecessary sonic information, stuff we, just by the way we're built, would never hear anyway. It thereby reduces a standard digital audio track to about $\frac{1}{12}$ of its original size, usually without any appreciable loss of sound quality. It's a tiny, tidy package, perfectly suited to our current Internet bandwidth limitations. You can upload or download MP3s as quickly and easily as you download a Flash movie: Start the download, grab a beer, read the headlines of the paper, return to your computer, and there it is—a CD-quality song occupying about 4 MB of disk space. And that's where the trouble begins.

In the News

You've probably heard of, if not heard, MP3 by now, particularly given the furor it has raised among record company advocates. The lawsuits are flying, which is having an unintentional effect of spurring interest in MP3. In any case, MP3 owns the music-download scene. Although MP3 is both useful and legal, many do use it illegally.

> *MP3 stands for MPEG-1, Layer 3, and is but one of three bears you can sic on Goldilocks. MPEG-1 audio compression comes in three flavors, Layer 1, Layer 2, and Layer 3. Each layer is based on the same encoding premise but is more sophisticated and feature-laden than its precedent. Layer 3 compression is the most complex: With its large set of compression tools, it yields the best quality audio at the smallest file size. Layer 1 and Layer 2 compression can and do yield CD-quality tracks, but those tracks occupy substantially more space on your hard disk than those produced by Layer 3 encoding.*

But, well-known artists do release their albums in the MP3 format. Among the first was Frank Black and the Catholics' album *Pistolero*, which you could download back in early 1999 for $8.99 or you could pay $.99 a track and make your own compilation. Frank Black, as you may remember, used to go by Black Francis when he headed up one of the coolest and most innovative bands of all time, The Pixies. You can still download *Pistolero*, as well as a thousand other albums and tracks we've all heard of, over at www.emusic.com, for exactly the same price: It's still ninety-nine cents a track, and the whole thing remains $8.99 (see **Figure 10.1**).

So it has happened that many of us have downloaded a bunch of cool MP3s to our hard disks and enjoyed them for many hours in front of our monitors, using jukebox software. And some of us have even made a bunch of MP3s from our CD collections and organized them into killer playlists on our PCs. The thing is, what we'd really like is to listen to these tracks and playlists far away from the din of our CPU. So what then? Easy answer: Burn them to CD. It's possible to decode an MP3 to a standard CD track. You can then burn these tracks and have a nice compilation to listen to on any CD player anywhere. That's what we'll show you how to do in this chapter. If you've never heard of MP3 before, we'll even show you how to go about obtaining MP3 files.

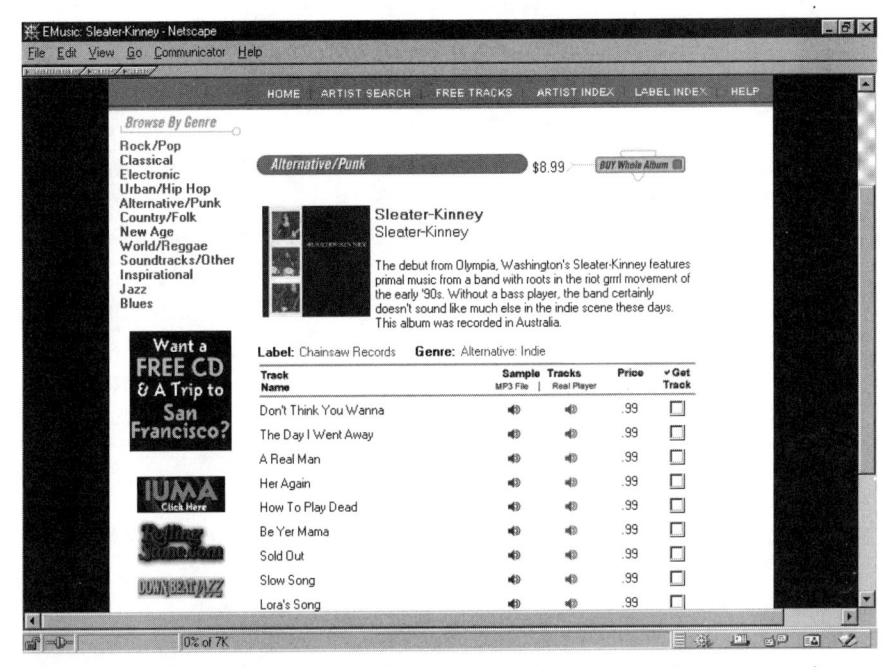

Figure 10.1 This is Sleater-Kinney's page over at www.emusic.com. Here, you can download whatever track you like for ninety-nine cents or download the whole album for $8.99.

> Read chapter 14, "Legal Issues: A Quick Overview," for a look at copyright law. For now, we'll tell you it's perfectly legal to download MP3s if you have the assent of the copyright holder—you're guaranteed assent if you download from a legitimate music site such as www.rioport.com and www.mp3.com.

> It's also legal to post MP3s to the Internet with the assent of the copyright holder. If your unsigned band cut a monster track and you want everyone to hear it, you can post it to the Internet with complete impunity.

Now Let's Go Get Some of These Things

All you need for this step is a current Web browser, and you know us, we like Netscape, not because it's superfantastic, but rather because it's not Microsoft. And we say *current* because some of the older browsers aren't audio-savvy.

Now we're going to shoot over to MP3.com (www.mp3.com; see **Figure 10.2**).

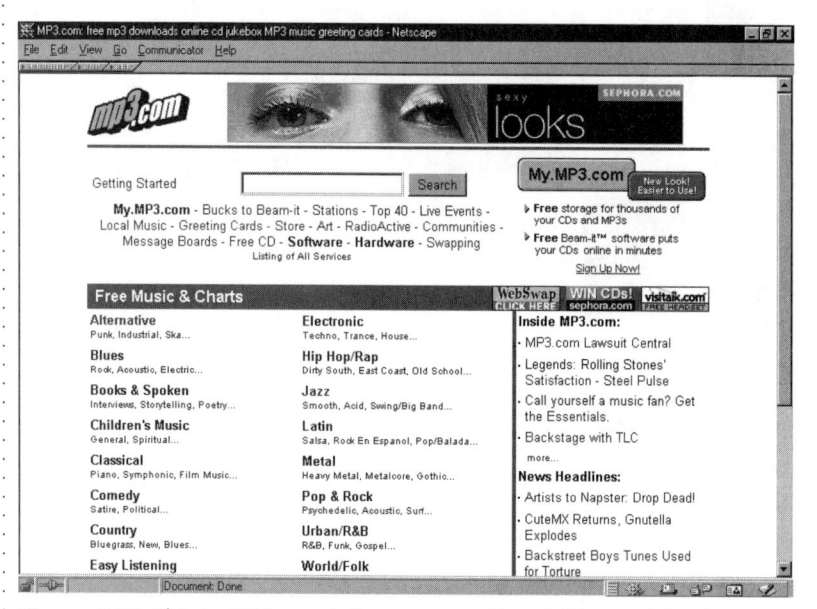

Figure 10.2 This is MP3.com's home page, the starting point of your initial foray into the world of MP3. But remember, MP3.com isn't the only place for free legitimate MP3s on the Internet, not by a long shot.

We picked MP3.com because it's a legitimate MP3 site, and it, in its short existence, has helped along thousands of independent artists. It also features a broad and varied selection, so if you don't dig the stuff we go after, you can go to your favorite genre and download something from that area. Many sites like MP3.com have sprung up, and lots are devoted to a single genre, so go out and have a look when we're done here.

There it is, the home page. Today we're feeling pretty good, so we'd better temper that with some Shoegazer music. Yes, "Shoegazer" is a genre, although we didn't know that until just recently. That rubric didn't exist when we were out buying music by pigeonholed outfits that are now considered "Shoegazer" bands. To be honest, we're still not quite sure what defines Shoegazer: We know, though, that it's not obtrusive—it's ethereal, even, and dreamy—and a melancholy pang surfaces time to time. The pang tickles Bob but good—he's got that thing where he sees his somber soul reflected in art, and he can't help but be happy, like a baby in a mirror.

Since we've done this before, we know we'll find Shoegazer somewhere in the Brit Pop section in the Alternative area, unless the site underwent a reorganization while we were away. Aha, right where we left it.

Now we're faced with a whole bunch of tracks, arranged in order of popularity. Just so you know what you're getting into, MP3.com gives you the option of playing the files before you download them. The way we generally do this is click the track title—this most often takes us to another page featuring the track we want to play and download, an artist biography, and other tracks by the artist. Scrolling through the list, we come across a track entitled "I Hate Paul Reiser" by a band called Poingly—odds are, this isn't Shoegazer, per se, as one might have to look up from his shoes to proclaim hatred for Paul Reiser, but judging from the title, it should delight us. We click the track to move into the bio area and begin playing the hi-fi version of "I Hate Paul Reiser," which does, in fact, delight us (see **Figure 10.3**).

If you can't play the file or save it to disk here, there are quick remedies. On a PC, get into you browser's Preferences area, and in the Applications area, find the file extension you're looking for (in this case, MP3 or MPEG Audio). Check the box next to "Always ask before doing anything with this kind of file." That should give you the option, whenever you click to download an MP3, to open the MP3 file or save it to your hard disk. If you're on a Mac, it's a little easier: If you want to play the MP3, click it. If you want to download it, hold down Ctrl and click the MP3. Press OK in the window that pops up to save it.

Backing out of Poingly's area into the list area, we come across Mira, a cool Shoegazer outfit that we know got signed to the cool Projekt label. We go in and grab all the band's stuff—same way we grabbed Poingly's—and notice that Mira has an album coming out here shortly, which is handy knowledge, as we'll want to go buy that when it hits the shelves. Happy for Mira, we take our leave from MP3.com, comfortable in the knowledge that everything we've just done is not only completely legal but openly encouraged by the copyright holders themselves.

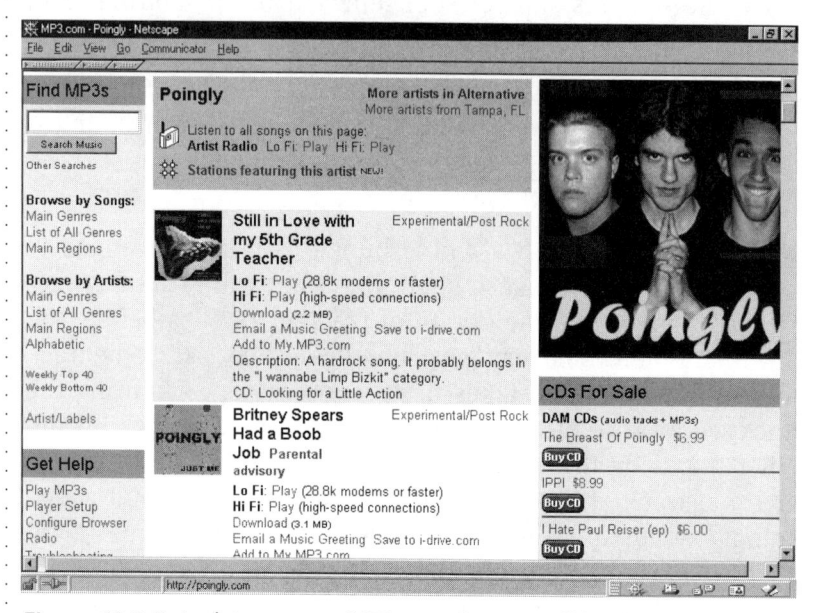

Figure 10.3 Poingly's area on MP3.com features all kinds of information, from their influences to downloadable tracks.

> ### By the numbers
>
> By default, the MP3s you acquire from sites such as MP3.com will be encoded to 128 kbps, or kilobits per second. That means, practically speaking, that one second of those MP3s will occupy about 128 kilobits (not kilobytes, mind you) of hard disk space. By comparison, one second of CD audio occupies about 1400 kilobits. That's the ultimate beauty of MP3: the compression method MP3 utilizes—this removal of Bird's breath—retains CD quality sound at a really low "bitrate" (that is, the number of bits constituting one second of audio) and saves us all that space on our hard disks. MP3 will only take you so far though. You can compress CD audio all the way on down to 32 kbps with MP3, but below 128 kbps, some important digits—stuff you would hear, unlike Bird's breath—must be removed to get the bitrate that low. The result doesn't sound so good, or as good as 128 kbps anyway. Conversely, a bitrate larger than 128 kbps may be of slightly higher fidelity, but the size of the MP3 will increase too.

Napster

Besides our browsers, we've also used Napster to acquire MP3s. Today anyway (there's litigation ongoing), you can download the Napster client for the PC (see **Figure 10.4**), free of charge, at www.napster.com, and you can get its Mac counterpart, Macster, at www.macster.com (see **Figure 10.5**).

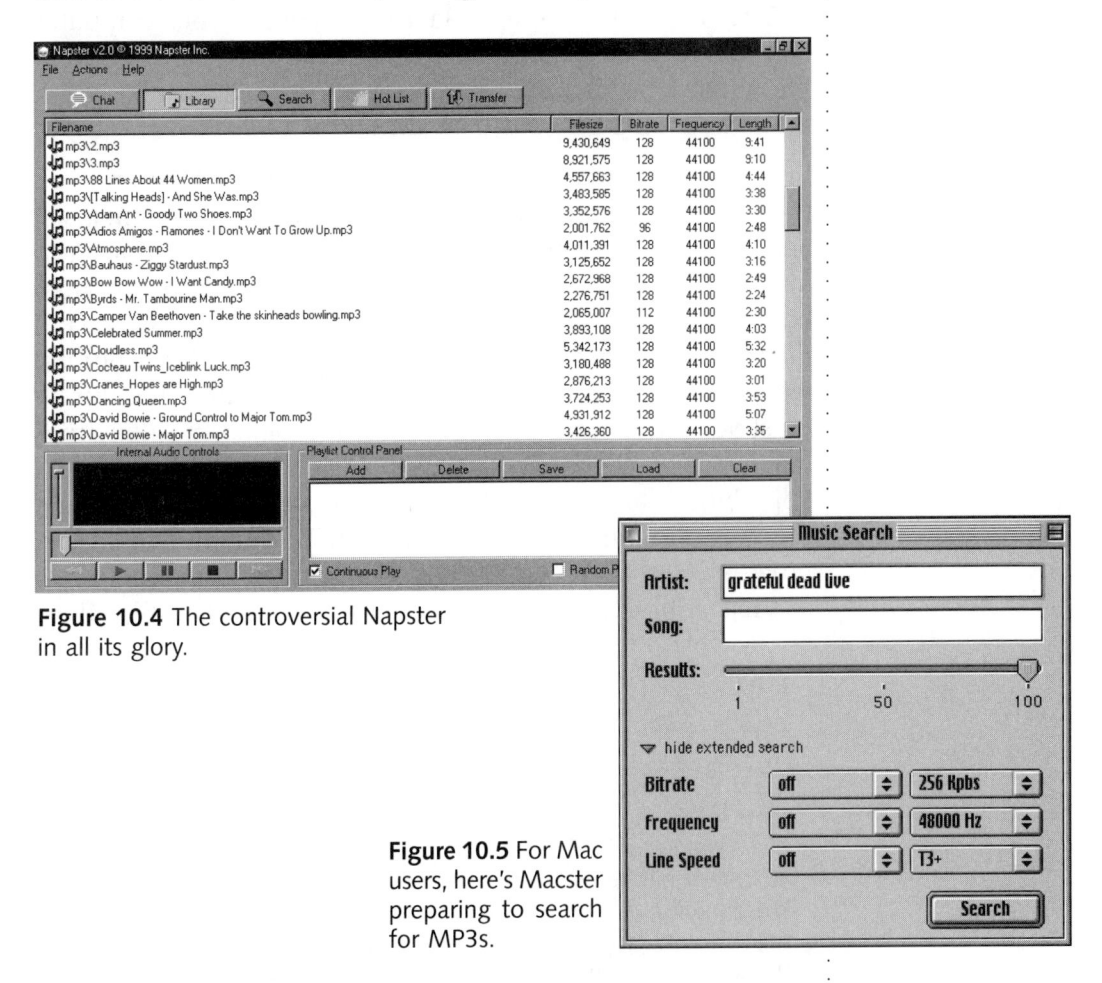

Figure 10.4 The controversial Napster in all its glory.

Figure 10.5 For Mac users, here's Macster preparing to search for MP3s.

The Napster and Macster clients are something akin to Web browsers, in that they facilitate communication between you, your computer, and a server. The servers involved here, though, as opposed to Web servers, don't offer public files for viewing or download; rather, these servers simply enable file sharing between the computers connected to them, like and including your own.

Using Napster, you'll lay out a few search terms, such as the name of the song you're looking for and what bitrate you prefer. This request will then be relayed to the server, which will proceed to look around in all the computers connected to it and then get back to your client with what it finds. From these search results, you select the MP3 you're looking for and tell your client to instruct the server that you wish to download it. The server establishes a data link between your computer and the computer that has the MP3 you're looking for, and file transfer begins, user to user. Soon enough, you've got a brand new MP3 on your hard disk.

In Napster's search area, you type the name of the artist or track you're looking for—in the Artist and Song Title fields—and define a few other search criteria (see **Figure 10.6**). You may want to fill in the Bitrate must be and Frequency must be fields, located just to the right of the Artist and Song Title fields, just to narrow things down, qualitywise. For a bitrate, we suggest you select Equal to and 128 KB/S from the Bitrate must be drop-down menus. From the Frequency must be drop-down menus, choose Equal to and 44100 Hz. MP3s with a 128 kbps bitrate and a 44.1kHz sampling rate generally will be the most diminutive of CD-quality MP3s. Sound quality gets progressively worse with lower bitrates and sampling rates, and higher bitrates and sampling rates make for really big MP3s.

> **MP2**
>
> What 128 kbps is to MP3, 256 kbps is to MP2 (MPEG-1, Layer 2). Layer 3, having more compression tools at its disposal, is more adept than Layer 2 at encoding to these low bitrates. If you find in some weird place an MP2 file you want—the odds of which are slim—you'll want it encoded to 256 kbps because you lose quality at a lower bitrate with MP2 files. This MP2 file encoded to 256 kbps is going to be substantially larger than the MP3 file encoded to 128 kbps, so given that the two files will be of almost exactly the same quality, we'll opt for the MP3, if it's available.

Once you press the Find It button directly beneath the Artist and Song Title fields, the Napster client shoots your search terms up to the server. In turn, the server proceeds to scan all of its users' MP3 collections. Everyone connected to the Napster server has access to everyone else's designated MP3 directory, and you may discover that some MP3s are being downloaded from your hard disk as you search.

Often, Napster finds many instances of the MP3s you're looking for. In **Figure 10.6**, you'll see that a search for "William Shatner" produced several results. When this happens, Napster decides, according to itself and the criteria you've stipulated, which instance will cause you the least hassle in downloading and places a small green icon beside these. Additionally, Napster arranges the search in descending order of Ping time: This effectively means that the MP3s listed near the top of the results are on computers that transfer data quickly, as far as the server is concerned. Double-clicking one of the results listed initiates the download, and you'll automatically be taken to the Transfer window, where you can watch the download progress.

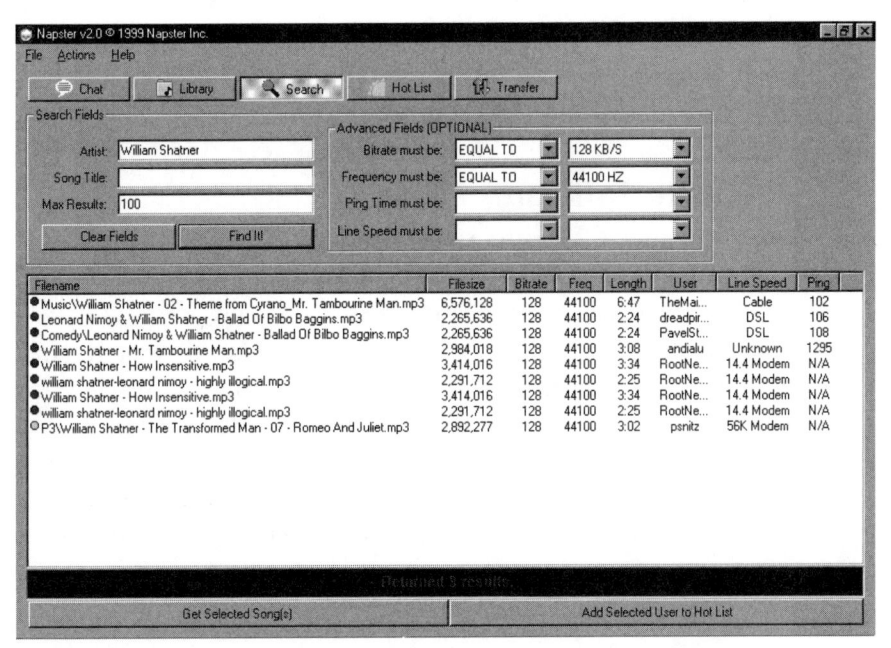

Figure 10.6 Having completed its search, Napster determines which file will cause you the least problems during download and offers a synopsis of vital information about the track, such as file size and encoding bitrate.

That's how easy it is to acquire MP3s. With a browser or a client such as Napster, you can have all the new, high-quality music you want without ever leaving you computer. Given that, it's not too difficult to see why MP3 is all the rage: There's no haul to the record store, your selection is virtually infinite, and above all, MP3 sounds great. That's the future of digital music, friends, in all of its permutations.

> *Broadcast radio, even, is soon to be challenged by IP-multicast MP3s, which will pump out of your PC's speakers at that same CD quality. Regular folks like us have already erected thousands of independent, commercial-free Internet radio stations, at no cost to themselves or their users. There's an astonishing lack, too, of legal issues around these stations. One notable restriction is you cannot announce what songs you'll play, only the ones you have played. You can cuss until Caligula gets upset, play whatever songs you like, and remain totally legit. But we'll leave that for another book.*

Now we should do some things with these high-quality MP3 files we've acquired, huh?

Requisite Software

Hoorah! More free stuff! Nearly all the best and coolest MP3-related software won't cost you a dime. Not only that, you can choose from hundreds of nifty software packages, so if you grow tired of the one you get, it's easy enough to switch. And with many packages it's no big deal to simply swap what are known as skins, or the software's user interface. By putting a new skin on your software, you can change the look and feel of your MP3 software's interface. Some packages even feature a skin editor, letting you design your own software interface.

We intend to turn our MP3s into CD-suitable material, so one thing our software must offer is some kind of MP3 "decoder." "Decoder" is in quotes because the process of transforming an MP3 into a CD-ready track isn't exactly decoding. It's more like inflation or padding. Once an MP3 track is encoded, there's no going back. The information pulled out is gone forever. And "decoding" goes by many names and will not be consistently referred to as "decoding"—the utilities and features that decode are also called disk writers or something similar.

Mac users might be a little disappointed when they see the selection of MP3 software, especially when compared to million choices PC users have. You're limited further by how many of these MP3 programs will decode MP3s. Toast 4.0 will automatically decode MP3s you line up in a burn queue, but problems arise in automated decoding, such as you're not able to hear the resulting AIFF before it gets burned. If automation unnerves you, you can download a tried-and-true MP3 decoder for the Mac called Mpecker Drop Decoder for free over at www.anime.net/~go/mpeckers.html. You decode MP3s with Mpecker simply by dragging whatever MP3 you wish to decode onto the Mpecker icon. That brief movement sets Mpecker in motion. In short order, you'll have an AIFF file ready for a burn. However, we suggest you listen to the decoded track before you proceed to burn it, just to make sure it sounds OK.

Our PCs, on the other hand, endure many MP3 software changes. Three MP3 software packages, however, invariably remain on our machines while many others—good ones even—fall by the wayside. The first is Winamp, by Nullsoft. Winamp serves as a touchstone of the MP3 software world (see **Figure 10.7**). The language Winamp uses often becomes the standard way of talking about MP3-related things, and many software developers create applications around and for it. Since it has been around awhile and has seen a version or two, Winamp tends to be less buggy than a lot of other packages. It's smooth, and many people have found bliss with it, so we're comfortable saying Winamp is well worth a look.

We keep MusicMatch Jukebox, or MMJB, around too (see **Figure 10.8**). You do have to pay for this one, but it's worth the 30 or so bones. Jukebox does it all, and does it all well. It has two noteworthy cool features: an automated link to CDDB (Compact Disc

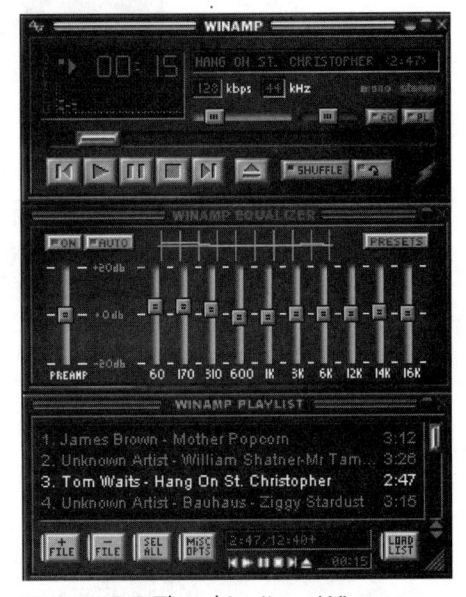

Figure 10.7 The ubiquitous Winamp ain't that great, but it's achieved industry-standard status.

Database, a supercomprehensive online database of artists, album titles, and album contents, found at www.cddb.com) and a convenient Export Playlist to WAV feature. If you happen to be ripping and encoding tracks from your music collection, MMJB will go out to CDDB, get the information on the CD you're ripping, and name the tracks accordingly—you never have to punch in track title, artist, or album information. Then, when you're preparing to burn a compilation CD out of MP3s, all you have to do is put together your intended compilation in MMJB's playlist editor and hit Export Playlist to WAV. The only thing left to you then is to open your CD-R software, queue up your tracks, and burn or use MMJB's built-in burning utility.

Figure 10.8 Look at the size of that thing! MusicMatch JukeBox is easily the finest playlist organizer going, and features such as Export Playlist to WAV make it worth the money.

Finally, there's our favorite MP3 software, Sonique (www.sonique.com). Sonique, like Winamp, was recently acquired by a larger company and may suffer for that in the future. For now, however, Sonique is our choice for coolest MP3 software around, although our reason has little to do with technical or functional stuff, though those aspects of Sonique are impressive. We like Sonique because of the immense amount of thought that went into the aesthetics of the interface, and the importance the guys who wrote it seem to place on aesthetics in general. What are we looking for in MP3 if not cool aesthetics, right? That hypothetical guy who took LSD by accident that one time, the one who was hearing all the stuff we don't ordinarily hear, might sometimes miss those aspects of hearing. With Sonique, he's compensated for that loss by the general interface and by a searing collection of visuals, these small interfaces-within-interfaces that dance along with the playback of your MP3s. Sonique is a kind of poetry, postmodern synaesthesia, magic for free. Can't beat that. So there's the frank version: Sonique looks cool (see **Figure 10.9**). And it does everything we need it to do.

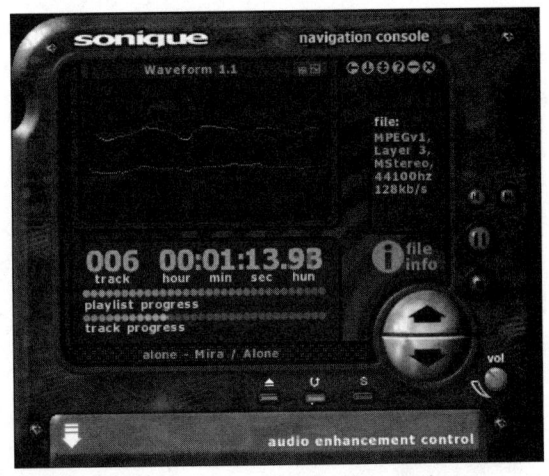

Figure 10.9 Sonique is, hands down, the prettiest piece of MP3 software around. And pragmatically speaking, Sonique does everything you need it to do, from playlist management to MP3 decoding.

Getting Your MP3s Ready for CD

It's the trend among CD recording software manufacturers to include automated MP3 decoding in their products. With these, all you have to do is line up your herd of MP3s, or even in some cases a mix of digital audio formats, and hit burn. The software will do all of your decoding for you on-the-fly, during the burn process.

In many cases, though, this might not be the most comfortable way to go about getting your MP3s onto disc. For instance, when you allow a CD recording program to automatically decode and burn your MP3s, you will not be able to hear the file resulting from the MP3 decoding process before it gets burned to the disc. For all you know here, you could be burning garbage wrought of a malfunctioning decoding procedure. Imagine burning a perfect disc, except for one track poorly decoded or otherwise mangled—you may have to scrap your whole project. If you had decoded your MP3s and reviewed them while they were on your hard disk and then gone ahead with the burn, you could have averted that tragedy. Some people, too, are leery of having two system resource hogs (MP3 decoding and CD burning) operating simultaneously: Whether or not the CD recording package successfully achieves happy negotiation between decoding and burning—allotting to each its share of resources—some still find it frightening. If you are uncomfortable using this kind of utility, crack open Sonique, and we'll show you another, safer way.

As we mentioned, Sonique isn't anything like any other MP3 software programs or, for that matter, anything you've probably ever seen on your desktop before. You interact with Sonique via a series of screens, or windows, that replace one another, and the options presented therein. There is a main window (see **Figure 10.10**) of sorts within Sonique, and it's through this that you'll be accessing the other windows, where you'll configure Sonique for decoding. You'll also get to windows from within other windows: Each window presents you with a series of options, some of which will lead to yet other windows. If you're somehow lost within Sonique—which, as you see, may very well happen from time to time—you can always get back to the main window by punching the left-pointing arrow in the upper-right corner of whatever window you find

Figure 10.10 This is Sonique's main screen, or window. You'll be selecting a couple of items from here at various times, specifically playlist editor, setup options, and visual mode. Here, we're selecting playlist editor.

yourself in (see the pointer in **Figure 10.11**). Your playback controls—for example, Play and Fast-Forward—reside outside the window, in the gray border of Sonique.

Let's first compose a playlist in whatever playlist editor your software offers. In Sonique, you get to the playlist editor by clicking the words *playlist editor* in the main window—when you move your pointer over the assorted sets of words in the main window, they pulsate, just so you know what you're selecting. When you click, the main screen vanishes in a slick animation, and in its place the Playlist Editor window appears (see **Figure 10.11**). The playlist you devise here will eventually be used to build your CD. Remember that standard CD-R media will hold only about 74 minutes of music, so be sure that your play time doesn't extend past that. Sonique will tell you exactly how many minutes of music you've got queued up, so you don't need to do any math.

Figure 10.11 This is Sonique's Playlist Editor. The pointer is just beneath the left-pointing arrow that returns you to the main screen.

The playlist builder controls are located at the bottom of the Playlist Editor (see **Figures 10.11** and **10.12**) and offer you four playlist controls (sort, shuffle, reverse, and clear) and three building controls (add, remove, and save). To build a playlist, click the word *add*, which will open a familiar Open File window—and then pick the tracks you want in your playlist by holding down the CTRL key and selecting them, one by one. Hit Open in the Open File window, and you're done. The tracks you selected should now appear in the Playlist Editor, and you should see a

Figure 10.12 Sonique's Playlist Editor, where we've built the playlist that will become our CD. Notice, in the lower-right corner, that Sonique calculates the time, in minutes, of your playlist.

total playing time near the bottom of the window. If the playing time is 74 or fewer minutes, you're good to go; if it's more than 74 minutes, you're going to need to remove a track or two.

Remove a track by selecting the track you wish to remove and clicking *remove* at the bottom of the window. Now, if you don't like the order of the tracks, don't worry—you can adjust them right before you record. The playlist we built consists of those six Mira tracks we got over at MP3.com, so we've got about 28 minutes of music in the queue, all told. We're doing OK here.

Once you've got your playlist built, return to the main window by clicking that left-pointing arrow in the upper-right corner of the window. From the main window, click the words *setup options*. In Setup Options, you'll find two navigation bars, one at the bottom presenting you with general and plug-in options and another at the right with a whole array of options (see **Figure 10.13**). Select the *general* option at the bottom of the window and then the *audio* option on the right.

This will lead to a screen with two fields: the Select Output field and WAV disk writer path field, where you'll enter the path for the files you'll later be burning to CD. When you're filling in the path, be sure to include the whole path (in **Figure 10.13**, D:\AudioFiles\WAV is the path we've entered). You also must have enough room on your hard disk for these WAV files. Figure approximately 10 MB of disk space per minute of music. Knowing that we've got about 28 minutes of music queued up, we anticipate needing about 280 MB of disk space, which we happen to have available.

Figure 10.13 This is the Setup Options window, with the *general* and *audio* options highlighted. The pointer is placed over the arrows with which you select your output. Remember to change it back to your sound card when you're done decoding.

In the Select Output field, click the small arrows to the right of the field to navigate to WAV disk writer (see **Figure 10.13**). Remember that you've done this. If you don't change it back to your sound card's output when you're done decoding, you'll end up making these huge WAV files out of every MP3 you queue up and play, even if you're only checking out a track you may never want to burn.

Now, from the navigation bar at the bottom of this same window, select *plug-ins*. This will change the bar off to the right. From this new bar, select *StarDust* (see **Figure 10.14**). *StarDust* is your decoder proper. Configure it to your tastes. Ours is optimized today for Best Quality, and we've set both the buffer and prebuffer to somewhere in the middle. The buffer and pre-buffer are something like the buffers you use when recording CDs. Big buffers occupy a lot of your CPU's processing and memory resources, but they usually result in smoother and more reliable operation. We also like to select the high priority option—this allots a bunch of system resources to the decoding process, which will also result in better operation. All this is going to take awhile and will naturally retard other applications we may be running, but that's an easy sacrifice today, as we'll be watching an Ingmar Bergman movie and eating a pizza while our MP3s decode and subsequently won't be using any other applications. If you're in a hurry, make small buffers, deprioritize Sonique, and optimize for fast performance.

Figure 10.14 This is the Setup Options window, where we've selected the *plug-ins* and *StarDust* options. StarDust, your decoder proper, can be configured in many ways, some resulting in fast and perhaps reckless operation, others resulting in slow but careful operation.

Return once more to the main window, and get back into the Playlist Editor. See to it that no looping of the playlist will occur by clicking the Repeat Modes button (it's one of three little buttons outside of the main window, toward the bottom; see the pointer in **Figure 10.15**) until any repeat mode is off—you'll see a message in the little window of the screen informing you of an off status. If you happen to loop your playlist, you risk initiating an endless decoding cycle, and all those WAVs you wrote the first time around may be written again in some fashion. (We don't know whether this will overwrite the first-round WAV you recorded or produce a second duplicate WAV, and we don't particularly want to find out.)

After confirming there's no unwanted looping going on, hit play—that biggish green button off to the right of the screen, on the thick gray border. You'll get a message that decoding is about to occur, and the option to proceed. Proceed. You can check the status of your decoding by returning to the main window and selecting *visual mode*: This window will register both track and playlist progress, so you have an idea of when the decoding will be finished (see **Figure 10.16**).

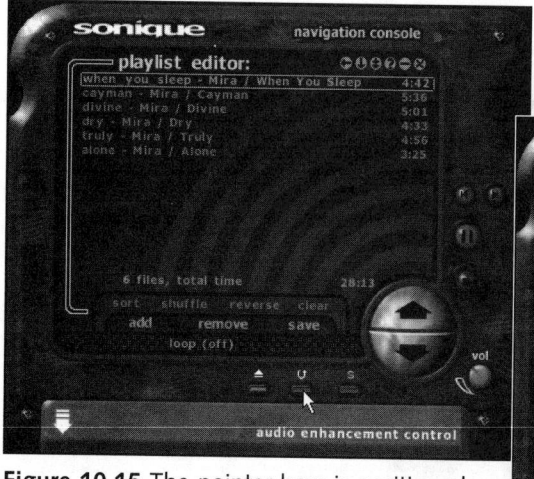

Figure 10.15 The pointer here is positioned over the Repeat Modes button. Notice the off message in the small window directly above it.

Figure 10.16 Watch your MP3s become suitable for burning in Sonique's visual mode.

Since we've chosen to optimize for quality, the decoding process is going to take awhile. You can do many things as your tracks decode. We're going to watch *Persona* and eat a pizza, but you may choose to go shopping, speak with your children about some hazards they may encounter during adolescence, call your Mom, or start reading that series of interviews with Michel Foucault you've been meaning to get to.

About 45 minutes into *Persona*, right near that classic Brechtian moment of alienation from film as medium, and ultimately of film as ideological apparatus, our MP3s are done cooking, and our idea of recorded music as a physically packaged, over-the-counter phenomenon is forever altered. We have now a directory full of WAV files almost ready to be burned to CD. We say "almost" because, listening to the WAVs (right-click wav > properties > preview, you remember), we've found one WAV is marred with a common MP3-related problem: Not enough bass. This is caused by the Minimal Audition Threshold component of MP3 compression, which reduces track size by removing imperceptible low-frequency sounds. Sometimes, encoders are a little indiscriminate in what they remove at these frequencies. Users of MP3 software yelled about this a lot, and developers evidently heard them, because it doesn't happen so often anymore. If you are lacking bass, fear not! Another great use of those digital audio editing programs we talked about in Chapters 7, "Highway 61 Revisited," and 8, "Restoring and Recording Cassette Tapes," on record and tape preparation is that you can also use them to mend the WAVs that MP3 encoding or decoding wrought. This is most easily accomplished with the equalizer function of whatever package you decided on. Simply do a bass boost, and that should fix most of what's ailing you (see **Figure 10.17**).

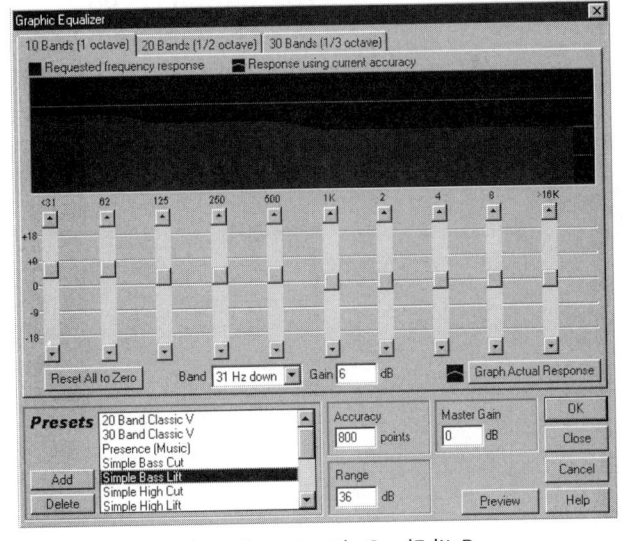

Figure 10.17 A bass boost with CoolEdit Pro.

While you're in your audio editing program you may want to normalize your tracks, especially if they're coming from widely disparate sources. Normalization adjusts the gain of your tracks so that they meet a kind of standard loudness. It sets whatever peak amplitude it finds in your track to around 0db and adjusts everything else accordingly. This has the effect of making all of your tracks equally loud during playback, so you won't be jarred by a superloud track appearing on the heels of a track you were listening to at a comfortable level. When we're making compilation CDs from all manner of material, gain normalization is a must. Today, we could normalize Mira's stuff but we don't really need to, judging from our listening.

Happy with our WAVs, it's time to burn.

Burning Your Former MP3s to Disc

Nothing will happen here that's spectacularly different from the other burns we've done. Shut off your computer's automated stuff, such as active screensavers or power management features, and quit any open programs. Open your CD recording software, make sure it knows you're burning an audio CD, queue up the tracks, and burn. Now you have in your hand the future of music distribution—you won't be buying CDs at Corpco Inc. Records for very much longer. Odds are good that this is the way we'll all be getting music from now on. Aren't you proud to find yourself on the frontier like that? Sure you are, or you should be, anyway.

Compilation Discs

You've been recording compilation discs all through this book, and you're very good at it now. To be honest with you, because you're already good at it, we even talked about nixing this chapter altogether. You know how to get a track from whatever source to your hard disk, you know how to alter your tracks until they suit you, and you know how to burn tracks to CD. Knowing those things, you already know how to make a compilation CD, and we don't really need to elaborate further on this subject, right?

You're absolutely right, we don't need to elaborate any further on these things. You're fully equipped now to burn a good compilation CD. You figure, though, we can all use a few pointers from time to time, so what we thought we'd do here, in this chapter, is take four songs, each from a different medium—tape, LP, MP3, and CD—and record a compilation from them. Along the way, we're going to show you a couple things you can do to hone your compilation further. And we have a few as yet undisclosed tricks we want to show you.

We'll begin here with brief descriptions of the four tracks we'll use and then end with getting these four tracks to happily commingle on a CD.

Track 1, from a CD

Imagine our dismay when track 1 of our favorite CD would skip interminably in all CD players. We tried everything to remedy this: We wiped down the CD, we cleaned lasers left and right, and we attempted to get a decent signal from a good solid stereo component, all to no avail. We even tried some toothpaste trick we'd heard about, just to see if it would work.

> *It's said that if you wet your finger with toothpaste and rub that finger over a scratched or otherwise mauled CD, the toothpaste will fill the flaws in. Wiping the excess toothpaste away, then, you can place your CD in your stereo, and everything will work just fine. That's not the case, don't buy it: The toothpaste thing does not work. We don't know where that idea came from, but it's a bad one. Our bet is that this toothpaste trick originated with that same guy who said, "your adolescent years are the best years of your life," thereby crushing the spirits of billions of 15-year-olds.*

On a whim, we tried to play this track on a computer, in a Plextor CD-RW drive, no less, and we encountered the same skipping problem. Now, witness the raw power of Audiograbber, the ripper we discussed in Chapter 9, "Copying CDs"—somehow, some way, Audiograbber and the Plextor device were able to extract a perfect copy of this track to hard disk, even though this Plextor couldn't perform playback (see **Figure 11.1**). We're not sure what they did, but we're not asking any questions either.

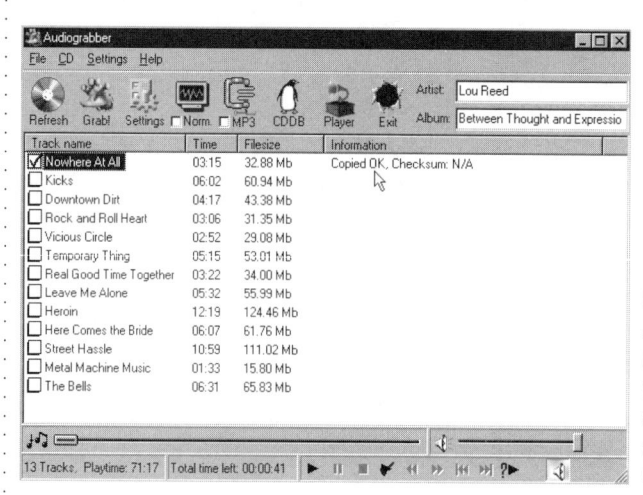

Figure 11.1 Audiograbber reporting its success in extracting an unplayable CD track.

Track 2, from a Tape

Oh, man, this thing was hissing something fierce and might've been played a time or two in the past. Fortunately, removing the hiss was all we needed to do to get the signal back.

You remember from Chapter 8, "Restoring and Recording Cassette Tapes," that tape hiss, or the annoying part of it anyway, is relegated to a pretty specific part of the sound spectrum (see **Figure 11.2**) and is constant throughout a sample, making it pretty easy to spot and remove using a digital audio editor.

Now, remember that dehiss curve we saved in Chapter 8, in Diamond Cut's Continuous Noise filter? Handy thing we did there, because all we had to do to dehiss this track was summon that curve we saved (see **Figure 11.3**), make a few slight adjustments, and save our new curve as a new preset. Soon, we'll have an army of dehissing presets to call upon, and we'll achieve a high degree of dehissing precision for our tapes.

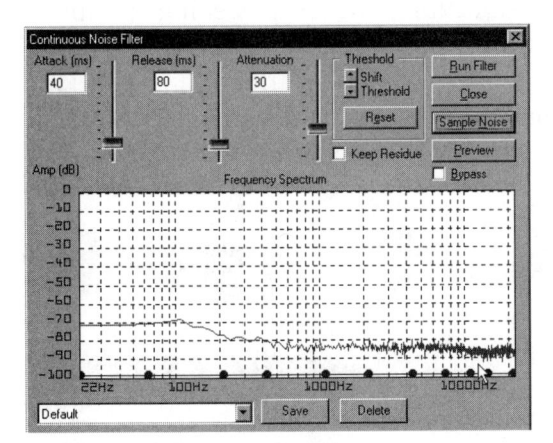

Figure 11.2 The noise print from our tape—observe the ugliness by the pointer.

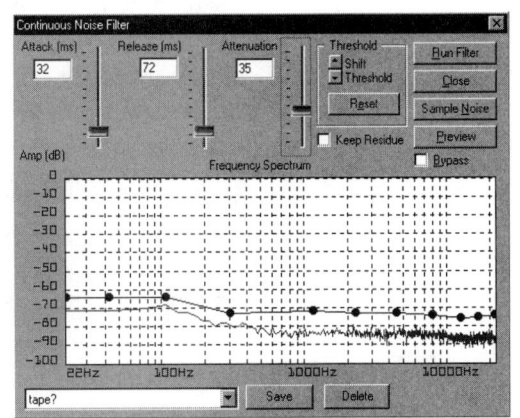

Figure 11.3 Our saved preset noise reduction curve, slightly modified for this tape.

Track 3, from Vinyl

Surely you've bumped into the Great Bummer of Analog Material after all these projects we've done: Your favorite songs on analog media are also the most trashed songs, because you listened to them most often and wore them out. In the sense that our computers can recover these tattered treasures, we have to chalk up a point for digital in the analog vs. digital debate.

Case in point: our favorite record. When this record first came out, it was one of these deals where we knew, for indisputable fact, that what we were hearing was the coolest thing ever in the history of humankind, even cooler than electricity and the printing press. That being, we forced all of our friends to listen to it. Of course, after enough playing for enough friends, let alone all those times we listened to it by ourselves, we wore our record down to gurgling, crackling, muffled misfortune.

Much crackling and popping was afoot on this track (see **Figure 11.4**), underscored by that long silence preceding the initial beat of the drum. Nothing hosts noise better than silence, eh? As luck would have it, though, our favorite album is a loud album, and the loudness drowns out most of the noise intrinsic to the medium, so we've got that going for us.

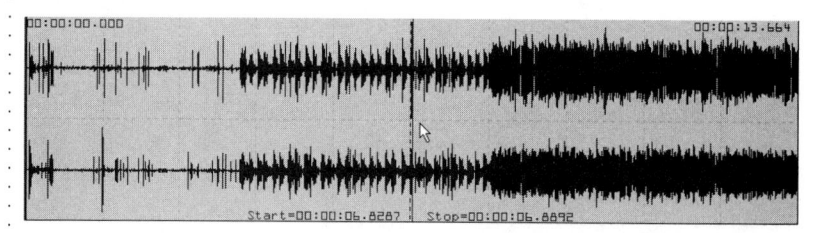

Figure 11.4 A close-up of the noise on the best record ever made in the history of humankind. The pointer here is directly next to a click we're about to mute. Notice all the impulse spikes all over the place.

Nonetheless, during the quieter moments, the crackling and popping become pronounced, and something must be done. We tried an assortment of impulse noise filters, but found that these did nothing to eradicate the pops and clicks without beating on the song itself. We had to get serious, and tedious, as serious implies tedious, you know: Using Diamond Cut, we went into the waveform, located every single noticeable click, and muted each of them (see **Figure 11.5**). Sometimes that's the only way, you remember. Long, long day, but we finally arrived at a satisfactory product.

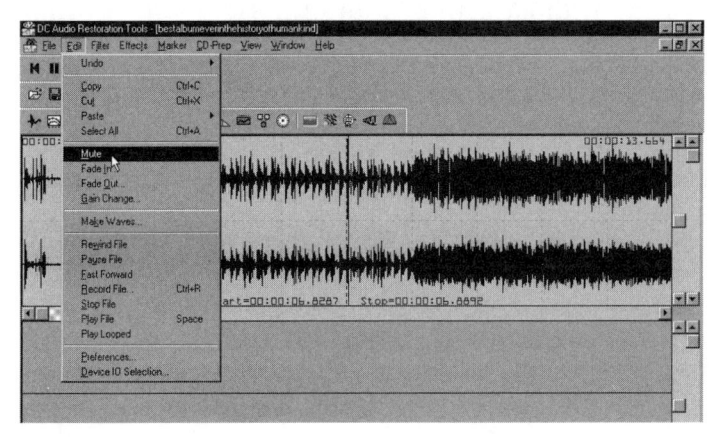

Figure 11.5 Gonna mute it.

Track 4, from an MP3

We went out looking for a dirty MP3, one that lacked sufficient bass or had been poorly encoded. We couldn't find any, probably because the popularity of the format has led to accessible high-quality encoding technology. You may never have to worry about altering decoded MP3s ever again—these days, they're coming out great. But there was that one song we bumped into in Chapter 10, "Recording MP3s to CD," that sat shakily atop tenuous bass.

That bass-bereft Mira track shall now be called by name: "Dry." Yes, laugh

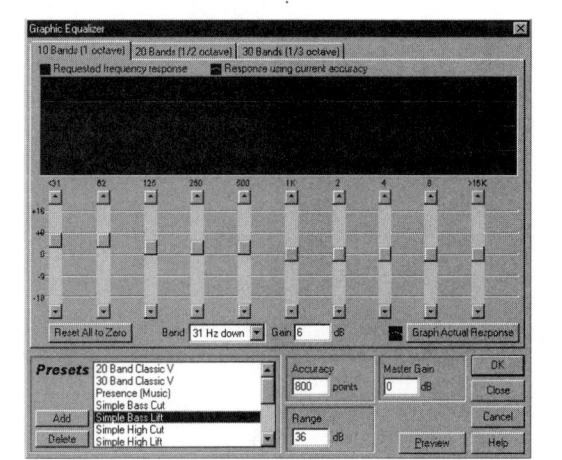

Figure 11.6 Mira getting a bass boost in CoolEdit.

along with us at the bitter coincidence. You'll remember too, from Chapter 10, that all we had to do to "Dry," once we decoded it, was boost the bass using CoolEdit's graphic equalizer. Easy enough. Now "Dry" is pretty near good to go.

So there they are, our tracks, resting on our hard disk, ready to be burned. What further issues could possibly arise?

Equalization

Because of the nature of the medium we talked about in Chapter 5, "General Hardware," you can't get too much treble response from vinyl without getting a lot of noise too, that being one of the reasons the RIAA Curve was implemented (see **Figure 11.7**). Even with the treble enhancement during master cutting, though, the treble of vinyl is still a little weaker than the treble of a CD—or other digital media. In fact, CDs evince such incredible treble response, analog guys commonly complain that CDs sound "too crisp and tinny." This is because you can get all kinds of treble onto CD without worrying about noise.

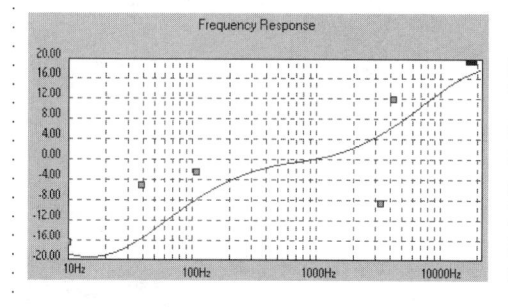

Figure 11.7
The equalization curve applied to an audio signal during the cutting of a master record. The treble boost still often cannot match the treble response of digital media.

When you burn a CD with tracks ripped from digital media and copied from analog media, as we are doing here, you might find that you don't particularly like this contrast between the vinyl and CD sound—it's just another thing to distract you from relaxation or getting your groove on, whichever it is you do when you listen. Once again, this is a pretty easy thing to fix.

You have two ways to fix this, if you have a graphic equalizer in your digital audio editing software: You can either cut the treble on the tracks you ripped from a CD or boost the treble on the track you copied from vinyl (see **Figure 11.8**). We figure, since the vinyl signal has already been equalized twice—once during recording and again in our preamp during playback for recording—that maybe we should leave it alone now. We opt most times to cut the CD treble as well as the treble of any decoded MP3s we're burning because, you remember from Chapter 10, MP3s are most often CD tracks without the unnecessary sonic information. As for tracks from tapes, whether you equalize them or not is going to be up to your ear.

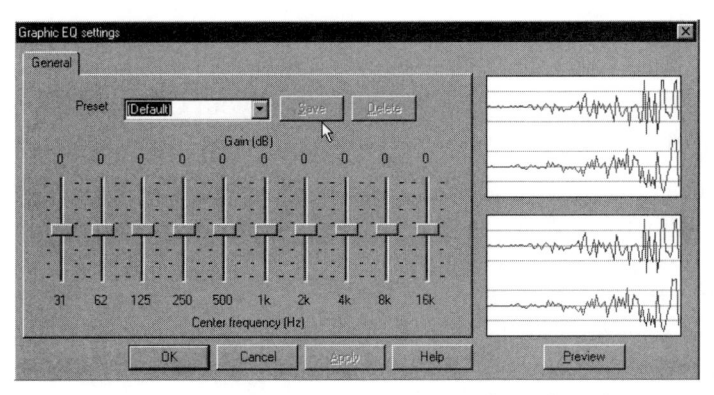

Figure 11.8 Easy CD Creator's graphic equalizer, found in its Sound Editor utility.

Open your CD track in your digital audio editor. Locate the graphic equalizer, and open that. We're still in Diamond Cut here. Its graphic equalizer is in the Filter drop-down menu—select and click it. You probably recognize the window that pops up: It looks like a graphic EQ you hook up to your stereo. It functions in precisely the same way. You're probably only going to have to tamper with three bands: the bar beneath 16,000 Hz, the bar beneath 8000 Hz, and the bar beneath 4000 Hz. That's the treble range we're going to reduce. Hit the Reset Levels button (see **Figure 11.9**) to get all the sliders in a row in the middle—this is called a flat response and simply means that no equalization will be placed on to your CD track just yet.

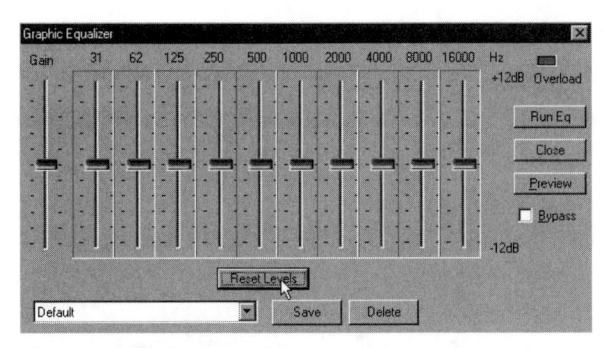

Figure 11.9 Diamond Cut's graphic equalizer, shown here with a flat response.

You're going to have to do this by ear and memory. Minimize Diamond Cut, and find the track you copied from vinyl. Listen to it (we'll naturally do that right-click > Properties > Preview thing we've been doing). Remembering what it sounds like, return to Diamond Cut, and press the Preview button off to the right in the graphic equalizer window—your CD track will start playing, and a progress meter will appear.

Now, move any of those three sliders downward—you'll hear the effect of what you're doing on your track as you do it—until you think you're close to the vinyl sound. Press the cancel button in the progress meter (see **Figure 11.10**). Return to your vinyl track, listen to it again, and then go back to Diamond Cut and alter some more, in the way we just described. Keep doing that until you believe your vinyl and CD track will happily coexist on the CD you're about to burn (see **Figure 11.11**).

Repeat this process with decoded MP3s. That's it.

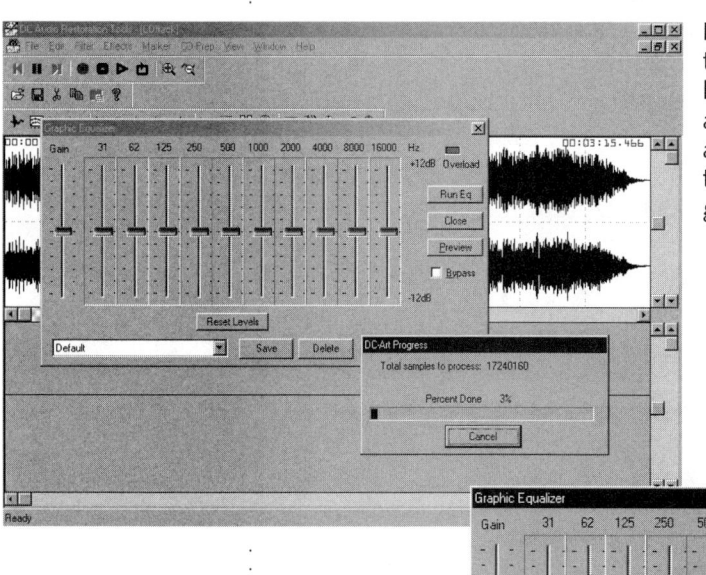

Figure 11.10 After pressing the Preview button, we're able here to hear our track playing and the effects of what we do among the sliding bars. Notice the progress meter below the graphic equalizer window.

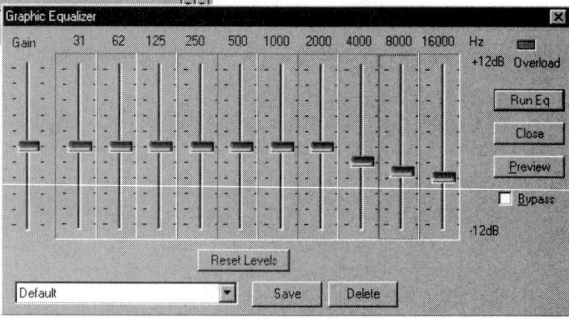

Figure 11.11 This is what we finally come up with. Our CD track and our vinyl track shall now happily cohabitate on our upcoming compilation disc, according to our ears anyway.

Fade-Ins and Fade-Outs

Sometimes a fade-in or fade-out is called for. Studios are typically pretty good at discerning when to implement fade-ins and fade-outs, but you may disagree with an engineer's choice and wish to add them where he or she did not. You can also remove them if you don't like them, but that usually results in a strange intro and outro, so we don't recommend it.

A fade-in gradually increases gain from a quiet, soft starting point, or silence even; conversely, a fade-out decreases gain from a loud point to softness or silence. Traditionally, folks put a fade-in at the beginning of a song and a fade-out at the end (see **Figure 11.12**), but you can do whatever you want.

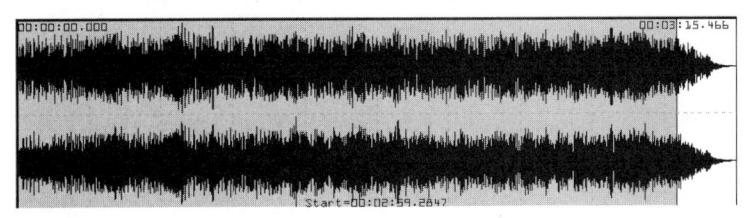

Figure 11.12 See how this waveform tapers off at the end, in the highlighted area? That's a fade-out down there.

In Diamond Cut, open whatever track you wish to add a fade-in or fade-out to. Listen to it by pressing the Play button in the task bar, and figure out where you might like to put a fade. Then, select the area you wish to add the fade to by left-clicking your waveform (don't release your mouse button) and dragging your pointer over the waveform—this will highlight a segment of your track (see **Figure 11.13**). Let go of your mouse button. Now you've selected part of your waveform for editing.

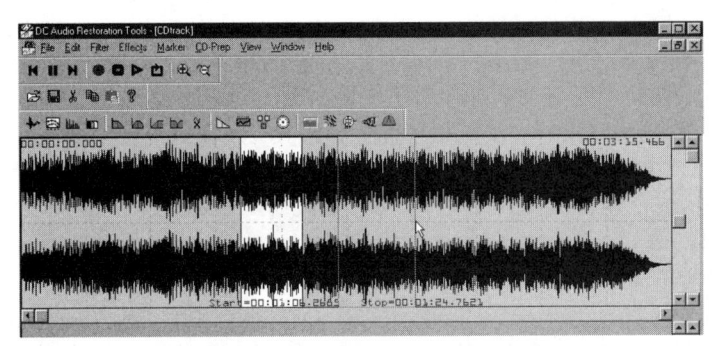

Figure 11.13 Selecting a segment of song in Diamond Cut.

You'll notice when you move your pointer over the boundaries of your selection, your pointer becomes a horizontal line with an arrow at either end. This is how you adjust the size of your selection. When your pointer becomes that horizontal line, left-click and hold your mouse button and move your mouse side to side—you'll notice that the selection increases and decreases. That's how you select precise areas in Diamond Cut: Move either end of your selection where you want it to go using the horizontal pointy thingy (see **Figure 11.14**).

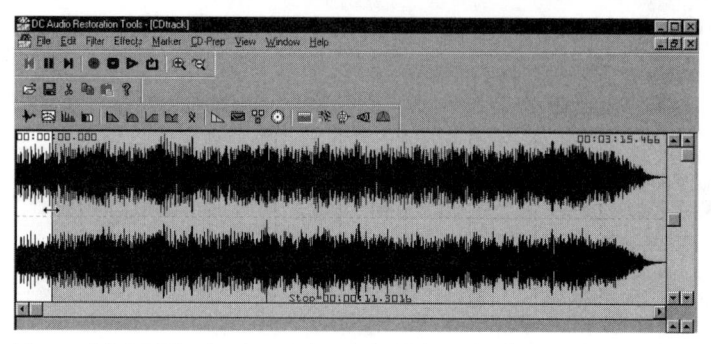

Figure 11.14 The horizontal pointy thingy is sharpening our selection here.

Now, select with as much precision as you can the area of your track you wish to add a fade-in to. Click the Play button in your task bar—this will play what you've selected, not your whole track. Make further adjustments to your selection if you need to here.

From the Edit menu, select Fade-In. The Gain Change window will appear. The first thing you'll probably notice here is the graph occupying most of the window (see **Figure 11.15**). The y axis here represents gain, or loudness, 0 being the gain at the end of your selection. The x axis represents time, 100 being the end boundary of your selection. So this line you're looking at—the one Diamond Cut places there by default—represents the sonic path your selection will travel over time. In this instance, our selection will, at 0 seconds, be virtually silent, -20dB. As the song plays in time, over the two seconds we've selected for our fade in, it will become progressively louder until, at the end of our selection (represented by 100 on the x axis of this graph), the song will play as it would have, at the same loudness it was before we applied a fade-in (represented by 0 on the y axis). That final loudness is sometimes referred to as unity gain.

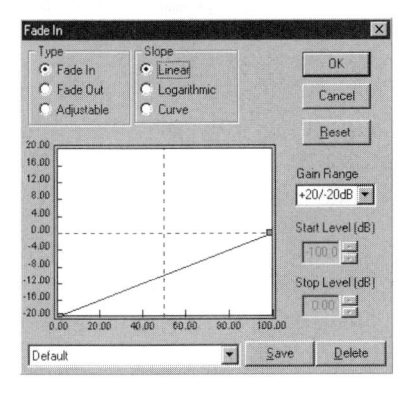

Figure 11.15 Here's the Gain Change window. If we go with what's on the graph, our segment of song will begin softly and get progressively louder, just as the line begins low and ends high on the graph.

You can do all this work, but you may find that Diamond Cut's default fade-in is fine for most purposes. You could just run the filter here if you like.

You can adjust this line, to hone your fade in or to make some bizarre fade-ins. For illustration, we're going to make a weird fade-in for you. In **Figure 11.16**, we selected the radio button next to Adjustable in the Type box and the Curve radio button in the Slope box. This presents us with, as you might imagine, a curve that we may adjust in that graph. Off to the right, we selected +20/-20dB from the drop-down menu beneath the words "Gain Range." All this does is changes the range of values of the y axis so you can play either beneath or above the unity gain line.

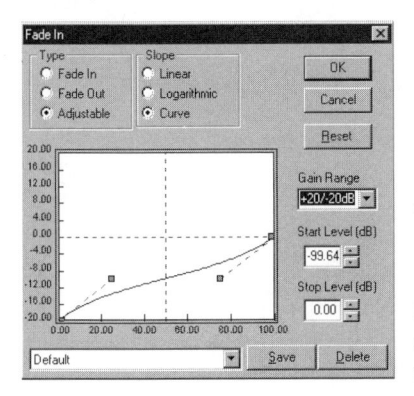

Figure 11.16 Here's our adjustable curve, before adjustments.

Just below the Gain Range drop-down menu are the boxes where you select your beginning and ending decibel levels by way of a pair of arrows attached to the boxes—clicking the up arrow raises the value and clicking the down arrow lowers the value. We're starting at -20dB—silence—and we're ending at 0, or unity gain.

Now we're going to adjust our curve by clicking the green boxes attached to it and dragging those boxes. **Figure 11.17** is what we came up with.

That's a wild sonic path. During playback, the volume of our selection will progress quickly from silence to the unity gain (0) line. From there, our selection will get really loud for an instant—as we've gone above unity gain—and then come back down in volume to the unity gain line, where our track will then proceed as normal.

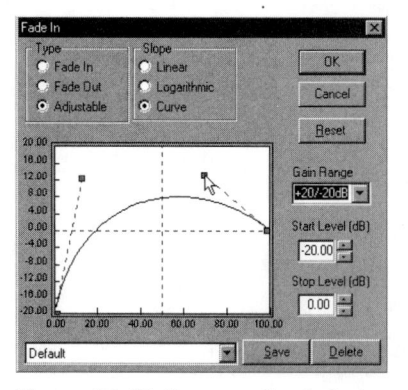

Figure 11.17 Our peculiar fade-in, created by clicking and dragging the green boxes (see pointer).

Applying a fade-out is exactly the opposite of fading-in but ultimately the same procedure. You'll select the end of your track, in the same way we selected the beginning. Select Fade-Out from the Edit drop-down menu, as we did a second ago with Fade-In. Then, you'll return to the Gain Change window. You'll see, in **Figure 11.18**, that here in the graph, you begin at unity gain and then fade out to wherever you want, -20dB or -100dB, whatever you like. If you feel like adjusting the line or the curve, adjust it. These lines and curves are things you're going to have to experiment with, as there's no way to describe what they sound like, and what sounds good to us may not sound good to you at all.

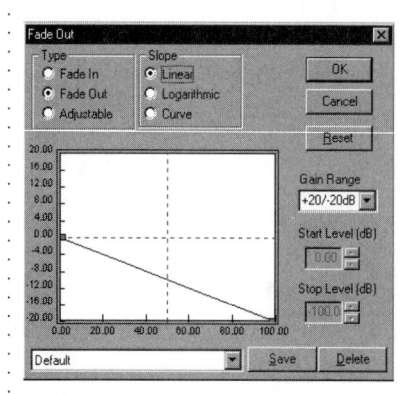

Figure 11.18
A typical fade-out.

Normalization

Next to our CD track, everything sounds timid: The vinyl, tape, and MP3 tracks are too quiet by contrast (see **Figure 11.19**). So, if we burn our tracks now, one loud track will appear among several soft ones. This is not conducive to listening pleasure at all. We'll be loudly shocked out of our chairs, right as we were beginning to relax with our freshly burned CD.

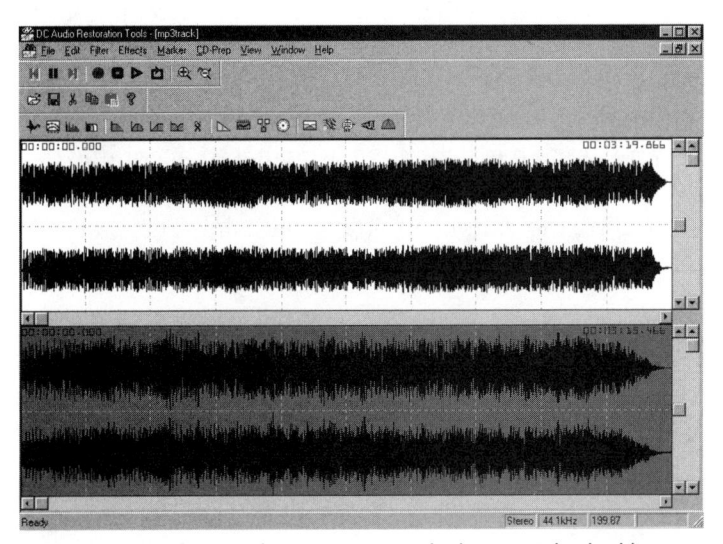

Figure 11.19 This is what our CD track (bottom) looks like next to our MP3 track (top, highlighted). Slightly discrepant peak levels, we'd say.

This discrepancy in volume happens all the time when you're making CDs out of tracks you pulled from all different sources. Maybe your recording levels were low during the transfer of analog material to your hard disk, maybe the levels were low during the original recording, or maybe the CD was mastered at high levels—could be just about anything. The good news is, this is easy to fix.

All digital audio editing software and some CD-R software packages feature a normalize function. Sometimes it's called Normalization and other times it's called Gain Normalization, but they all do just about the same thing. They bring digital tracks to a kind of standard normal loudness, so that no loud tracks jump out at you from amidst soft ones.

Normalize last, because tampering with frequency response, as we did just a second ago, also alters gain. If you normalize a track first and then apply equalization, you might alter the gain so pronouncedly that you must normalize again.

In Diamond Cut, the tool is called Gain Normalize, and it's accessible from the CD Prep menu up top (see **Figure 11.20**). After you've opened a track, all you have to do is click CD Prep, select Gain Normalize, and click again. That initiates normalization. What happens, while Diamond Cut is churning away there, is that the loudest moment of your track is located and pumped up to a fixed point, 0dB, in this case. Then, the rest of your track has its loudness increased according to how loud it is compared to the loudest moment. You're essentially just increasing the volume of your track here. That's all there is to that. Repeat this process with each track you intend to burn.

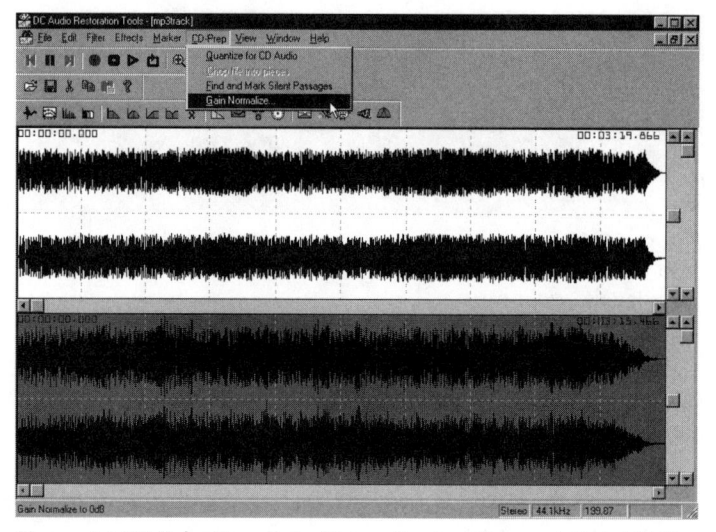

Figure 11.20 Selecting Gain Normalize in Diamond Cut. We'll do this to each of our tracks.

There, done, now everything is pretty smooth, sonically. Now we're going to proceed with the burn. Nothing new or spectacular here about burning—we're just lining our slightly altered tracks up in our CD-R software and hitting record. Once this CD is done cooking, we're going to throw it into the stereo and have a listen. Bob's itchin' to get his groove on.

Mixed Discs 12

Perhaps you've noticed, as your computer shakes off its utilitarian fetters and takes its rightful place among your home-entertainment equipment, that bands and their agents are releasing what they call Enhanced CDs, discs that not only play in your stereo system but also function in your computer as CD-ROMs. Open them, and you'll see pictures, videos, messages from the band—a whole promotional apparatus right there on your monitor. We have an Enhanced CD sitting right here, a very precious one: Galaxie 500's enhanced version of *On Fire,* which contains all 13 original tracks as well as the video for "When Will You Come Home." We're fairly certain that if we sat in front of MTV for a million hours of broadcasting, or even if we sat through a million hours of more progressive and socially redeeming programming, we'd never see that video. Now, with this miracle of optical storage, we have access to this video any time we like: We can cringe at the agony of a bunny maimed by beauty products yet be delighted by the tinkling arpeggio accompanying the montage.

But CD-enhancing isn't just for bands and their record companies anymore. You can make these kinds of discs yourself, at home, using your burner. As with the other recording projects we've talked about, your Enhanced CD will come out better than anything a record company could release: Those guys are blighted by problems we regular folks don't have to face—namely, we don't have to concern ourselves with who gets what money when we make our CDs in this way. In fact, we're kind of surprised Rykodisc released *On Fire,* considering what it had to deal with. In any case, we're glad it did.

The Making of Multisession

Out here in consumer computing land, almost all CD-R software will allow you to burn multiple sessions, which is basically all you need to do to make one of these audio/data discs. Think of it like this: Instead of closing a disc, as you do when you're burning a plain-vanilla audio CD so that you can play it your stereo, you'll be closing a session, using your CD-R software. These sessions resemble whole closed discs, in that you write your lead-in, then your data, and then a lead-out. You do each ensuing session in exactly the same way, writing a lead-in after the lead-out of the preceding session, then your data, and then another lead-out. So, if you look at it that way, you'll be burning two separate discs, but on the same piece of media. No sweat, right?

Things just got easier. Because of the way they're built, audio CD players—even software ones, since they're based on the same principles—read only the first session of a multisession disc, stopping at the first lead-out. Contemporary CD-ROM drives on contemporary computers, on the other hand, read the final session of a multisession disc first, which can contain information about where to find all the stuff written in prior sessions, but we don't need to include that particular information here—all we need to put there is our data stuff, such as a music video, which will then be accessible by most CD-ROM drives.

Our job, then, is necessarily a simple one. All we have to do is see to it that the first session we burn consists of music and that the second session we burn consists of CD-ROM type data, which can be anything from a text file to a QuickTime movie. As you'll see at the tail end of this chapter, you can even include in the data session a small, simple file that will automatically launch whatever application is needed to view your data.

Before we roll, keep in mind that we're working with limited space here (74 minutes and 650 MB, you remember), so if you were thinking you'd do a thirty-song tribute to Elvis, including rare footage of that time he shot his television while chewing on a slab of bacon dipped in mayonnaise, think again. Audio/visual data sucks up a lot of space: You know how big standard digital audio data is, just imagine setting some moving pictures on top of that. Another resource concern we'll address here in a second is that this conglomerated lead-in and lead-out area between your two sessions occupies some space too: 22 MB, to be exact, about two minutes of audio. Our limits in mind, let's do this audio session.

> **Extra? Extra?**
>
> We're going to lay a couple clarifications on you. The kind of CD we're talking about here—this meshing of CD-Audio and CD-ROM—is indeed an Enhanced CD, as we'll habitually refer to it, but sometimes it's more properly called a Blue Book CD or a CD-Extra. Enhanced CD refers to a whole group of CD types that includes, but is not limited to, Blue Book CDs. The Blue Book, like the Red Book, is named for the color of the binder in which the standard for this kind of audio/data disc was published. It lays down specifications for creating a CD with a single discrete audio section that will play on your stereo and a single discrete CD-ROM data section accessible with a CD-ROM drive, arranged in an order that precludes playback of CD-ROM data on your stereo.
>
> The kind of CD we'll show you how to make in this chapter functions in precisely the same way a CD-Extra does, but it lacks one small irrelevant thing, specifically, a file named info.cdp in sector 75 so you cannot carry the "CD-Extra" logo on your jewel case. You probably wouldn't want to have CD-Extra associated with your CD anyway: You'd have to cough up royalties if you did. We're going to be burning what's called a multisession CD—but a specific kind of multisession CD. We'll burn an audio session first and then a data session after that.

The audio session

Preparing your audio session for the burn is exactly the same thing we've been doing through the course of this book—we've told our software that we intend to make an audio CD, and we've lined up our audio files, you know the story. Here, though, there's one tiny exception. Instead of closing, or finalizing, the disc, we're going to close only the audio session, which simply means we can add another session after it later.

Remember to pay attention to how much audio you burn here. Add 22 MB (or to be on the safe side, 32 MB) to whatever amount of audio data you've queued up (remembering that 1 minute of song equals about 10 MB), and then subtract that number from 650 MB. The resulting number is approximately how much space you have left after the audio session for your data session.

When you go to burn the files you've lined up, you're given a few burn options by most CD-R software: Close session should be among them somewhere, near the other burn options, such as recording speed and DAO/TAO. For instance, in Nero Burning ROM (a shareware version is available at www.ahead.de), we've got all our WAVs queued up (we're burning from our hard disk here, and we'd advise you to do the same, for the reasons we discussed in Chapter 9, "Copying CDs") and have proceeded into our Write CD window by pressing the Burn icon in the task bar (see **Figure 12.1**).

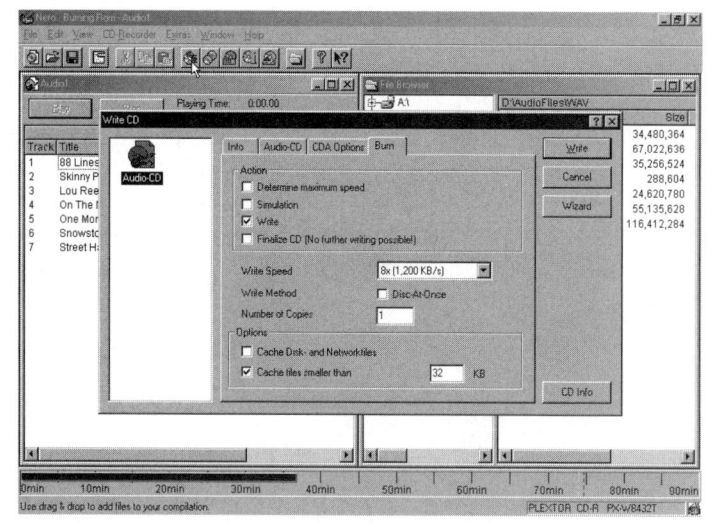

Figure 12.1 Nero's Write CD window, superimposed on the program proper. The pointer hovers over the Burn button we just pressed.

Under the Burn tab, we find our flock of burn options. The first thing we'll draw your attention to here is the Disc-At-Once box next to the words "Write Method." Notice we've left that box unchecked (see **Figure 12.2**). As you remember from Chapter 9, disc-at-once burning writes a whole disc in one fell swoop—there's no stopping that laser for anything, and it produces a final, closed product. We don't want that here, as we intend to close only the audio session, leaving the disc open for our data session.

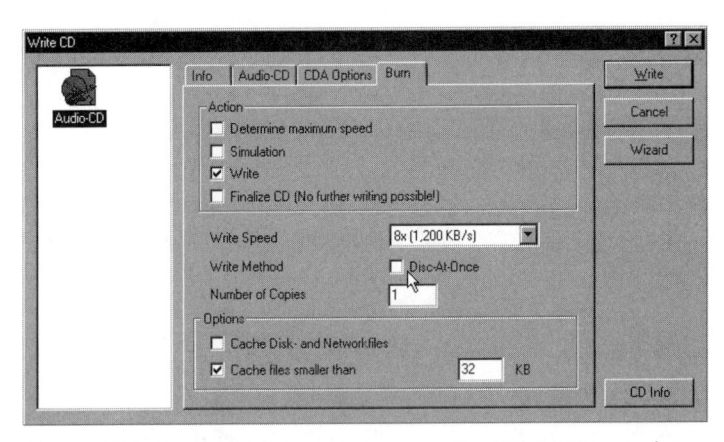

Figure 12.2 Now we're in real close on the Write CD window, where we've left unchecked the Disc-At-Once box, right next to the pointer there.

Like us, you'll need to turn off disc-at-once writing in your software, or select track-at-once writing, in whichever way it's presented to you: You'll either encounter this option right before you burn, in your comparable Write Options window—as we have here in Nero—or as a option in a menu or in the program window itself. In Easy CD Creator 4, for instance, you'll see in the lower-right corner of the program window either the letters DAO or TAO (standing for disc-at-once and track-at-once, respectively) occupying a small box. If the letters TAO appear there, all is well; if not, right-clicking the letters DAO will produce a small pop-up menu, providing you with two options, Disc At Once or Track At Once. Select Track At Once (see **Figure 12.3**).

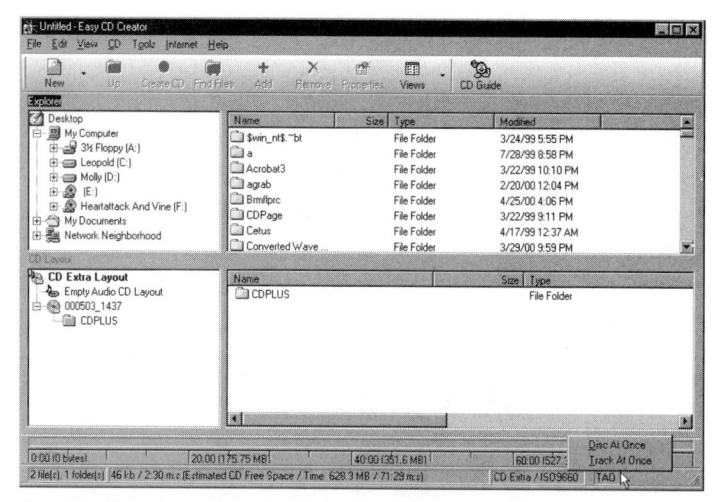

Figure 12.3 Here, in Easy CD Creator 4, we've loaded up the CD Extra Layout. We've right-clicked the letters TAO to illustrate how to get from Disc At Once to Track At Once, in case you need to do that.

*Easy CD Creator 4 and Toast 4 each offer you the option of writing a CD-Extra from the start (see **Figure 12.3**), so you don't have to mess with any of this session stuff. Select CD Extra from the File > New CD Layout menu. This brings up the familiar drag-and-drop windows, a file browser window, and a CD layout window. You then simply drag your music to the window that says Drag and Drop Your Audio Files here, drag your data to the data window, and burn. If you want, go ahead and do that, and forego this whole session thing—you'll end up with the same thing we ultimately do here.*

Nero is peculiar in that it works by way of assumption. If you deselect Disc-At-Once, Nero assumes that you want the opposite method implemented, Track-At-Once; if you deselect Finalize CD, it assumes you wish to leave the disc open for further writing. Fair assumptions, to be sure, as disabling one thing necessarily implies enabling the other. CD recording has a definite binary nature, pun fully intended. We imply to Nero, by not checking the box next to Disc-At-Once, that we wish to write Track-At-Once; Nero accepts this and allows us then to uncheck the box next to Finalize CD, which will leave the disc open for further writing after our audio tracks have been burned.

We spoke, in Chapter 9, about how track-at-once burning, by nature, adds additional silence between audio tracks, so you may wish to clip any silence at the beginning and end of your audio tracks before you burn them here.

We've unchecked the box next to Finalize CD (see **Figure 12.4**). This is key. By doing that, we've told Nero that we do not want a closed, finalized, disc at all, and Nero is quite happy to oblige: Nero will merely close our audio session now, after it has burned our audio tracks. Unlike Nero, many CD-R programs will offer a box or radio button next to a phrase such as Close Session. That's what you'll want to select here, that and only that; do not select anything such as Close Session and Disc or Close Disc. Close only the session.

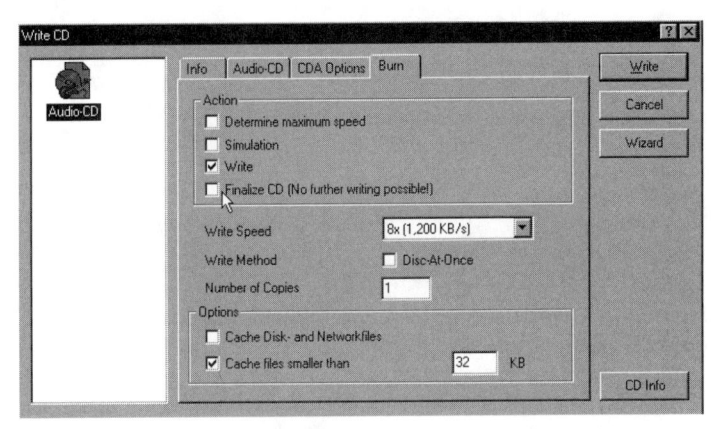

Figure 12.4 We're back in Nero's Write CD window now. We've unchecked Finalize CD, next to the pointer. It's imperative you do that, as this will leave your disc open for the data session.

Finally, you'll notice we've checked the Write box—we're going to go ahead and burn these tracks now. The other options Nero offers here we leave up to you: You can run a simulation or write at 1x or whatever else you like to do. Just make sure there's no check in the box next to Finalize CD. We initiate our burn by pressing the Write button in the upper-right corner of this window. Moments later—you probably noticed from **Figure 12.4** that we burned at 8x—our CD-R drive ejects a half-done multisession disc, which we promptly reinsert into that same CD-R drive. We're not done yet. Now it's time to write the data session.

The data session

Instead of telling our software that we intend to burn an audio CD this time, we're going to tell it we want to burn a CD-ROM. In Nero, you accomplish this by Selecting New from the File menu. A window appears—it looks exactly like the Write Options window above—and we select CD-ROM from the scrolling window off to the left (see **Figure 12.5**). Then we click the New button in the upper-right corner of this window, having fooled with nothing among the tabs.

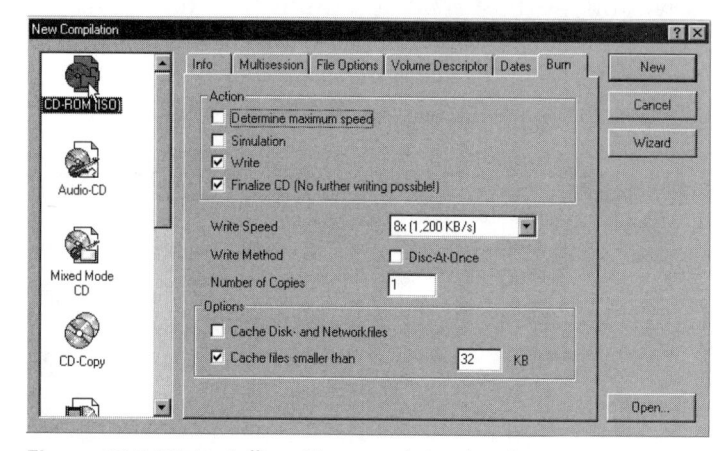

Figure 12.5 We're telling Nero we intend to burn a CD-ROM by clicking the graphic representation of a CD-ROM in the scrolling window.

That done, the two traditional windows appear: a file browser and the CD Layout window. Drag-and-drop whatever data you like from the file browser to the CD Layout window.

Once we're happy with what data we'll burn in this second session, we click the Burn button on the task bar. The Write CD window appears, just as it did before, but with options unique to CD-ROM this time (see **Figure 12.6**). You don't have to concern yourself with configuring any of these options, not even under the Multisession tab, as you'll see in just a second. Nero's default settings for CD-ROM are all fine for our purposes. All you need to do here is return to the Burn tab, which you'll immediately recognize as exactly the same thing we were just in, when we were getting ready to burn our audio session.

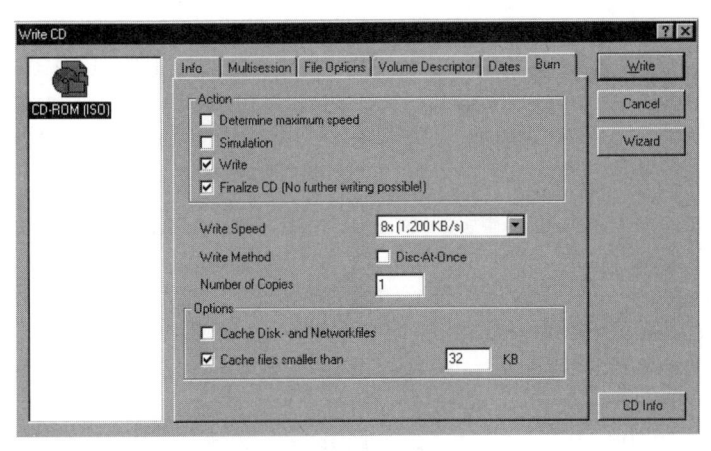

Figure 12.6 Nero's Write CD window, same as before, except we're burning a CD-ROM session this time.

This time around, in one simple motion, we're going to check the box next to Finalize CD (see **Figure 12.7**), that very same box we strictly avoided checking during the audio session. After the software burns your data session, it closes your disc and can't write any more data to it. That's exactly what we want here: When this burn is done, we'll have a fully operational multisession CD, ready to be played on our stereo or read by our CD-ROM drive.

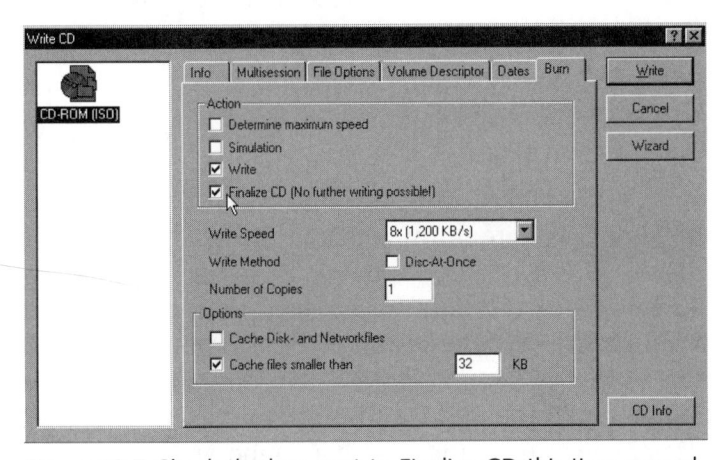

Figure 12.7 Check the box next to Finalize CD this time around.

Now, when we click the Write button in the upper-right corner, or when you click your comparable Write button, your software, if it's pretty current, will begin conversing with itself. The conversation is transcribed as follows: "What the... I asked for a blank disc, and I get this disc that already has data on it. Oh, I see, my user left his last session open, and he wants to append a session here. That's just fine, but I better say something before I burn the new session, just in case."

Most times, you'll get a simple dialog box that says, "You know you're burning a multisession disc now right?" In that case, you just click Yes, the burn will proceed, and shortly, you'll have a shiny new multisession disc. Sometimes, your program will proceed without mentioning anything, kindly assuming that you know what you're doing. Yet other times, you'll be taken to the utility in your program that does multisession stuff, and the burn will proceed from there. Nero gets down and dirty with its user, as you'll see in **Figure 12.8**.

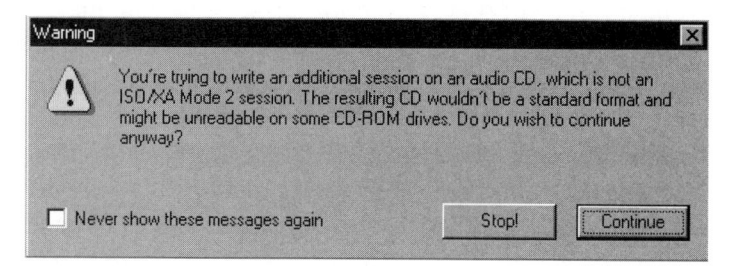

Figure 12.8 Eek! Er, wait a minute...what we're hearing from Nero here is sorta wrong.

We're slightly alarmed by what Nero has to tell us, until we realize that what it's telling us is somewhat mistaken. What Nero is getting at here, essentially, is that this CD we're making isn't on the books anyplace, and since this is some weird new kind of CD we're burning, some CD-ROM manufacturers and the drives they make won't be able to handle it. That may have been the case several years ago, back when operating systems and drives didn't support Blue Book discs or many other kinds of multisession discs. Today, though, this disc we're making will be compatible with just about everything—at the very least, your stereo and your contemporary Mac or PC will support it. Knowing that, we click the Continue button in the alert box. The burn moves forward.

The CD that our CD-R drive ejects this time is a finished product, containing music for our stereos and data for our computers. We congratulate ourselves, and reach for a beer. We must have beer now, as we're about to disclose something we find insidious and evil, and you may perpetuate this scourge, finding it convenient rather than demonic. Naturally, if it's evil, it has something to do with a PC, so you Mac users don't have to concern yourself with this.

The deleterious autorun.inf file

Surely you've witnessed this: You stick a CD or a CD-ROM in your PC and the thing either starts playing or starts installing something even though you didn't tell it to. That's what's known as Auto-Insert Notification. Very insulting to our intelligence, if you ask us, and very annoying—as if we couldn't have gone into the contents of our CD-ROM and double-clicked a setup icon. (Fortunately, we can turn this feature off on our CD-ROM and DVD-ROM drives. From the Start menu, go into Settings > Control Panel. Double-click the System icon. In the System Properties window, hit the Device Manager tab, find your CD-ROM drive in the list of devices, and select it. Get into your drive's Properties window by clicking the Properties button at the bottom of this window. In the Properties window, select the Settings tab, and when you get there, uncheck the box marked Auto-insert notification [see **Figure 12.9**]. Reboot. Now you're done.)

We'll assume Auto-Insert Notification is enabled on your computer.

Your computer launches these things without your permission—that is, when Auto-Insert notification is enabled—because Windows automatically looks at whatever CD you put in your drive, detects a file called Autorun.inf, and executes the instructions contained therein. Sounds complicated, right?

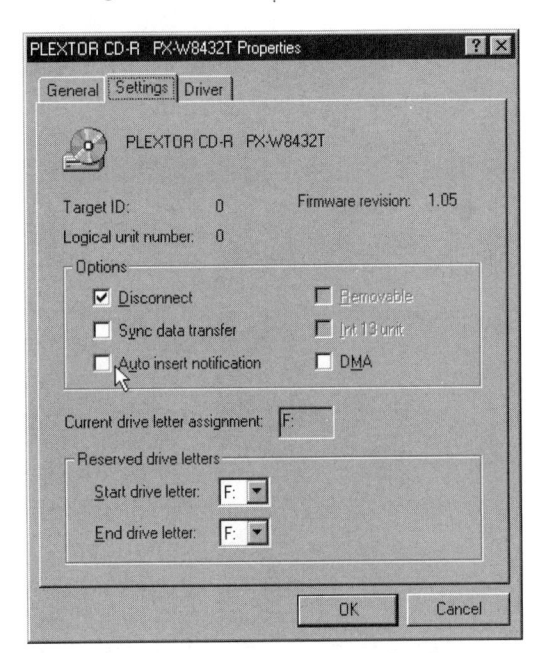

Figure 12.9 We've struck a blow for the forces of good: Auto-insert notification has been disabled.

It's not, and that's why the Autorun.inf file is ubiquitous now. Here's the very basic one we just wrote:

[autorun]
open=start index.html

That's it. Save that as Autorun.inf in an ASCII text editor—Notepad is fine here—and that part is done.

Now you have to write a file called index.html. You can do this several ways. Bob likes to open Word—that is, Word 6.0/95 or later, PC or Mac—and compose a page complete with graphics and text. Then, in Word, he selects Save As from the File menu, which brings up the Save As dialog box. From the Save as type drop-down menu at the bottom of dialog box, he chooses HTML Document (see **Figure 12.10**). In the file name field right above the drop-down menu, he types index. Josh, in contrast to Bob, likes to write straight HTML.

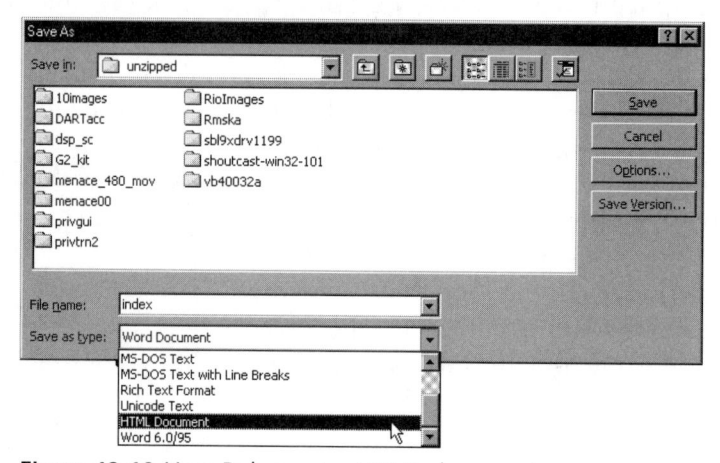

Figure 12.10 How Bob creates HTML documents.

During your data session, burn both the Autorun.inf and index.html files to the root directory of your CD—that is, don't go and put them in folders. Then, once you've stuck your finished product into your computer, an irritating blank DOS interface will pop up and promptly vanish (if you're a perfectionist and can't deal with having weird stuff randomly appearing, a swift little utility at www.phdcc.com/shellrun/index.html will prevent these annoying DOS windows from popping up). Once it's gone, the index.html file on the CD you've made will open up in your computer's default Web browser.

The good part about using HTML here is that you can either build a site on the disc itself (a very fast loader indeed, since it's local to your users' computer—you can totally inundate them with high-bandwidth media such as QuickTime, AVI, or RealVideo movies and MP3s) or direct people to an already existing site on the Internet. Since HTML is a universal language, too, both Mac and Windows users can enjoy the data on your disc.

So, what if you don't want to use HTML at all? Say you just want to launch an .avi file or something like that? Easy enough: Just write open = start video.avi instead of open = start index.html in your Autorun.inf file. Or if you want to launch an executable you've written, simply write open = whatever.exe. Just make sure that both the Autorun.inf file and the file or executable specified therein are both burned to the root directory in the data session of the CD.

> *You can, if you want, put the file you want to execute or open in a subdirectory, but you must say in your Autorun.inf file exactly where it is, for example, open = start fellini\roma.mov. If you ask us, that just complicates things.*

> *You can make your Autorun.inf files as simple or complex as you want—just zip over to www.microsoft.com, search on Autorun, and you'll find a truckload of stuff you can use in the Autorun.inf files.*

You can use this knowledge for good, but we also know that most people don't, so we turned off our Auto-Insert Notification so you can't get at us with your Autorun.inf files. We'll actually suggest you turn Auto-Insert Notification off, and leave it off, at all times, as it can really mess up some burn processes.

Home Recorders 13

Now you think we are trying to confuse you. We have been talking about home recording, and then we hit you with a chapter on home recorders. Are we insane? Let's not go there, but we will go somewhere else, and that is to distinguish home recording from home recorders. Once something gets a name attached to it, it is hard to pry it off, and so the components we cover in this chapter we will call home recorders because that is what everybody else calls them.

Home recorders are CD-R and CD-RW recorders that look like standard audio CD players with a few extra buttons, the most notable of which is the big red record button you have already seen on your computer screen. These machines don't need a computer to record audio discs, unless you consider the logic chips inside of them to be computers (see **Figure 13.1**).

Many of us use a computer all day at work and perhaps the last thing we want to do at night when we drag our wearied sedentary bodies home is to jump onto the computer to make a CD. A more relaxing, yet slower and less flexible, way to make CD copies or compilations is to use a home recorder. These recorders have been available for some time now, but only recently have their prices been low enough that the average person might be able to afford them. Only recently, too, have the retail electronics stores given them any shelf space.

Figure 13.1 Philips makes lots of models of consumer home recorders. This is a dual-tray model that will allow you to dupe discs at 2x.

Home recorders have lots of features; are easy to use; and do indeed rid you forever of those ghastly buffer underruns, track following errors, and other assorted lockups and glitches that you are likely to come across when recording a CD on your PC or Mac. But compared with the automated recording systems we can set up on our computers—using a combination of hardware and software—home recorders can fall short of their computer counterparts in flexibility and accuracy when performing automated recording.

Dig this: You load up your 100-disc audio CD jukebox, or even your five-disc changer, with your favorite music, program a playlist of your favorite tunes, attach a digital out cable to a home CD recorder from Philips, Marantz, or Pioneer. Then push CD Sync on the recorder and Play on the player. Leave the room and come back in an hour and pluck your compilation disc out of the tray, load it in your car stereo, and hit the road for a tune-filled joyride. But that ride can be a joy bus hell ride if you are not careful and don't understand the basics of home recorders and why they are so different from computer recorders (see **Figure 13.2**).

Figure 13.2 Pioneer and Pioneer-based home recorders are excellent for automated copying. The autosync feature works every time. That may not be the case with all home recorders.

Home Burning Basics

When you look at the comprehensive manuals and all the features you can use on these units, you might think it will be just as difficult to use a home recorder as it was to learn the software to record an audio CD on the computer, assuming that you found that difficult at all. Generally, though, you only need a few more functions to record, and therefore, the units have a few more buttons than you will find on a normal compact disc audio player. In addition to the playing controls, you'll find buttons for Input Source, CD Sync, Record, Erase, and Finalize.

Home recorders will record both CD-R and CD-RW media, although special audio-only media is necessary for models designated as consumer recorders. This is because these recorders fall under the definition of a digital audio recording device in the Audio Home Recording Act of 1992 (AHRA). Home recorders incorporate the Serial Copy Management System (SCMS), as required by the AHRA. SCMS is a firmware feature and serves two functions: First, it enables the recorders to recognize copied SCMS CDs and prevents them from being copied, and second, it prevents them from recording on non-SCMS-enabled media so the can't-copy-a-copy principle will be preserved and the royalties built into the cost of the media will be paid (see the section on the AHRA later in the chapter).

Professional audio recording models from Marantz, Tascam (TEAC), and HHB will record to standard, inexpensive CD media. As the prices for these more flexible professional CD recorders continue to fall, they are becoming an ever popular alternative to SCMS-enabled consumer recorders.

Figure 13.3 Marantz, like Philips, offers a dual-tray home recorder. It will record compilations at 1x and make copies at 2x.

Figure 13.4 HHB makes the coolest-looking professional recorders around. Although you can't tell from this picture, it's purple.

Figure 13.5 The Marantz professional recorder lets you turn SCMS on or off. Professional recorders are excluded from the AHRA.

Home recorders are available in a variety of configurations. Most have a single drive and expect that your source material will come from an external source, usually another CD player or CD changer. Philips and Marantz make dual-tray models that allow you to dupe audio discs directly with a single machine, although making a compilation obviously requires a lot of disc swapping and attention to the process (see **Figure 13.3**). Pioneer makes a recorder with a three-CD changer and a recorder, so you can draw from three source CDs without swapping discs. We don't know if that is enough flexibility at the source, so we prefer to use a 100- or 200-disc changer as the source. We can program the changer to play the songs we want in the order we want, and simply plugging it into the home recorder and pressing play allows us to make a compilation CD without a lot of trouble, albeit in real time.

That, of course, is one of the drawbacks of these machines—recording speed—which is pretty much confined to 1x, except for the Philips and Marantz dual-tray models, which can dupe discs at 2x but record compilation discs at 1x only. So if your need is for speed, stick with computer recording.

> *The core of the Philips and Marantz consumer units is a slightly modified Philips CD-R/RW drive. The controller, however, is modified for home-recording applications and is designed for a standalone mechanism with SCMS copy protection.*

Home recorders can record from both digital and analog audio sources. To record digitally, of course, you need a digital output on your CD player. Some CD players have digital out ports, but many do not. You can do digital recording through an RCA jack or a digital optical connection. And you can use analog inputs if your CD player does not have a digital out jack or if you are recording from tape or vinyl. CDs that are input this way, though, will not be digital copies.

You can automate the recording process or do it yourself. In manual mode, the recorder is under your control, obviously, and you need to start and stop both the recorder and the source. In automatic mode, the recorder will, hopefully, detect track starts and stops for you.

When you insert a disc into a home recorder, the first thing that happens is Optimal Power Control (OPC), which we discussed in Chapter 4, "CD-Recordable and CD-Rewriteable Drives," and the recorder displays OPC for several seconds. To record, you simply press Record on the unit and then Play on your source device. For automatic recording, you can use the CD Sync function. CD Sync allows the recorder to begin recording as soon as it senses the beginning of a track from the source device.

The Philips-based recorders need 150 to 400 ms, or milliseconds, to recognize the start of a track. In theory, this should give you a fair chance at not having the beginning of the tracks chopped off. But if the logical track start is within this time window, a portion of the beginning of the audio will not be recorded. You may find this occurring much too frequently on the Philips-based consumer models (Philips and Marantz) to rely on the CD Sync function to produce quality, listenable discs. You may need to start the process yourself to get completely reliable tracks. Copying full discs on the dual-tray machine, however, creates fully formed tracks and a perfect dupe of the original. So in that sense, Philips-based consumer home recorders can match the results of PC recorders (if not the speed), but at tremendous cost in terms of flexibility.

Pioneer's consumer recorders, which are not based on the Philips mechanism, do not have that limitation because they use a different method to sense the beginning of an audio track on the source device. The Pioneer recorders and the HHB professional models based on them start recording at the instant the recorder detects an ID flag or a signal level at the input of less than -90 dBfs. Using these models, automatic recording can safely be used to copy CDs and make music compilations without the worry of an incomplete track.

If you insert a computer CD-R or CD-RW disc into the consumer Philips, Marantz, or Pioneer units, the recorder will just ignore it, disabling the record button or displaying "no audio." Forget the trick some sly users tried with some of the early models: Place an audio-only disc in the recorder, allow it to register, then open the tray manually and replace it with standard computer media. The manufacturers caught on and made this workaround history.

Music-only media

Consumer home recorders must use a special media, generally called "music-only" or "audio-only" media (see **Figure 13.6**). This is a misnomer as these discs can be used in a computer recorder to record data (or music). They are really the same as the blank CDs we have been using so far for recording except that they have an extra little bit of information on them that prevents a copy of a copy, at least on a consumer home recorder. If you need to copy one of these discs, just throw it into your computer recorder. No problem. But putting a computer blank into a home recorder will result in a "no disc" message, and the recorder will refuse to use it.

Many people get confused, and we don't blame them, about the differences between the two media types. It surely is not ever clearly explained anywhere. Music-only media costs two to three times more than standard media, and there are a couple of reasons for that. First, much less music-only media is manufactured and sold than standard media. Second, since the manufacturer must pay a royalty on every piece, that is passed on to the user, too.

We'll give you just the basics here, a couple rules that you need to know to differentiate the media so you won't run into trouble. Don't buy music-only media for your computer recorder. There is nothing special about it sonically and it will not make your recordings sound any better. The only thing it will do is cost you three bucks a piece rather than one. Don't try to use computer media in a consumer home recorder. It won't work. Do use computer media in a professional component recorder such as those from Marantz, HHB, and Tascam (Teac's professional audio division). It will save you money and unless you actually need to use SCMS for some reason, there is just no reason to do it. Do be careful, when buying media, of ignorant salespeople who will take everything we just said and twist it around to where you don't have a clue anymore and can't figure out what to buy. A good rule of thumb is this: Never pay more than a buck and a half for a piece of CD-R media. That kills two birds with one stone. You are unlikely to get music-only media at that price, and even if you do, that's cheap enough that it doesn't matter.

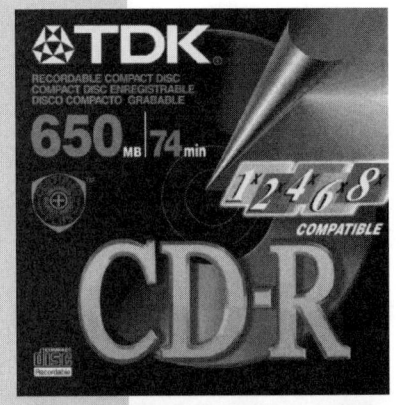

Figure 13.6 Standard computer media is fine for making audio discs (top). Media marked "for music only" or "digital audio" is meant for home recorders with SCMS (bottom). There is no reason to use it for computer recording.

Is rewritable media right for audio recording?

One feature highlighted by Philips and some of the other manufacturers of home recorders in their efforts to market them is rewritability. Magic as this may seem to the uninitiated, what we're talking about here is plain old CD-RW, the same discs that you can record and erase on your computer recorder, except that like music-only CD-R media, they cost more. That's fine, and we suppose that it may be useful in some cases to be able to erase a compilation disc or a copy and write it again, but the main problem with using RW media for music is that almost no CD audio players will read and play it, although a few new ones are starting to, notably new models from Philips. DVD players have a mixed record when it comes to playing either CD-R or CD-RW audio discs. All DVD players will play pressed audio discs. Some will play CD-R but not CD-RW. Some will play both. If you are shopping for a DVD player and plan to play your recorded CDs on it, take a CD-R audio disc and a CD-RW audio disc with you to the store. Let the salesman pitch you, and then ask him to play the discs you brought. Watch him squirm. More fun than a Wesley Willis concert.

CD-RW does have some advantages in audio recording. You can erase a track and replace it if you desire. But the erase function necessarily only goes so far. Only the last track written to the disc can be erased. So, on a ten-track disc, to erase track 5, you must first erase tracks 10, 9, 8, 7, and 6. If you really want or need truly malleable content, you should use MiniDisc, which allows you to erase, move, add, and delete tracks at will without the limitations of CD audio's linear format. MiniDisc uses magneto-optical (MO) technology, so it is much like a hard disk in logical layout; it can always make room for something by moving other things to other places on the disc.

The Audio Home Recording Act of 1992 (AHRA)

Let's give you a little background. Most of us have recorded a cassette tape of our favorite songs from other tapes and CDs. Some of us have recorded from CD to digital audio tape (DAT), and a few of us have used a home CD recorder, such as those you see in this chapter, to copy an audio CD or to make a CD compilation. But we noticed in that case that we couldn't copy the DAT or CD to to another DAT or CD. This is because DAT recorders and home CD recorders are equipped with the Serial Copy Management System (SCMS), a copy-protection technology used on DAT recordings and mandated by Chapter 10 of the Copyright Act of 1976. This 1992 addition to the Copyright

Act, titled Digital Audio Recording Devices and Media, and generally referred to as the Audio Home Recording Act (AHRA), was added to establish copyright structures for digital audio tape.

SCMS encodes a copy of an original digital recording with information that prevents users from making a copy of the copy. Its implementation in DAT systems manifests itself by allowing the DAT recorder to copy from a CD to a DAT, but that first-generation tape cannot be subsequently copied to another DAT.

The AHRA provides that the importer, manufacturer, or distributor of any digital audio recording device or digital audio recording media must file quarterly statements and pay, with those filings, royalties on each recorder or piece of media distributed in the U.S. The royalty is two percent of the manufacturer's selling price for recorders and three percent of the manufacturer's selling price for recordable media. The royalty minimum for recorders is one dollar, and the maximum is eight. There are no minimum or maximum royalties for recording media.

The popularity of home recorders will put some more money into these funds, since home recorders and their media (remember that they use special media) is hit with a royalty on distribution or importation. In return for the royalty, the AHRA gives consumers immunity from copyright infringement if they use a device that is covered by the AHRA, provided that the use is noncommercial.

Legal Issues: A Quick Overview

As you can imagine, home recording has its advocates and detractors. The Home Recording Rights Coalition (HRRC) is an example of the former, and the Recording Industry Association of America (RIAA) is an example of the latter. In the middle stands John Q. Citizen, who wants to make a mix CD for his wife and doesn't understand what the big deal is. Home recording sounds small—you are, after all, in your home, almost the smallest cultural unit we know. But most material out there is copyrighted, so when you engage a commodity with an intent to duplicate it home recording becomes a big issue.

The current debate over home recording focuses on two questions: Should a machine such as a CD-R drive be condemned because it could, despite its wealth of legitimate uses, bestow material gain on thieves and pirates? And what uses of CD-R drives constitute piracy, anyway? Let's look at what the law says.

The Law

Any time you duplicate copyright-protected material you need to know what is OK to do and what is not.

> *Our look at copyright laws in this chapter and elsewhere in this book is provided for your information but does not constitute legal advice. Copyright is a complicated area of the law and cannot be covered in any real depth in this short overview. In addition, this area of law is evolving quickly and may have changed by the time you read this book. This overview focuses on U.S. copyright laws. Your home recordings may also be subject to international copyright laws, which this book does not address. If you want copyright advice, talk with an attorney versed in copyright laws, who can give you guidance.*

U.S. copyright law is grounded in the U.S. Constitution and codified in Title 17 of the U.S. Code (USC). In Article I, Section 8, the Constitution empowers Congress "to promote the progress of science and useful arts, by securing for limited times to authors and inventors the exclusive right to their respective writings and discoveries."

Parts of Title 17 are known by other names, including the Audio Home Recording Act (AHRA, 1992), the Digital Millenium Copyright Act (DMCA, 1998), and the No Electronic Theft (NET, 1997) Act. The courts have handed down thousands of cases that have interpreted these laws. All apply in some way or another to your rights and responsibilities when it comes to making copies of copyright-protected musical works.

Think Practically

Sometimes the best way to get a sense of what your rights are is to think of things in a practical and ethical manner. But a lot of copyright law is complicated, unsettled, and counterintuitive, so let's look at what you *ought* not to do, for sure, because it is fairly obvious. Later we'll discuss some of the areas that are not so clear-cut.

Now that you know how to make multiple copies of a compact disc, you've probably also figured that if you sit at your computer and make a hundred copies and then go out on the street corner and sell them, you're doing something wrong.

It's just common sense. The artist, or his record company, or both, own the material on that original disc. The artist created it, and he has a right to profit from its distribution. The copyright law gives him several exclusive rights. These rights are specified in Section 106 of the Copyright Act of 1976, and what it gives to the artist and all the other recording artists is clear. The artist can make a bunch of copies for distribution and sale. This is called the "Right of Reproduction." The artist can prepare derivative works—a remix of a song, for example—and distribute the remixed version just as he would the original. The artist can sell, rent, lease, or lend the CDs to the public and can perform the music in public, such as at a concert. The artist can present the music publicly by playing it from the CD.

But what about you? Can you loan your compilation discs to your brother or to a friend? Can you give copies to several friends? Can you distribute copies to strangers? Can you play the copy in public? The answer to the question is no.

If you make a disc for yourself on a CD recorder covered under the Audio Home Recording Act of 1992 (AHRA), such as the home recorders we covered in Chapter 13, "Home Recording," you are immune from suit for copyright violation. You paid a royalty on that disc and recorder when you bought them, and the RIAA has thoughtfully distributed that royalty to copyright holders to guarantee them remuneration for just this situation. As we'll discuss later, we think you are OK making discs for yourself using a computer recorder. But in either case, giving them away to friends and family violates copyright law.

Let's take a look at the players in this fast-changing debate.

According to the RIAA

Determining what U.S. copyright law has to say about using CD-R in a home-recording context requires research, interpretation, and time. What's clear right now, however, is that the proliferation of user-friendly tools for copying audio to CD has got the record industry up in arms. The tools also give those who don't respect the rights of music copyright holders new opportunities to create pirated discs for subterranean sale and deprive those copyright holders of deserved royalties.

To get an idea of how the RIAA views home copying issues, visit its Web site at www.riaa.com (see **Figure 14.1**).

Member companies of the RIAA trade association create, manufacture, and distribute approximately 90 percent of all legitimate sound recordings produced and sold in the U.S. and include Warner Bros., Columbia, Motown, RCA, Geffen, and Capitol as well as many lesser-known labels.

According to Cary Sherman, the association's senior executive vice president and general counsel, the RIAA takes the position that any time you copy unauthorized music to CD using your computer, you infringe copyright.

Figure 14.1 The RIAA Web site.

The association recognizes that the AHRA gives home users who perform noncommercial copying immunity from copyright infringement actions, provided that the copying is performed on a digital-audio copying device as defined by the AHRA—a home recorder using a serial management system or equivalent technology. We mostly discuss computer recorders that don't use serial copy management, and the use of these recorders for copying audio discs or tracks is not protected within the definitions of the AHRA. So you are not immune to a lawsuit for copyright violation when you copy an audio disc using a PC.

According to the HRRC

On the other side of the issue is the HRRC, which believes that making compilations of songs you purchased is a fair use of those purchases. The HRRC is a coalition of consumers, consumer groups, trade associations, retailers, and consumer electronics manufacturers dedicated to preserving the consumer's rights to purchase and use home audio and video recording products for noncommercial purposes. The HRRC was founded in 1981, after a U.S. Court of Appeals had ruled that time-shift videotaping of television broadcasts—taping a show to watch it later—was copyright infringement. The U.S. Supreme Court later overturned that decision—Sony Corp. v. Universal City Studios, commonly known as the Betamax case—finding that time-shifting was not copyright infringement. To explore further the HRRC's position on CD copying, see its Web site at www.hrrc.org.

Figure 14.2
The Home Recording Rights Coalition supports the right of consumers to make copies and compilations of material that they own for their own use.

The effect of the Betamax case on CD burning

We think it is easy to see the similarities between using a CD-R to record copyrighted audio material and using a VCR to record copyrighted video material, which the U.S. Supreme Court approved of in its decision in the Betamax case. The road to the Betamax decision began in 1976, when Universal City Studios and Walt Disney filed suit against Sony, the manufacturer of the Betamax recorder. They charged Sony with contributory copyright infringement, arguing that home taping of television shows and movies for later viewing violated Universal's and Disney's copyrights in those properties. The U.S. District Court ruled in favor of Sony. In 1981, the U.S. Court of Appeals for the Ninth Circuit reversed the District Court's decision and sided

> **Copyrights in music, and how they are constituted**
>
> Most music discs contain copyright-protected material. Each disc even has a copy-protection bit that can be set to show that the owner of the material claims copyright and wants to disallow copying. Some of the recording programs we discussed in Chapter 3, "Audio Recording and Ripping Software," will let you set this bit on the discs you make too. Unfortunately for the record industry, the bit is informational only. For it to prevent copying, recorders and recording software would have to look to it for guidance and refuse to copy a disc just because the bit is set to "on." In the absence of products that recognize it in this way (we have yet to encounter one for computer recording), this protection scheme does not impede copying or ripping.
>
> Even though a copyright gives its owner the exclusive right to reproduce the music on a CD, copyright law also limits this exclusive right by addressing "fair use" of protected materials.
> The act lists some of the situations that may be considered fair use—quoting or excerpting for criticism, comment, news reporting, teaching, scholarship, and research—but it certainly does not exclude other uses, such as home recording for personal use.

with Universal and Disney. The court found that time-shift home recording was copyright infringement and Sony could be liable as a contributory infringer. In 1984, the Supreme Court overruled the decision of the Ninth Circuit. Associate Justice Byron White ("Whizzer" to you football fans) said that he was "not at all convinced that Congress intended each home recorder of copyrighted works to be an infringer, whether he records sound or video."

In its opinion, the Supreme Court stated, "The sale of copying equipment, like the sale of other articles of commerce, does not constitute contributory infringement if the product is widely used for legitimate, unobjectionable purposes. Indeed, it need merely be capable of substantial noninfringing uses." The Court found that private, noncommercial time-shifting in the home was just this sort of substantial noninfringing use. As a result, the Court held that the VCR itself could not be prohibited. Quoting the District Court, the Supreme Court made a point we believe applies just as well to CD-R drives: "Whatever the future percentage of legal versus illegal home-use recording might be, an injunction which seeks to deprive the public of the very tool or article of commerce capable of some noninfringing use would be an extremely harsh remedy, as well as one unprecedented in copyright law."

Go to Jail?

So far, we have been talking about civil liability. What about the criminal side? When is copying so egregious that criminal penalties apply? Section 506 of the copyright law addresses this, and we will reprint it here so we can examine it closely:

- (a) Criminal Infringement.—Any person who infringes a copyright willfully either—

    (1) for purposes of commercial advantage or private financial gain, or

    (2) by the reproduction or distribution, including by electronic means, during any 180-day period, of 1 or more copies or phonorecords of 1 or more copyrighted works, which have a total retail value of more than $1,000,

    shall be punished as provided under section 2319 of title 18, United States Code. For purposes of this subsection, evidence of reproduction or distribution of a copyrighted work, by itself, shall not be sufficient to establish willful infringement.

So what do we really have here when we make a compilation or duplicate CD for our own use? First, we actually have to

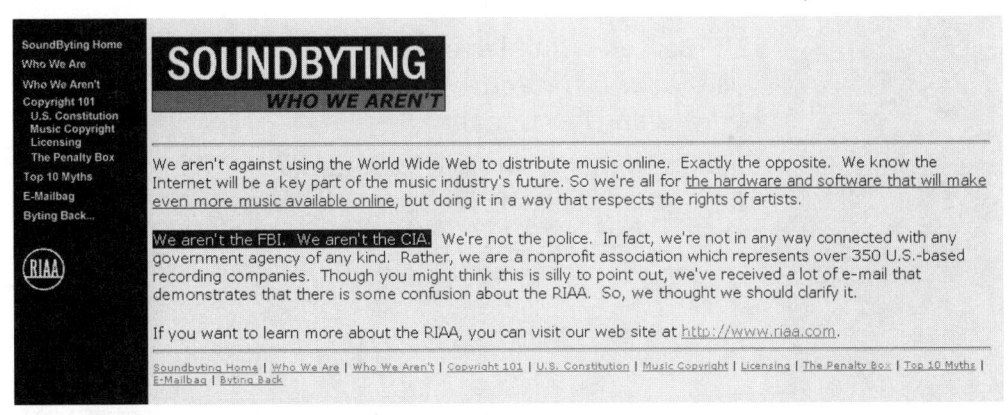

Figure 14.3 Besides its main Web site, the RIAA runs www.soundbyting.com, a site designed to educate college students in the ways of copyright law.

infringe a copyright. Second, we had to do it willfully, that is, deliberately. Well, we did that. Third we must do it for commercial advantage or private financial gain. We didn't do that. Fourth, we have to make $1000 worth of reproductions in a four-month period to be criminally liable.

So, are we in trouble when we make CDs for our own use? The Department of Justice hasn't shown much interest to date in coming after individuals. Instead, it has focused on large-scale commercial piracy. But this could change at any time.

Where Are We Now?

We think the courts will treat computer recording devices the same way they did the Betamax and allow their use. So when we make compilation discs on a computer recorder for our own personal use, from material we have purchased with the understanding that we can listen to it anytime or anywhere we want, and in any order we want, we don't lose any sleep worrying that the RIAA or the Feds or Metallica is going to drop the hammer on us. We just enjoy the music. And we hope you do, too.

However, we keep up with developments, and you should too. To learn more about copyright, go to the U.S. Copyright Office Web site at www.loc.gov/copyright/ or check the following resources:

- **Electronic Frontier Foundation's Campaign for Audiovisual Free Expression**
  www.eff.org/cafe/indexcenter.html

- **UC Berkeley Intellectual Property Resources**
  www.sims.berkeley.edu/resources/infoecon/Intellectual_Property.html

- **Yahoo Digital Copyright Law Links**
  http://fullcoverage.yahoo.com/Full_Coverage/Tech/Digital_Copyright_Law

CD Recorder Manufacturers

You'll see lots of companies selling CD recorders and bundles. But they all will be manufactured by one of companies listed here.

If you are trying to figure out who actually made a recorder, before you buy, take a good look at the faceplate and then check these Web sites to try to match it up with the pictures there. Sometimes the faceplates are a different style, but you can usually tell by the locations of the lights, the open/close button, the headphone jack, and volume control.

LG Electronics www.lge.co.kr/english/index.html

JVC www.jvc.com/ds2

Mitsumi www.mitsumi.com

Panasonic www.panasonic.com

Philips www.pc.be.philips.com/cdrw

Plextor www.plextor.com

Ricoh www.ricohcpg.com

Samsung www.samsungelectronics.com

Sanyo www.sanyo.com

Sony www.ita.sel.sony.com

Teac www.teac.com

Yamaha www.yamaha.com

What Are MP3s?

There are sounds we, with our specific biological makeup, never hear. If suddenly we were able to hear all the things, the world would become pretty cacophonous, so cacophonous, in fact, we'd probably go insane. Every time you spoke with your neighbor, you might hear every single projectile particle of saliva crash against the roof of his mouth and likely your face, too, if he's a spitter. A sneeze could sound like the Fourth of July. And listening to Charlie Parker, you'd hear, in addition to every note he played, the rush of breath producing the note. Now, of course, if our ancestors had heard all these things, they'd have found pleasant ways of working with it, just as they did find their wonderful ways of working with what we do perceive.

These sounds we never perceive do cause mechanical responses in your ear—the fibers in your cochlea vibrate with the stimuli, and the whole sonic picture is there, breath, spit, and all. There is a moment, though, before conscious perception, when your brain processes the whole sonic picture and filters out a great deal of stuff. Your brain then passes on a signal mainly devoid of breath and spit to your consciousness: A second moment of hearing, as it were, the auditory experience we know as genuine human hearing. This is why you don't hear Bird's breath, or so much of it anyway.

A theory, like this one, of the way hearing works is known as a psychoacoustic model. You'll often hear that tiny phrase invoked in conjunction with MP3. When a model like this is applied to digital material with the aim of compressing the material, it's called Perceptual Coding, meaning simply compression, or coding, according to the way human senses are thought by science to work.

MP3 encoding works basically by emulating your brain in the process we just described, or at least by beating your brain to the sonic punch. The encoding process removes the sonic information your brain would have filtered out if the nonencoded sample were hitting your ear, thus reducing the amount of information in a sample and subsequently reducing the amount of space a sample occupies on your hard disk.

Speculation and empirical evidence suggest that one of the things your brain filters out is a weak signal directly next to a strong signal. Imagine Bird blowing through his saxophone, just blowing, producing no note. You can hear that, right? Now imagine him blowing a note. Though that blowing you could hear before remains—albeit in a different form—it's barely detectable, if at all, beside the note he's blowing. Your brain admits the strong note Bird produces into conscious perception but censors his relatively weak breath, though his breath is distinctly there, producing the note. This filtering is known as Signal Masking, Frequency Masking, or Auditory Masking. MP3 encoding is sound discriminating in much the manner of the human ear, removing the digital information that comprises these weak signals and leaving the strong signals in place.

MP3 also removes very, very low frequency sounds, sounds we most often don't hear. These occur below what's known as the Minimal Audition Threshold. A nice mathematical curve describes this threshold, making it easy on encoding software developers.

An MP3 encoder does one last thing: Huffman coding. Say you wrote an important letter that's three and a half pages long, but you're broke and have only one stamp and can therefore send just three pages. You get it in your head that if you turn the phrase "Would that it were, dearest sweetest belovedest," which occurs commonly in your letter, into simply "01" you could save a lot of space. Then, you see that if you turn your oft-repeated "beware that infernal Goya" into "11" you could save even more space. After that, you see that, though you only say it a handful of times, by reducing the epithet "stinking swine" to "0011," you could compress your tome further still. Pretty soon, you've gone through your whole letter, which now reads something like 010101010110011 and is 20 percent thinner. So lick your one remaining stamp and fire that bad boy off.

That's pretty much what Huffman coding does: It goes through the data produced by the first part of MP3 encoding, finds commonly occurring stuff and assigns it a small tag, then finds less common stuff and assigns it a larger tag, then finds even less common stuff and assigns it an even larger tag, and so on. It's not much different from a video compression scheme that identifies common visual elements between frames, such as the background behind a talking head, and gives it a single value to exploit its redundancy and reduce the video's typically cumbersome file size.

So that's how MP3 encoding works. The Fraunhofer Institute started working on this in 1987, with the goal of satisfying the requirements of a digital broadcast project—they probably had no idea that this way of encoding would come to rule the Internet and perhaps didn't even see the Internet explosion on the horizon.

In 1989, the Moving Picture Experts Group (MPEG)—a subgroup of the International Standards Organization (ISO), which produces standards for both the digital and nondigital world—was charged with finding somewhere in the world a way to compress digital audio and visual content for storage as well as the accompanying way to decode this information for playback. The call for proposals went out. The Fraunhofer Institute's idea was declared the winner in 1992, and its way of encoding and decoding (well, sort of anyway) came to be designated MPEG-1, and was adopted as a standard. MPEG-1 came in three flavors: MPEG-1, Layer 1; MPEG-1, Layer 2; and MPEG-1, Layer 3.

MPEG-1, Layer 3, is particularly bitchin' where audio compression is concerned: You can get a supersmall file with superhigh quality, where the other layers produce files of similar quality but of larger size. Perfect for the Internet right? Files compressed according to the MPEG-1, Layer 3, scheme have ".MP3" as an extension, and since "MP3" is by a long shot easier to utter than "MPEG-1, Layer 3," these files came to be referred to as "MP3s."

That's the long and short of it.

Web Resources for CD Recording C

- **About.com CD recording resources (informational)**
  www.homerecording.about.com/entertainment/homerecording/msub25.htm
- **Adaptec CD-R Central (vendor)**
  www.cdrcentral.com
- **Andy McFaddens's CD-R FAQ (informational)**
  www.fadden.com/cdrfaq
- **CDPage (informational)**
  www.cdpage.com
- **CDR Media World (commercial)**
  www.maxtarget.com/hardware/cdrom/cd.shtml
- **EMedia Magazine (magazine Web site)**
  www.emedialive.com
- **MP3.com (commercial)**
  www.mp3.com

- **Octave Systems (vendor)**
  www.octave.com

- **Optical Sciences Center, University of Arizona (educational)**
  www.optics.arizona.edu

- **Optical Storage Technology Association (OSTA) (trade organization)**
  www.osta.org

- **PC Technology Guide (informational)**
  www.pctechguide.com/09cdr-rw.htm

- **SIGCAT (organization)**
  www.sigcat.org

- **Sonic Spot (commercial)**
  www.sonicspot.com

Glossary

Our great thanks go to Leo Pozo, the mastermind, who has compiled and kept up the best glossary on compact disc technology. We appreciate his kind permission to allow us to print a much-abbreviated version here. You can view the full glossary at www.cdpage.com.

A

Access Time Amount of time it takes a CD-ROM or DVD drive to find and read the requested information and make it available to the CPU. Although many vendors cite this number, use access times with care because there is no measuring standard. Faster hard disk drives claim access speeds of 12 milliseconds or even faster, most CD-ROM drives claim access times of about 80 to 120 milliseconds, and some DVD drives claim slightly faster access times.

Analog A type of signal that reflects the variation in the phenomenon being measured or represented, such as voice, temperature, pressure, intensity of light, electrical flows. To be used in computers, analog signals, such as those in communications, must first be modulated into digital code strings.

Analog-to-Digital Conversion Analog-to-digital conversion, or ADC and also known as modulation, uses special ADC chips to convert analog signals to digital strings. In CD and DVD players, DAC, or digital-to-analog conversion, chips convert the digital stream to an analog audio wave stream. Conversion is necessary to send computer data through regular telephone lines, to use analog audio and video in digital systems (and vice versa), for computerized telecommunications, to display computer data on analog monitors, and so on.

ASPI Advanced SCSI Programming Interface, or ASPI, is a driver that helps the operating system (and software) communicate with the hardware—such as SCSI devices and CD-Recordable drives.

ATA Short for AT Attachment, ATA is a disk-drive implementation that integrates the controller in the disk drive itself. There are several versions of ATA, all developed by the Small Form Factor (SFF) Committee. ATA is known also as ATAPI (AT Attachment Packet Interface) and IDE (Intelligent Device Electronics). ATA-2 is known as EIDE (Enhanced IDE, Western Digital's implementation) and Fast-ATA (Seagate's implementation). ATA-3 is known as Ultra ATA and Ultra IDE (UIDE). ATA-3 supports data transfer rates of 33 Mbytes per second.

ATAPI. *See* ATA.

Audio Traditionally, audio signals were recorded and played back as analog signals. Today, digital audio is becoming prevalent. The quality of digital audio depends on the sampling rate and the sample size. Humans hear sound in the range of 15 to 20,000 Hz.

AutoPlay Also known as autorun, this feature starts up a file automatically when the user inserts a CD (or other removable media). For this to work, Windows and the media must support the Auto Insert Notification feature and must include the Autorun.inf file in the media's root directory.

B

Block Error Rates Block Error Rates indicate the number of logical blocks that contain erroneous bytes detected during a read from the CD-ROM. Block Error Rates, or BLERs, are measured in errors per second. They also serve to gage effectiveness of mastering, replication, and CD-R encoding processes—aspects of quality of a CD-ROM.

Blue Book Released by Philips and Sony in 1995, the Blue Book is also known as the CD-Extra format (CD-Extra is Sony's trademark for its Blue Book products). Blue Book, CD-Extra, and Enhanced CD are often used interchangeably, and the specifications are in the Blue Book, which call for a replicated multisession disc. Blue Book CDs can be played by CD-Audio drives and by drives in PCs. CD-Plus was a somewhat similar specification but is no longer used much.

Buffer A small amount of memory that holds instructions or other information and is available to the CPU. Buffers should not be confused with memory cache. Buffering is used to overcome factors that affect direct access of instructions or data to the CPU, such as speed differences and interface delays between a device and the CPU. Buffering is important in audio and video compression-decompression processes and especially when recording CDs and DVDs, because it can prevent the dreaded buffer underruns.

Buffer Underrun During recording, a CD-Recordable drive requires data in an uninterrupted stream, at a specified rate. If the stream is interrupted and the buffer fails to cover the interruption, the recording stops—reporting a buffer underrun, ending the session, and ruining a disc. Adequate buffering and the packet-writing option help reduce buffer underruns.

Bus In a computer, the route that data is transferred through between the CPU, the system memory (RAM), and the peripheral devices. Among the more common buses are the USB, or Universal Serial Bus; the IEEE 1394 bus, also known as FireWire and i.Link; and the PCI, or Peripheral Component Interconnect, bus. Each has a different specification for how fast it can transfer data and how many devices can be connected on the bus.

C

Capacity of CD-ROM Refers to the storage of a standard CD, measured in megabytes of user data. CDs can hold 63 or 74 minutes of data (although some companies claim to have squeezed in a few extra minutes—without bad results). For CD-Recordable media, 74 minutes was considered the maximum design capacity, but one company has announced 12x recordable media with a capacity of 80 minutes. CD-ROM normally hold 650 Mbytes of data.

CD The compact disc was developed by Philips and Sony. The specifications for the 12cm disc, now known as the CD, were issued in 1981 in the now famous Red Book and have become an international standard. The CD is mass-replicated and is made up of a polycarbonate substrate, a thin reflective metallic layer (its mirrorlike appearance comes from aluminum), and a lacquer coating. The encoded data track is a continuous spiral track of about 1.6 to 2.2 microns wide, and the pits are about 0.6 microns wide. Any other size or type of disc is not a CD.

CD Digital Audio Philips and Sony developed the necessary technology for storing digital audio signals on a compact disc and introduced the CD Digital Audio in 1982. This new product was based on the Red Book. CD Digital Audio was designed to hold about 60 minutes of audio data in as many as 99 tracks.

CD-Extra. *See* Blue Book *and* Enhanced CD.

CD-Plus. *See* Blue Book *and* Enhanced CD.

CD-Recordable CD-Recordable technology allows production of CD-ROMs on a personal computer. It requires a CD-R recorder or drive, appropriate software, and recordable media. CD-R media is sold pregrooved in 63- or 74-minute capacities. Once recorded, the CD-R disc is read the same as a mass-reproduced CD.

CD-Recordable Recording Modes Initially, there were two options: Disc-at-Once (DAO) and Track-at-Once (TAO). DAO records 1 to 99 tracks in one pass, without interruptions. TAO records in more than one pass. Some recorders provide for session-at-once recording, which allows recording various tracks but leaving them unclosed, allowing another track (usually data) to be recorded before the disc is closed.

CD-ROM The Compact Disc-Read Only Memory is the standard CD. Although its physical characteristics and track structure are the same as that of Red Book CD Audio, CD-ROM was designed for computer data and uses additional layers of error detection and correction (the CD-ROM specification is defined in the Yellow Book).

CD-ROM Drives The original CD-ROM drives had a transfer rate of 150 Kbits per second, required their own controller card, and had no audio plug. Recent CD-ROM drives work at 56x, and 72x drives are now appearing on the market.

CD-RW Developed by Philips and Sony, CD Rewritable, or CD-RW, technology implements the Orange Book, Part 3, specifications. Although the specifications require that RW media be rewritable at least 1,000 times, most manufacturers claim to surpass that minimum hundreds of times over. There are 12x CD-RW drives. According to some figures, CD-RW drive production has surpassed that of CD-R.

CD-Text This function, used mostly in CD-Audio applications, involves placing as much as 5K of text in the disc's Table of Contents. That text can be displayed by players that support this function.

CD-WO CD-Write-Once specifications (as defined in the Orange Book) came out rather late. A write-once hybrid disc contains an area where read-only files can be placed. The rest of the disc is the write-once area, which can be written to in one or more sessions

Constant Angular Velocity and Constant Linear Velocity Magnetic and optical storage drives can rotate with constant angular velocity (CAV) or constant linear velocity (CLV). CAV, used mostly by magnetic drives and record players, is measured in RPM and means that the read head sweeps the same angle, for the same amount of time, at all radii. CLV, used in CD-ROM, allows the head to read the same length of track at all times and all radii. This is also called reference speed or scan rate. CLV requires that the disc spin slower as the head moves to the outer edge of the disc, and a 1x CD-ROM spins from 539 RPM at the inner edge to 210 RPM at the outer edge. Recent high-speed drives combine CAV and CLV.

D

DAT Digital Audio Tape, or DAT, is generally high-quality, small 4mm magnetic tape that in the computer arena has been used mainly for archiving and back up. For CD-ROM, it is used as a transfer medium. For DVD, which deals in gigabytes, DAT has been replaced by Digital Linear Tape (DLT).

Data Transfer Rate The reading speed of the drive. The first CD-ROM drives had a transfer rate of 150 kilobytes per second. Now, 40x drives are common, and faster drives are becoming available, as fast as 72x.

Digital Contrasted to analog, digital refers to the use of digits (0 to 9), in specific code schemes. The binary coding scheme uses 1s and 0s and is the basis for binary digital computers.

Disc-at-Once (DAO). *See* CD-Recordable Recording Modes.

Disc Format Mass-reproduced CDs are stamped to reproduce the coded tracks of the master. CD-Recordable and CD-Rewritable blanks, however, use formatting to add functionality to the encoding technology.

Disc Read Head/Disc Write Head Storage drives (magnetic and optical) have a read/write head, or heads, that float over the recorded area. CD-ROM drives have only a read head, which uses a low-intensity red laser diode, lenses that focus the laser on the track, and others lenses that redirect the reflections to one of the photodiodes for appropriate decoding. Some Write-Once and Rewritable optical drives use two heads (to read and to write), and other drives, including CD-Recordable, use one head to do both—employing a high-intensity laser for the write function. Recently, Kenwood introduced a 40x drive with a read head that uses seven laser beams to sweep seven tracks at once. The drive's electronics performs the appropriate decoding.

DMA Direct Memory Access, or DMA, is a data-transfer process, usually from device to system memory. MS-DOS implements a table of DMA channels for that purpose.

Driver A program that controls a hardware device, such as a hard drive, printer, and mouse. A driver helps a hardware device and an application that wants to use that hardware device talk to each other.

Dyes Recordable and rewritable media use a layer of colored dye to record data. Improved dyes make possible higher speed discs. The color of recordable and rewritable media depends less on the color of the dye used and more on the reflective coating of the media. Some claim that the silver coating (which results in bluish discs) shows higher ratings in longevity and reflectivity as compared to the gold coating (of the well-known greenish discs).

E

Enhanced CD The Enhanced CD has old roots and is a multi-session disc based on the Blue Book with audio tracks in the first session and data in the first track of the second session. (CD-Extra is Sony's name for these discs.) The data track can be read by a CD-ROM drive, but it remains invisible to CD-Audio players. This solves the old problem of mixed-mode discs that had data in the first track and CD-Audio in the remaining tracks. Players would try to play the data and produce awful noise.

Erasable An erasable disc with an optical drive lets the user write and erase at will—just as with magnetic hard drives. The preferred term is rewritable, as in magneto-optical rewritable and phase-change rewritable technologies.

F

FireWire. *See* Bus.

G

Gap Gaps (also known as intertrack pauses, pregaps, postgaps, and separators) are two or three seconds of mostly 0s at the beginning of a track. Gaps are used to separate tracks of data, audio, and video in the same session.

I

IDE Intelligent Device Electronics, IDE, is an interface for storage devices that includes most of the circuitry previously found in the interface card. The growth of multimedia was also helped by IDE controller cards that supported CD-ROM, CD-R, and other drives.

IEEE 1394. *See* Bus.

Injection Molding A common industrial process used to produce plastic products of all shapes and vinyl for music records. CD mastering and replication plants use injection molding machines fitted with stampers to stamp, or press, the molten polycarbonate into CDs. Once stamped, the replicate (or substrate) is allowed to cool before it is moved for metallizing (the shiny surface), and then it is given a coat of protective lacquer. Machines produce seven to ten replicates per minute; some newer models claim even higher rates.

ISO The International Standards Organization, or ISO, is composed of scores of international committees and is the accepted source of standards for electronic and computerized data communications and information processing.

J

Jewel Case The plastic shipping and storage case for CDs.

L

Label CD-Audio, CD-ROM, and other optical discs are usually labeled on their back side. The labels of mass-replicated discs are generally screen-printed at the replication plant in as many a three colors.

Lands Optical discs have a spiral track that contains pits and lands. Lands are the clear spaces between the pits. When reading a replicated disc, the laser light reflects at a higher intensity from the lands than from the pits. The transitions between lands and pits are coded as 1s (or 0s).

Lead In/Lead Out A CD-ROM uses small lengths of track before the beginning and after the end of the coded part. In single-session applications, they serve as markers. The lead-in includes the Table of Contents, and the lead-out can include code to stop the player.

M

Mastering The production of a glass master disc. Encoders use a high-power laser beam to burn pits on a large glass disc coated with a sensitive recording layer. Once treated, or developed, the glass disc is referred to as the master, or positive. Next, a metallic master is created, generally known as the father (or stamper, if it is used for reproduction of small runs). For large mass-reproduction jobs, the father is used to produce intermediate mother molds used to produced the necessary metal stampers (sons, or production stampers). These then are fitted in the injection molding machines. Mastering and reproduction are usually done at the same plant.

Media Also called storage media. Optical technology uses various types of media, or discs. Mass-reproduced CD-Audio and CD-ROM involve a stamped (injection-molded) polycarbonate substrate (the core), which is given a reflective coating and a protective lacquer coating. DVD is similar but with thinner substrates that are bonded together.

Metallic Coating After injection-molding and cooling, each disc undergoes metallizing—a process that gives the CD a metallic coat and its shiny surface. This shiny surface reflects the laser light during the read process. For mass-reproduced CDs, this coating is generally aluminum. CD-Recordable, Write-Once, magneto-optical, and Rewritable discs are manufactured with a silver or gold reflective layer in their sandwich of layers and coatings.

Mixed-Mode Disc A CD that contains CD digital audio and CD-ROM tracks. Generally, the CD-ROM data is in the first track, and the digital audio portion takes up the remaining tracks. The earlier CD-DA players tried to play that first track, producing loud, harsh sounds. The Blue Book specifications brought some order in that area, since there were various mixed-mode formats. Blue Book (or Enhanced CDs) are now the better-known mixed-mode discs.

Modulation Modulation generally refers to analog-to-digital conversion. There are, however, various other modulation schemes. For example, CD-Audio players use a digital-to-analog converter to produce the stereo analog music signals. To produce the appropriate mix of sounds in the signal, the system uses Pulse Code Modulation (PCM)—although Adaptive Digital Pulse Code Modulation (ADPCM), and others, have been implemented in audio applications.

MP3 A digital audio format popularized by audiophiles using the Internet. It is a compressed digital audio format (MPEG-1, Layer 3), and MP3 players are software decompressors. There are portable players (such as the Rio PMP300) that store and play 60 to 480 minutes of MP3 audio, depending on the quality. MP3 users generally equate 1 MB to one minute of high-quality sound. There is considerable interest in digital audio in compressed and secure formats, and various digital audio options besides MP3 are being considered. Philips, one of the major players in the industry, has announced an MP3 player with security options.

MultiRead The MultiRead specifications, approved by the Optical Storage Technology Association trade group in July 1997, addressed the capability of drives to read recordable and rewritable discs.

Multisession A disc that has been encoded in more than one session. Therefore, the disc has more than one volume, so it is also known as multivolume.

O

Orange Book Philips published the recordable compact disc standard in 1990, reportedly in a binder with orange covers. It defined two new CD products: magneto-optical (Part 1) and write-once (Part 2). Rewritable (Part 3) was released later. Part 1, CD-MO, defines CD media with tracks that can be erased and rewritten by drives using magneto-optical recording technology. Part 2, Write-Once, defines tracks that can be written but not erased and rewritten. Write-once is known mostly as recordable technology. Part 3, Rewritable (CD-RW), was developed by Philips and Sony. Until recently, CD-ROM and CD-R drives could not read CD-RW because CD-RW media has much lower coefficients of reflectivity. But those issues have been addressed. The specifications require that RW media be rewritable at least 1,000 times—but most media manufacturers claim millions of rewrites. *See also* Phase-Change Technology.

P

Phase-Change Technology This rewritable technology is used by CD products that implement the Orange Book, Part 3, CD-Rewritable specifications. The phase-change disc employs a grooved polycarbonate substrate and a stack of five layers whose composition determines the recording capabilities. In the recording layer, the laser pulse heats a spot above its melting point, and the spot shifts phase, from crystalline to amorphous. To erase, a laser beam of higher power reheats the spot, which then cools to its original crystalline state and is ready to be written again.

Pits During optical encoding, pulses of a high-power laser beam burn microscopic pits on the recording layer. The untouched spaces between pits are called lands. During the read process, the laser light focuses on the spinning spiral track, and since the pits reflect light less intensely, the read head detects the changes in reflectivity. Those changes are processed as 1s, and the lands represent the 0s.

Program Area This term, introduced in CD-Audio production, refers to the area of the disc where the user's files, or songs, are stored. In CD-ROM, all the files of the application go in the program area.

Protective Coating Optical discs have a clear plastic or lacquer coat that seals and protects the substrate and metallic layer. Even with this coating, small scratches, dirt, and other markings can make the disc unreadable. This coat must prevent air from reaching and oxidizing the metallized layer—which would render the disc unreadable. Some new CD-R media claim additional protection with a special coating.

R

Recording Layer This is the sensitive layer of a disc, and it reacts in a specific way under the pulse of an laser beam. Each recording technology uses a disc with an appropriate recording layer.

Red Book Philips and Sony published their specifications for CD-Audio in 1980—reportedly in a binder with red covers—and addressed the specifications for the CD. The now-famous Red Book was key for the high-quality sound of CD-Audio.

Reflectivity A measurable property of a surface, also called reflectance. In optical technology, baseline reflectivity refers to the reflectivity of the lands—the clear spaces between the pits in the track (the pits have lower than baseline reflectivity). While reading the track, the changes in reflectivity are detected and decoded. The differences in reflectivity between rewritable and mass-reproduced and one-off discs can be substantial.

Replication Duplication using injection-molding equipment, as for CD-Audio and CD-ROM. Mass replication made CD-Audio a competitive product. Later, since the same CD-Audio mass-replication plants could produce CD-ROMs, they made possible low CD-ROM production costs—which were certainly crucial during the first years of the CD-ROM industry.

Rotation CD and DVD drives rotate clockwise. All single-layer discs are read from the inside out. In double-layer discs, DVD reads both layers from the same side, and there are two ways of doing so. Opposite Track Path (OTP) reads the top, or outside, layer (layer 0) radially from the inside out and the inside layer (layer 1) radially from the outside in—after transferring at the transition area (which makes it seem that the tracks are running in opposite directions). OTP reading is used to provide for reading continuity—important for video applications. Parallel Track Path (PTP) reads both layers nonsequentially during a session—the tracks run in the same direction. For text and data applications, PTP is preferred, because it allows random access to data anywhere in the tracks.

S

Sampling Sampling is part of analog-to-digital conversion. The analog signal is sampled at an specific rate and quantized—which means that a numerical value is matched to each sample and that value is converted to binary code. Although the frequency of sampling is important for continuity, the size of the sample (in bits) is important for depth of quality. CD-Audio involves sampling rate of 44.1 kHz and sample size of 16 bits, but DVD-Audio specifies various sampling rates and quantizing for even higher quality sound.

SCMS The Serial Copy Management System, or SCMS, for consumer devices is part of the Copyright Act of 1976. In 1992, an addition, known as the Audio Home Recording Act, established a copyright framework for recording to tape, which is applied to optical discs. The SCMS, essentially, mandates all hardware and software covered by the Act to include a method to prevent unauthorized copying of a copyrighted product—thus precluding piracy. The SCMS can incorporate any method to accomplish this, including a royalty structure for using the material.

SCSI The Small Computer System Interface, or SCSI, was introduced as the "intelligent interface for intelligent devices." SCSI cards can connect to 8- and 16-bit buses and link devices in a daisy chain. The interface issues commands to the chain, and each SCSI device recognizes the commands addressed to it.

Stamper A metallic mold (usually nickel) produced during the mastering process. *See also* Mastering.

T

Termination Resistors Small plastic contraptions placed at each end of the chain of devices in a SCSI configuration. Their role is to signal there are no other devices beyond that point and prevent excess signal noise on the SCSI bus.

TOC Table of Contents is a list of the files and addresses of the entire disc. In CD-ROM, the TOC is in the lead-in area and can hold 99 addresses (the number of tracks that a CD can have). In current multisession applications, each session uses its own table of contents and the application scans the disc and begins to read the last table of contents first.

Track Ninety-nine tracks can be coded in the program area of a CD. Each session can have multiple tracks, and each track is preceded by a gap (2 to 3 seconds) and can contain data, audio, or video. Usually, audio tracks are contained in one session.

Track-at-Once. *See* CD-Recordable Recording Modes.

Transfer Rate The player's capacity to deliver data to the bus. The first CD-ROM drives were designed to read 75 sectors of data per second, providing a transfer rate of 150 Kbytes per second. This basic transfer rate became the baseline and is now referred to as 1x. Drives identify their speeds accordingly. For example, a 24x drive is 24 times faster than the first 1x drive. Recordable and rewritable speeds will always be much lower. In DVD, the base transfer rate is about 1.2 Mbytes per second (equivalent to that of an 8x CD drive).

U

USB. *See* Bus.

Leo F. Pozo, who created this glossary, is a consultant and previously worked for the Department of Defense, developing and supporting CD-ROM applications. He is a member of the board of SIGCAT (Special Interest Group on CD/DVD Applications and Technology) and has participated in various industry conferences. His full-fledged "Glossary of CD and DVD Technologies" and other writings are also published on various Internet sites. He can be contacted at leopozo@yahoo.com.

Copyright © Leo Pozo

Index

45s 4-5

A

a2b music 17-18
A/D conversion. *See* analog-to-digital conversion
Adaptec 2, 33, 34, 36-38, 95-96
adapters 108
Advanced SCSI Programmer's Interface. *See* ASPI
Advansys, setting automatic termination 95-96
AES/EBU 77
Ahead Software 34
AHRA. *See* Audio Home Recording Act
AIN 89-90
albums
   arrangements of tracks 54
   cleaning 119
   importance of saving 4-5
   production of sound from 78-82
   recording 103-133
   type of audio produced by 6
Alien Connections 114
analog audio 6
analog cards 74-75
analog-to-digital (A/D) conversion 76-77, 110
applications. *See* specific applications
Aptiva 60
Arboretum Systems 112
ArtistDirect.com 22
Asimware Innovations 34
ASPI 97
Astarte 37
AT&T 17
AT Attachment (ATA) 51
AT Attachment Packet Interface (ATAPI) 51, 60, 84
ATA 51
ATAPI. *See* AT Attachment Packet Interface
AtomicPop 22
attack 152
audio blocks 160
audio controls, configuring 120-124
Audio Engineering Society/European Broadcast Union (AES/EBU) 77
Audio Home Recording Act (AHRA) 227, 232-233, 236-237, 238
audio-only media 231
audio sessions 213-217
audio-only recording software 40-41
AudioCatalyst 42-43, 166-175
Audiograbber 42, 166-168, 171-174
Auditory Masking 246
Auto Insert Notification (AIN) 89-90, 221
autoexec.bat 93
automatic termination 95-96
autorun.inf 221-223

B

Basic Input/Output System (BIOS) 31-32, 94-97
Beelzebubba 132
belt drives 106
Betamax case 239-241
BIOS 31-32, 94-97
bitrate 182
blanking 55
Blue Book 213
bmdrivers.com 92
Brainwave Synchronizer 115
Brio 60
buffer underruns 57-58, 91, 98-100, 161-162
Buffered Burst Copy 172-173
buffers 193
burning. *See* recording
busmastering drivers 92

C

C/S jumper 51
cable modems 27
Cable Select (C/S) jumper 51

265

cables, Small Computer System Interface (SCSI) devices 96, 98. *See also* specific cables
caching, read-ahead 93
Cage, John 132
calibration of CDs 65
capacity. *See* storage
Capitol 238
CardDeluxe 75
cassette tapes 5, 135–155
CD Copy 42–43
CD Creator 33
CD Speed 46
CD Spin Doctor 34–35, 165
CD Sync 229–230
CD-Audio 61, 63–65, 160
CD-DA 61, 160
CD-R drives. *See* recorders
CD-rewritable (CD-RW) drives 11, 49–69
CD-RW drives. *See* CD-rewritable drives
.cda files 44–47
CDDB 42, 187–188
CDFS.VXD drivers 44–47
CDNow.com 23
CDR Identifier 46
CDRWin 33–34
CeQuadrat 33, 36
chains, Small Computer System Interface (SCSI) 95
chamois 119
Charismac Engineering 2, 38
checking device status 88
choosing recorders 53–54
CIRC 55
cleaning
   albums 119
   cassette tapes 137
   CDs 198
clicks, filtering 126–128
CLV 54
colors of CDs 9, 68
Columbia 238
Command Software 34
Compact Disc Audio files (.cda) 44–47
Compact Disc Database (CDDB) 42, 187–188
Compact Disc File System 44–47
Compact Disc–Digital Audio (CD-DA) 61, 160

compact discs. *See* CDs
compilation discs 197–209
compressed audio formats 16–17. *See also* MP2; MP3
Concerto Grosso 132
config.sys 93
configuring audio controls 120–124, 137–138
connecting
   recorders to Macintosh computers 52
   tape decks to computers 136–137
   turntables to computers 109–111
connections. *See* adapters; cables
Constant Linear Velocity (CLV) 54
Continuous Noise Filter 143–145, 148–155
conversions, analog-to-digital (A/D) 76–77
converting WAV files to MP3 44–47
CoolEdit Pro 115–116
copying compact discs (CDs) 157–176
copyright infringement 232–233, 235–242
Corel 33
Corelli 132
Count area 65
crackles, filtering 128
Creative Labs 74–75
Cross Interleaved Reed Solomon Code (CIRC) 55
cue sheet 66
CuteMX 20–21
cyanine 9, 68

D

DAE. *See* ripping tracks
DAE Speed drop-down menu 173–174
DAO. *See* Disc-at-Once recording
Darla sound card 75
Dart Pro 98 117
Dartech 117
DAT machines 76–77

DAT. *See* digital audio tape
data sessions 218–221
daughter cards 74
DCC 6
Dead Milkmen 132
declick filters 126–128
decoding MP3s 186–187
defragmentation 85, 167
dehiss, denoise filters 129, 143
dehissing 148–155
dehum, debuzz, notch filter 129–130
deleting tracks 69, 192
DeNoiser 143
derivative works 237
Detect Silence 132
Diamond Cut Audio Restoration Tools
   adding fade-ins and fade-outs 205–208
   described 82, 117–118
   equalizing tracks 203–204
   recording and restoring audio
      from albums 122–123
      from cassette tapes 140–155
Diamond Cut Productions 82, 117
Diamond Rio 25
Digital Audio Extraction (DAE). *See* ripping tracks
digital audio 6, 15–27
Digital Audio Labs 75
Digital Audio Recording Devices and Media. *See* Audio Home Recording Act
digital audio tape (DAT) 6, 232–233
digital audio tape (DAT) machines 76–77
digital compact cassette (DCC) 6
Digital Millennium Copyright Act (DMCA) 236
digital sound cards 75
direct drives 106
disabling read-ahead optimization 91
Disc-at-Once (DAO) recording 64, 66, 169–170

INDEX

DiscJuggler 34
disconnect command 90
Discribe 2, 38
discs. *See* specific discs
disk utilities 88
Disney 239
distorted tracks, repairing 123
DMCA 236
Dolby Noise Reduction (NR) 139
downloading music 26–27
driverguide.com 92
drives. *See* specific drives; recorders
DSL modems 27
duplicating compact discs (CDs) 157–176
DVD 12
dyes 9, 68
Dylan, Bob 103
Dynamic Synch Width 173–174

E

EAC 43
Easy CD Creator 30, 34, 165, 216
Easy CD Pro 33
Easy CDDA Extractor 42
Echo Digital Audio 75
Edison Shop, The 105
Egosys 77
EIDE 51
electronic chips 81
Emagic 39
Emusic.com 24
encoding, MP3s 245–248
Enhanced CD 211, 213, 259
Enhanced Integrated Device Electronics (EIDE) 51
equalization curve 79–82, 202
equalization, tracks 202–204
equalizers, 131. *See also* graphic equalizers
erasable discs 69
error correction 55, 162
Exact Audio Copy (EAC) 43
exporting MP3 to WAV format 45
extracting tracks. *See* ripping

F

fade-ins and fade-outs 205–208
Fast Small Computer System Interface (SCSI) 97–98
file finders 20–21
File Transfer Protocol (FTP), downloading music with 19–20
filters, noise reduction 124–130. *See also* specific filters
FindFast 91
finding music 15–26, 183–186
FireWire 38, 50–53, 94
firmware 97, 227
Four Walls 132
fragmentation 85
frames 65
Franck, Jackie 166
Frank Black and the Catholics 178
Fraser, Liz 128
Fraunhofer Institute 247
Frequency Masking 246
Frequency Space Editor 114
FTP, downloading music with 19–20

G

G3s and G4s. *See* Power Macintosh computers
Gain Change window 206, 208
Gain Normalization 209–210
Gear Pro 34
Geffen 238
General tab 89
Golden Hawk Technology 33
graphic equalizers 110, 116, 202–203
grooves 79, 119

H

handling media 101
hard disks. *See* hard drives
hard drives 51–52, 83–85, 108–109
hardware. *See* specific hardware
head-cleaning kits 137

headphones 109
Hewlett-Packard 8, 10
HHB 227, 231
Hi-Val 8
high-pass filter 125–126
hiss, filtering 144–145, 148–155
home recorders 3, 225–232
Home Recording Rights Coalition (HRRC) 235, 239
Hoontech SB DB-3 daughter card 74
Hot Burn 34
HRRC 235, 239
HTML 222–223
Huffman coding 246–247
hums, filtering 129–130
HyCD Play and Record 45
Hyperprism 112, 118
Hypertext Markup Language (HTML) 222–223

I

ID numbers, Small Computer System Interface (SCSI) devices 97
IDE hard disks 84, 92
IDE recorders 50–51, 90, 92, 94
IEEE 1394. *See* FireWire
iMacs
  connecting recorders to 52
  connecting turntables and preamplifiers to 110
  limitations on recording 93–94
  sound cards 73
  Universal Serial Bus (USB) recorders 50, 94
iMesh 20
Imix.com 23
impulse noise filter. *See* declick filter
Incat 33
incompatibility, CD-recordable (CD-R) drives 67–68
independent record companies 19
index points 58
index.html 222
Information area 65
injection molding 61

installing CDFS.VXD drivers 44
Integrated Device Electronics (IDE) hard disks 84, 92
Integrated Device Electronics (IDE) recorders 50–51, 90, 92, 94
interfaces, recorders 50–53
International Standards Organization (ISO) 247
Internet Explorer 26
interpolation 55
Iomega 12
ISO 9660 image 10
ISO 247

J

jitter correction 171–172
Jornada 60
jukeboxes 41
jumpers 51
Just Audio 36–37
JVC 7, 10, 53

K

Kodak 100

L

lasers 59, 67
lathes 79
lead in and lead out 58, 64–66
legal issues on home recording 235–242
lens 59
LG Electronics 7
line-in ports 111
Linux, recording software for 2, 39
Liquid Audio 17–18, 22–23
Listen.com 24
logical standard 63–64
LPs. *See* albums
Lycos 20

M

Macintosh
 audio extraction software 167

configuring audio controls 121–122, 138
decoders 187
file finders 20
hardware requirements for recorders 60
MP3s
 decoders 187
 playing 181
Small Computer System Interface (SCSI) devices 97–98
software for
 recording 2, 37–39
 restoration 112
sound cards 72–73
troubleshooting
 music downloads 26
 recordings 93–98
Macster 20, 183
magneto-optical (MO) drives 12, 232
manufacturers of recorders 7, 243
Marantz 227–231
Massive Attack 128
master discs 66
Master jumper 51
Matsushita 54
Maxell 100
media 9, 67–68, 100–102, 231
Median filter 128
metal azo 9
Mezzanine 128
mic ports 111
MiniDisc 69, 232
Minimal Audition Threshold 195, 246
Mitsubishi 8
Mitsui 100
Mitsumi 7, 53
mixed discs 64, 211–221
MMJB. *See* MusicMatch Jukebox
MO drives 12, 232
modems 27
mono connections 108
Montego II sound card 74–75
Morita, Akio 6
Motown 238
Moving Picture Experts Group (MPEG) 12, 247
MP2 184

MP3
 converting from WAV to 44–47
 defined 12, 16–17
 encoding 245–248
 finding 20–26
 recording from 177–196
 support for 19
MP3 CD Maker 44–45
MP3.com 25
MP9060A 60
Mpecker Drop Decoder 187
MPEG 1, Layer 3. *See* MP3
MPEG 12, 247
MPEG-1, Layer 2. *See* MP2
multisession recording. *See* mixed discs
music only media 231
music. *See* tracks
MusicMatch Jukebox 41, 187

N

Napster 20–21, 183–186
Nero Burning ROM 35, 214–220
NET 236
Netscape Navigator 26
NewTech Infosystems 36
Ninth Symphony 6
No Electronic Theft (NET) 236
Noise Reduction 117
noise reduction filters 118, 124–130, 143
noiseprints 141–145
normalization 196, 209–210
NR 139
NTI CD Maker 36
Nullsoft 187

O

octave.com 163
OPC 65, 229
optical head 58–59
Optimal Power Calibration (OPC) 65, 229
optimization, read-ahead 91–92
Orange Book 62, 64, 67
Output 113

INDEX

P

packet writing 64
Padus 34
Panasonic 53–54
Partial Rip 170
Pavillion 60
PC Card 51
PCA 65
PCMCIA 51
Perceptual Coding 246
Performas 52, 73
Philips
   home recorders 228–230, 232
   as manufacturer of recorders 7–8, 10–11, 53
   releases audio compact disc 6
   releases CD standards 61–62
phonographs. *See* turntables
photodetectors 59
phtalocyanine 9, 68
physical standard 63
Pioneer 228, 230
Pistolero 178
pits 59
playback 160, 162, 196, 208
playing MP3s 181
playlists, building 191–192
Playstation 33
Plextor 7, 53
PMA 65
polycarbonate 9
pops, filtering 126–128
ports 111
Possible speed problems readout 175
posting MP3 179
power calibration 65
Power Calibration Area (PCA) 65
Power Macintosh computers 38, 50–52, 72–73, 94
power saving options 88
Prassi Software 36
preamplifiers 78, 82, 106, 109–111
pregroove 59
premastering software 31
preservation of audio
   from albums 103–133
   from cassette tapes 135–155
Preview mode 115
pricewatch.com 84
Primo CD 36, 162
Pristine Sounds Pro 114–115
Program Area 64–66
Program Memory Area (PMA) 65
programs. *See* specific programs
Prolinea 60

Q

QPS 52
Quadras 52, 73
Quantize option 118
Que! 52

R

radio 186
RAM 17
random access time 59–60
ratio servers 20
Ray Gun 112–114
RCA 238
RCA cables 106–108, 110
read-ahead caching 93
read-ahead optimization 91–92
RealAudio 17–18
record players. *See* turntables
recorders. *See also* specific recorders
   connecting hard drives to 51–52
   costs of 10
   interfaces of 50–53
   manufacturers of 7–8, 10–11, 53, 243
   media for 100–102
   parts of 58–65
   reasons for using 11–12
   selecting 53–54
   standards for 61–64
   X factor 11, 54–58
recording
   albums 103–133
   cassette tapes 135–155
   Disc-at-Once 66
   from MP3 177–196
   history of 9–11, 61–62
   software used for 29–47
   Track-at-Once 66–67
   troubleshooting and 87–102
   Universal Serial Bus (USB) limitations 52
   X factor 11, 54–58
Recording Industry Association of America (RIAA) 27, 235, 237–238
Recording Industry Association of America (RIAA) curve. *See* RIAA curve
records. *See* albums
Red Book
   74-minute rule 163
   described 53
   sample rate 122
   specifications for CD-Audio 63–65
   writing audio to CD 160
reel-to-reel tapes, finding equipment to play 5
reflective layers 68
releases 152
removing tracks 69, 192
repeat mode 194
replacing sound cards 73
restoring audio
   from albums 103–133
   from cassette tapes 135–155
reverb 131
RIAA curve 79–82, 202
RIAA. *See* Recording Industry Association of America
Ricoh 7–9, 53, 60, 100
Right of Reproduction 237
RioPort.com 25, 179
Rip Offset 170
ripping tracks 16, 29–47, 159–176
RMA 17
Rollingstone.com 26
Room Ambience filters 114
rumble filter. *See* high-pass filter
rumbling in records 119

269

S

S/PDIF 77, 110
Samsung 7
Sanyo 7, 53
SCMS. *See* Serial Copy Management System
Scournet 20–21
scratches, repairing 119, 198
screensavers 88
SCSI chains 95
SCSI recorders 50–52, 60, 84, 90, 94–98
SDMI. *See* Secure Digital Music Initiative
searching for music 15–26, 183–186
Section 506, Copyright Act 241
sectors 54
Secure Digital Music Initiative (SDMI) 27
seek time. *See* random access time
Select Output field 192
selecting recorders 53–54
Serial Copy Management System (SCMS) 77, 227–229, 231–232
servers, ratio 20
Settings tab 89
Sherman, Cary 238
Signal Masking 246
silence 124, 129, 142–143, 169
single-session recording 66
singles 4–5
skins 186
skips in records, repairing 119
Slave jumper 51
Small Computer System Interface (SCSI) chains 95
Small Computer System Interface (SCSI) recorders 50–52, 60, 84, 90, 94–98
software. *See* specific software
songs. *See* tracks
Sonic Foundry 117
Sonic Spot 30, 167
Sonique 188–189, 190–194
Sony
   Betamax case 239–241
   as manufacturer of recorders 7–8, 10, 53
   releases audio compact disc 6
   releases CD standards 61–62
Sony/Philips Digital Interface Format (S/PDIF) 77, 110
sound cards 72–77, 110–111
sound. *See* audio
Sound System Profiler 114
SoundBlaster 73–75
SoundForge 117
source materials 16
speakers 120
speed. *See* X factor
Spin Doctor 38
splitting tracks 132, 146–148
stampers 62
StarDust 193
stereo patch cables. *See* Y cables
stereo-mini adapters 108
storage 65, 84
storage media. *See* media
stylus 78–79, 108, 119
sync data transfer option 90
synchronization 171–172
Syntrillium Software 115
System Description CD-WO. *See* Orange Book
System Use Area 65

T

Table of Contents (TOC) 64–66, 160
Taiyo Yuden 100
tape decks, recording from 135–155
tapeless.com 75–76
tapes. *See* specific tapes
Tascam (TEAC) 7, 227, 231
TDK 100
TEAC 7, 227, 231
termination, Small Computer System Interface (SCSI) 95
Test area 65
testing
   applications 61–62
   recordings 10
Time est. tab 170
time-shifting 239–241
Toast 2, 37, 38, 165, 187, 216
TOC. *See* Table of Contents
tone arm 78
toothpaste 198
Toshiba 60
Track Splitter 132
Track-at-Once recording 64, 66–67, 169–170
tracks
   arrangement on albums 54
   copying 157–176
   defined 58
   equalization 202–204
   fade-ins and fade-outs 205–208
   finding 15–26, 183–186
   normalization 209–210
   removing 69, 192
   repairing distortion 123
   splitting 132, 146–148
   start of 230
   storage of 65
traditional recording software 31
troubleshooting
   music downloads 26
   recordings 87–102
turning off read-ahead optimization 91
turntables 5, 78–82, 105–106, 109–111, 120
Turtle Beach 74–75

U

Ultimate Band List 22
Ultra SCSI 97–98
Universal City Studios 239–240
Universal Serial Bus (USB) recorders 50–52, 60, 72–77, 94
upgrading hardware 72
U.S. Constitution 236
U.S. Court of Appeals 239–240
U.S. Supreme Court 239–241
USB recorders. *See* Universal Serial Bus recorders
USB sound devices. *See* Universal Serial Bus recorders

V

vacuum tubes 81
Verbatim 100
vinyl. *See* albums
virus checkers 88
visual mode 194
VQ 17

W

Warner Bros. 238
warped records, repairing 119
WAV files 17, 44–47
WaveBurner 39
waveforms 141–142, 146–147
Waveterminal U2A 77
White, Byron "Whizzer" 240
Wide SCSI 97–98
Winamp 25, 187
Windows
   recording software for 2, 33–37
   troubleshooting music downloads 26
   troubleshooting recordings 88–93
Windows Media Audio (WMA) 17, 22
windrivers.com 92
WinOnCD 33, 36–37
WMA 17
writing lead in and writing lead out. *See* lead in and lead out
writing modes. *See* recording

X

x axis 206
X factor 11, 54–58
Xing Technology 42, 166

Y

y axis 206
Y cables 82, 107, 110
Yamaha 7, 9–10, 17, 53, 73

Z

ZipCD 12

Take the burn out of burning CDs!

Professional CD-Maker 2000
Windows 95/98/NT 2000
Backup NOW!
As Easy As 1-2-3...
Take it from me, it's easy - you'll see!

Record your **favorite music** in the most popular formats – **MP3, WAV** and **CD-DA!** With the ability to encode and decode in all three formats, nothing is stopping you from **creating the music** you've always wanted.

TRY IT FREE!

Download a full version of CD-Maker 2000 and try it FREE for 30 days!

Accept No Limits
NTI
NEWTECH INFOSYSTEMS

Visit us at www.nticdmaker.com and start burning CDs NOW!

OCTAVE SYSTEMS INCORPORATED

The Intelligent choice...

504A Vandell Way, Campbell, California 95008
Phone: 408.866.8424 - Fax: 408.866.4252 info@octave.com
Washington State: 9645 - 160th Avenue N.E., Redmond, WA 98052
Phone: 425.895.8218 - Fax: 425.895.8768
To order by phone call 1.800.626.8539 (U.S.& Canada only) M-F 8-5 Pacific Time

CD Duplication Services

Octave Systems offers comprehensive, quality shortrun CD duplicating services without the expense of in house equipment or operators. With our high-speed, state-of-the-art CD-R duplication equipment, we offer fast, accurate short-run CD-ROM duplicating order turnaround with cost-effective pricing. All our products are from the biggest names in CD technology. Such as Yamaha, Sony, Teac, Plextor, Panasonic, and much more!

CD Duplicators, CD-R Printers & Disc Autoloaders

Octave offers a wide selection of duplication options for automated network-enabled CD-R duplication & printing systems, stand alone duplicating or autoloading duplication systems. Whether you want to duplicate a few disks or hundreds, we have a specific product to meet your needs. Octave also offers low cost, high performance autoloaders and CD-R Printers.

CD recorders

Whether you are looking for the hottest, fastest CD Recorder or a blazing read/write CD-rewritable, Octave has a CD recorder for you. With years of experience and many choices to chose from, Octave can offer you the CD duplication solution you are looking for.

Come visit us on the web at: **http://www.octave.com**

Padus
Panasonic
MediaFORM SMART TECHNOLOGY
SONY
YAMAHA

DIGITAL RECORDING 1Ø1:

EVERY TAKE COUNTS

Whether you're mastering a CD for duplication or just burning some MP3s, there's no room in the process for failure. That's why sound professionals and home recordists choose the legedary quality of TDK digital recording solutions. They know that TDK veloCD burners and 100% Certified CD-R deliver....

...The sweetest rips, The fastest burns, The most durable discs.

◈TDK ® www.tdk.com
The Digital Sweetspot of recording.